AN ALMOST
PERFECT
MURDER

AN ALMOST PERFECT MURDER

JOHN SUTER LINTON

HOW THE POLICE
CAUGHT ONE
OF THEIR OWN

ABC
Books

First published by ABC Books for the
AUSTRALIAN BROADCASTING CORPORATION
GPO Box 9994 Sydney NSW 2001

Copyright © John Suter Linton 2006

First published in August 2006
Reprinted August 2006
Reprinted April 2007

The National Library of Australia
Cataloguing-in-Publication entry:
Linton, John Suter.
    An almost perfect murder : the story behind the
    investigation into the murder of Ulrike 'Ricky' Conway.

    ISBN 978 0 7333 1927 3

    1. Conway, Ulrike. 2. Murder - Australia - Case studies.
    3. Murder - Investigation - Australia. I. Australian
    Broadcasting Corporation. II. Title.

364.15230994

Cover and internal design by Blue Cork Designs
Internals set in Janson Text by Kirby Jones
Printed and bound in Australia by Griffin Press, Adelaide

5 4 3

To the late, retired
Detective Superintendent
Ron Stephenson, APM

'It's not technology, it's people
WHO solve crime' — 2004

CONTENTS

FOREWORD

The murder of Ulrike 'Ricky' Conway was shrouded in betrayal, sex, drugs and deceit. Her lifeless body was discovered on 4 May 1997. But the events that would lead to her murder began almost a year earlier when her husband, John Conway, a Traffic Operations officer with the Australian Federal Police, pulled over a green Holden Gemini that was blowing smoke. The driver was Kathy McFie, and soon after she and John began an affair.

In a strange twist, Kathy McFie and Ricky also became good friends. The friendship, however, was one-sided. Ricky knew nothing of the relationship that had developed between her husband and her new-found friend. Kathy and John used the trust and love Ricky had for them to deliberately deceive her and erode her confidence and self-worth, dragging her down to her lowest ebb.

John Conway then abducted his son, and fought to keep custody through the Family Court. He told people that Ricky was an alcoholic and accused her of abusing their son. It seemed John would win, but he didn't. The battle, though, didn't end there. John was determined not to be beaten.

The day before Ricky was killed, she felt alone. She felt abandoned. She knew she had lost her husband, and she feared losing her younger son. Her pleas to John Conway went unanswered. He used his answering machine to filter Ricky's calls. It was all part of the deception, manipulation and control he exerted over her. Ricky believed she had nothing to live for.

She spoke of suicide.

The stage had been set. That night, Ricky was murdered. She didn't scream and she didn't fight. Her only protest came as she told the killers she was a mother, and not to hurt her. Her words were in vain. She had lost all reason for living. The assassins could not have found an easier target.

It would be an almost perfect murder.

Ricky's death was initially treated as being either the result of a suicide or an accident. It wasn't till after the observations of two detectives, Detective Sergeant Noel Lymbery and Detective Constable Ben Cartwright, that a whole new line of enquiry opened up. The observations were simple, but suspicious in the circumstances — a toilet seat left up, and an oversized needle mark in Ricky's arm.

There were suspects, but as the investigation narrowed, it became apparent that there was one person who had either committed the crime or had organised it. But there was little evidence to implicate John Conway. Even the Australian Federal Police hierarchy were sceptical of his guilt.

The investigation team, nevertheless, continued their search for evidence and called on help from the public. They got their help, but it came from an unexpected source. It wouldn't be the 'good citizens' of the general public that unravelled the mysteries, but rather drug addicts, dealers, petty thieves and wannabe hitmen.

There was also Ricky. She had kept a diary, having started it months before her murder. Ricky detailed her rocky relationship with John, her feelings of betrayal and her hope for a better future. The diary, the evidence of convicted felons and methodical police work would eventually bring down Ricky Conway's killers.

Some of the witnesses' names who gave police information have been changed. They have moved on from the events and associations that surrounded Ricky's death on 3 May 1997.

The investigation into Ricky Conway's murder was known as Operation Aquatic. This book is dedicated to the late, retired Detective Superintendent Ron Stephenson. The reason for the dedication is because in Ron's first book, *The Scent of Crime*, he writes in his foreword about an example of what police work is all about. He mentions a detective noticing a toilet seat having been left upright, and how from that, a murder investigation was launched.

As Ron wrote and other police have acknowledged, the success of Operation Aquatic came from the thoroughness and professionalism of its team, led by Noel Lymbery and Detective Constable Ben Cartwright. It was their doggedness and the tireless efforts of the entire team that saw them catch and convict all those involved in Ricky Conway's murder.

There is also a more personal reason for the dedication. I knew Ron, although briefly. We shared moments discussing mutual associates, and we also discussed what books we were writing. The last time we met before the tragic accident that claimed him and his wife, Gloria, he asked me what my next book was about. I said 'the Ricky Conway murder'. Ron immediately exclaimed, 'the upright toilet seat!' He knew the case well and would fondly refer to it as an example of the importance of 'the person conducting the investigation'.

AN ALMOST
PERFECT
MURDER

CHAPTER ONE

Friday 23 May 1997

More than they bargained for

Canberra is nestled inside the borders of the Australian Capital Territory (ACT) on the Federal Highway south-west of Goulburn. Being Australia's capital city it is the home of our democracy, where elected representatives from across the country gather to make law and debate issues affecting the nation.

The Australian Federal Government employs the majority of people living in Canberra, as is evident any weekday if one visits Civic Square in the centre of the city. Come lunchtime, the Square bustles with people criss-crossing from office to food vendor and back again. Their importance is identified by their ID cards and their lanyards, embroidered with the acronyms of various government agencies.

Another substantial element of the local community, though more transient in nature, is the student population. Home to various institutions of academia, Canberra acts as a beacon to students from all over Australia.

Though its population is just over 300,000, Canberra, like any larger city in Australia, has its social divides and social problems. In contrast to the aesthetically ordered tree-lined streets, grasslands and water features, the city possesses an inescapable dark side.

Irrespective of being the centre where the law of the land is agreed upon for the good of all. Canberra has its share of people who steal, deceive and commit acts of violence, sometimes even murder. While Civic Square is host to office workers during the day, it is also the place where illicit drugs can be bought under the cloak of darkness.

In the early hours of the morning on Friday 23 May 1997, detectives from Woden Police Station received information in relation to a person selling drugs in the area. Karen (not her real name) was known to police and was alleged to be supplying drugs from her apartment in the neighbouring suburb of Lyons. Both Woden and Lyons are located in the south-west of Canberra. A warrant was issued to search Karen's premises. The detectives executed the warrant, finding enough marijuana in Karen's flat to arrest her and charge her with possession and supply.

Karen was taken back to Woden Police Station for an interview before being formally charged. She cooperated with the detectives. She'd been charged before with the same crime and accepted the consequences, not that there was much else she could do in her situation. At the end of the formal interview the detectives offered her the opportunity to add anything she thought might help in her defence, or if there were just anything else she'd like to tell the detectives. It's a standard question all police ask at the end of an interview, giving the accused the chance to elaborate or to clear their conscience. Whatever the detectives thought Karen might say, they were about to get more than they bargained for.

Karen's thoughts whirled. Fear and anxiety filled her body. She didn't know if she could trust the detectives, or any police for that matter, because of what an associate had told her. That information had shocked and disturbed her. The confidence she shared made her feel uncomfortable and caused her to have sleepless nights. She had thought of telling the police before now, but she feared her life would be in jeopardy if she did. Karen didn't believe what she'd been told at first, not until she was in a taxi and heard the same news on the radio. While what Karen had been told made her fear for her own life, she knew she needed to tell someone. She couldn't bear the secret anymore. She needed to release her burden. If anything was to happen to her, at least she had done the right thing. Her conscience would be clear.

'Is there anything else you'd like to tell us?' the detectives asked again.

Karen took a breath. 'Yes. I know who killed Ricky Conway … the copper's wife.'

The news sent the detectives into a flurry. At 11.17 that morning they contacted their counterparts at Belconnen Police Station who were investigating Ricky's death. It was information the investigators had been waiting for.

Ulrike 'Ricky' Conway died early Sunday morning on 4 May 1997. She lay, at peace, in her bed. Friends, neighbours and police were unsure what had happened. There was no obvious cause of death. Her family, Ricky's mother, older sister and elder son had their suspicions and were quick to make accusations. Despite an exhaustive investigation by police, interviewing a myriad of people, including possible suspects, they were no closer to knowing who, if anyone, had had a hand in Ricky's death. They had their suspicions, but no proof.

By Friday 23 May, 19 days after Ricky's body had been found, police still weren't sure whether they were dealing with a suicide, as was first thought for what were very plausible reasons, or an accidental death, or worse, murder.

Everyone police interviewed had an alibi or was eliminated from suspicion. The investigation appeared to have stalled. It was likely officers could possibly be relocated to other duties. In fact, that Friday morning investigators were contemplating that the death of Ricky Conway would remain an open case, perhaps never to be solved. That was until they heard what Karen had to say. Her evidence would be the first piece of a complex puzzle that revealed the malevolent deception, planning and manipulation employed to commit what would have been the perfect murder.

And the motive?

Revenge?

Control?

Greed?

Recompense to satisfy a bruised ego?

To some people, another's life is cheap. Ricky's, it seemed, was worth little.

CHAPTER TWO

Suicide, accident, or ...?

It was getting dark and there was no light from the house. Phillip used his Zippo lighter to check he had the right key. There was something wrong with the front door lock. As much as Phillip tried he couldn't get his key to turn. It had happened to him once before, many years earlier when he was living in the house. The problem had been that his mother, Ricky, left her keys in the lock from the inside, which then prevented anyone being able to unlock the door from the outside. It was a peculiarity of the deadlock, and since that first time, Ricky always kept her keys in her bag. It had become a habit with her. Even though Phillip had moved out, he kept his key, as he would often call around to check on the welfare of his mother and younger brother.

Phillip's grandmother, Anna, had summoned him to check on Ricky. Anna was concerned after getting a call from Ricky's estranged husband, John Conway. She rarely ever spoke to John, even when he and Ricky were together. John had told Anna he had tried to contact Ricky several times during the day but the

5

phone had rung out. He had become concerned because Ricky usually phoned him. The reason he gave for needing to speak with Ricky was that he wanted to know what to do with his seven-year-old son's weekend clothes. John was taking Alistaire, not his real name, straight to school on Monday. Ricky had recently won custody of Alistaire, with John being awarded visiting rights. Anna remembered Ricky saying she was going to do some gardening on the weekend, and thought maybe she was outside and didn't hear the phone ring.

It was just after six in the evening when Phillip and his girlfriend called at his mother's house. Not being able to gain entry through the front door, Phillip looked to see if he could access the back yard over the side fence. There were too many obstructions, planks of wood and other debris for him to jump over safely. He went next door and scaled the fence to get to his mother's back yard. The lock on the rear door had been barrelled the same as the front. His key worked. Phillip stepped inside. The house was in darkness. His stomach cramped. He knew something was wrong. Phillip switched the lights on and walked through the laundry, into the living area and to the front door, finding his mother's keys in the lock, just as he'd suspected. Phillip opened the door to his girlfriend. A neighbour, who John also called, had turned up and entered the house with them.

Phillip led the way. He went first to his brother's room, but Alistaire wasn't there. He looked around for his mother, and entered her bedroom. There, on the double bed, Ricky Conway lay, eyes closed, seemingly asleep. The doona was neatly spread across her body, pulled up to her neck, and her head was exposed and resting on the pillow. No amount of calling her name or gentle rocking could wake her. Ricky was dead.

Anna had also contacted her eldest daughter, Gabby, soon after calling Phillip. Hans, Gabby's husband, arrived at the house. He walked in, finding Phillip squatting on the floor of his mother's bedroom. Hans comforted his nephew. He asked the neighbour to call the police, while he phoned Gabby, giving her the news. After collecting Gabby and taking her to her sister's house, Hans left to deliver the news to Anna in person.

John 'Ben' Cartwright was a detective constable with the Australian Federal Police (AFP), stationed at Belconnen in 1997. He is better known and introduces himself as 'Ben', having been given the namesake of a television character in the popular 1960s show *Bonanza* since school days. Ben Cartwright was the name of the paternal head of a family who owned a large property, the Ponderosa, in the American Wild West during the horse and buggy era.

Ben had spent his Sunday working the day shift, and come six o'clock he was home. Although he'd completed his shift, due to the rostering system, Ben was the 'on-call' detective for the area. That Sunday, Ben had just begun to unwind from a day's work when he received a call. It was the operations centre. They requested his attendance at 35 Gollan Street, Evatt, a suburb of Belconnen. 'Deceased female' was all he was told, not even a guess as to how the victim had died. Only minutes ago, it seemed to the weary detective, he had greeted his wife and kids with hugs, and now he was rushing back out the door, quickly giving his goodbyes. Experience told him he couldn't be certain when he would be home again.

In the Australian Capital Territory all deaths, whether suicide, misadventure or homicide, are investigated by the local detectives. While all police are officers for the Coroner, it's the detectives who have the training to ascertain if any foul play may have been involved. Uniformed officers are trained to secure and preserve the crime scene so no vital evidence is tampered with.

Ambulance officers and uniformed police, including the Belconnen Duty Sergeant on the day, John Collins, were the first to arrive at Gollan Street. They were greeted by a small gathering of people out the front. Friends and neighbours of Ricky's had lined the driveway. The mood was quiet and solemn, as they tried to comprehend the situation. There were more people inside the house, each consoling the other at their loss.

ACT Ambulance had been called in case there was a chance that Ricky could be resuscitated. While two ambulance officers, Ross Nulty and Adam Starr, began unloading their equipment, a third officer, Justin Hockley, went inside the house to assess the victim. The two officers hadn't even fully unpacked when Hockley returned and informed them that she was dead.

As friends and relatives milled in the living area and kitchen, police and ambulance officers examined the bedroom for any evidence that would indicate how Ricky had died. There was no obvious trauma on Ricky's body, no tampered doors or windows to indicate a break-in, so the assumption was that Ricky had died by her own hand. It wasn't only the lack of evidence pointing to foul play that prompted police to believe they had attended a suicide; only the day before neighbours called police fearing for Ricky's welfare.

The weekend beginning Friday 2 May was an emotional time for 42-year-old Ricky Conway. It was the first weekend, after an exhaustive Family Court battle only two weeks earlier, that Ricky would be without her young son, Alistaire. In fact, Ricky hadn't spent much time with Alistaire recently, after John had taken him from her a month earlier. John believed it was in Alistaire's best interest. So ensued the custody battle. The court had awarded Ricky custody and allowed John weekend visits. This was to be father and son's first weekend together after the court's ruling.

John drove to Alistaire's school to pick him up. Ricky was also there and walked Alistaire to his father's car. They then all returned to Ricky's house to collect his clothes and toys for the weekend. According to John, Ricky pleaded with him to stay at Gollan Street, as she would miss Alistaire too much. John declined and took Alistaire away, saying he would call on Sunday to arrange a time to drop off Alistaire's clothes.

Later that Friday evening, Ricky went to the local supermarket and purchased a bottle of Golden Gate Spumante. She told the sales assistant that she was having a quiet weekend at home to 'do a bit of gardening'. Ricky's drinking had been an issue in her relationship with John. He'd told people that Ricky drank excessively, that she had become reliant on alcohol as a crutch.

This weekend, Ricky was feeling abandoned and lonely. She had to deal with the knowledge that John was having an affair with another woman, and that that woman was taking care of her son. She felt Alistaire was being turned against her. She wanted her son back, and she wanted her husband back.

On Saturday afternoon, Ricky's emotions had got the better of her. According to John, she called 'a dozen times' during the day to speak with him and Alistaire, though Alistaire apparently didn't wish to speak with her. For whatever reason, and to what end, only Ricky knew, she went to her next-door neighbour's house with a peculiar request. It was a little after three in the afternoon and the only person home was a young teenage boy, Steve (not his real name).

Steve asked Ricky if he could help her. Ricky enquired if he or his mother had any rope around the house. The boy wasn't sure and asked why.

'To hang myself,' Ricky replied.

Steve froze for a few seconds, unsure what to say, but asked again to be clear, 'What do you want a rope for?'

'To hang myself,' Ricky repeated.

Steve, presumable not knowing what to do, left Ricky at the door and went looking for some rope. He returned empty handed, finding Ricky had walked inside and sat down on the couch. He explained to his mother's friend, 'Ricky, we don't have a rope … we've got an extension cord.'

'A rope would be better.'

There was silence. Steve wasn't sure what to do or say next.

'Do you have a tie?' Ricky broke the tension.

Steve went to his room and dutifully returned with a tie, handing it to Ricky. Ricky sat, feeling the fabric and observing the stitching, even commenting on it to Steve, although he didn't understand why. Ricky had been a seamstress, her father and mother were tailors, so the tie became an object of craftsmanship, not as a means to some other end.

'Thank you.' Ricky stood and left the house, returning to her home without any rope, extension cord, or the tie.

Steve thought for a moment about what had just happened. He knew it wasn't good. He couldn't wait for his mother to return home. He decided he needed to tell someone, to get Ricky some help. Steve went to a friend's house in an adjoining street and told him what had happened. They both went to Ricky's house and knocked on the door, but there was no answer. The friend jumped the fence between the garage and the house and continued knocking on windows and staring through to try and see inside. He banged on the rear door, but there was still no answer. Steve then went a couple of houses down from Ricky's, to the Dillon family.

Jacqui Dillon had known Ricky since she moved into the street, some 16 years earlier. Concerned for her friend, she phoned Ricky. After that, Jacqui went to Ricky's house. When Ricky opened the door, Jacqui immediately asked, 'What's going on?'

Ricky replied, 'Go away … can't a person die in peace?'

Jacqui brushed off Ricky's words and went inside the house. Ricky then confided in her friend, explaining how she felt. She even showed Jacqui a diary she had been keeping for the last couple of months. In it, Ricky recorded various incidents that had occurred between her and John, as well as conversations she had had with Alistaire after John had taken him away. The diary was a revelation.

The two women were interrupted when Constable Scott Clifton arrived, responding to a triple zero call: 'Attempted suicide.' Ricky became tearful and annoyed that the police had been called. She just wanted everyone to go away, and for the weekend to end. Shortly after Constable Clifton's arrival, the Duty Sergeant from Belconnen, Brian Sly, entered the house. Jacqui then left her friend with the two officers and made her way home.

Ricky explained the reason for her depression, that her marriage with John Conway was over, and that she felt John was turning young Alistaire against her. Even though she'd won in the Family Court, her son still longed for his father and Ricky was feeling left out.

Given that Ricky had mentioned to her neighbour, however unconvincingly, that she wanted to kill herself, Sergeant Sly felt it best to radio for the local Mental Health Crisis Team. Sergeant Sly received a radio message back, requesting he call John Conway. Arrangements were made to meet John later at the Belconnen Police Station.

Once the Mental Health Crisis Team arrived, both police officers left. Ricky made coffee for herself and the two members of the Crisis Team. The two healthcare professionals found Ricky to be cooperative and pleasant. She became teary when speaking of her relationship with John and Alistaire, and the failure of her marriage, but she didn't cry. The Crisis Team members observed Ricky holding her composure, showing them her depression had passed and that she was regaining her self-control. She assured them she didn't have suicidal thoughts, at least anymore. Ricky even attempted to see the humorous side to her afternoon's escapade. The Crisis Team took it as a positive sign. When they asked her what she planned to do in the coming week, she informed them she would return to work on Monday. Ricky had a casual position as a tailor at the Royal Military Academy. Ricky also informed the healthcare professionals that she had made an appointment with a drug and alcohol counsellor to try and rebuild her self-esteem and get her life back on track.

After spending an hour with her, the two Crisis Team professionals decided Ricky was not a risk to herself. They left their cards on the dining table and she promised to call them if she felt suicidal or became depressed again.

John Conway caught up with Sergeant Sly as arranged at Belconnen Police Station. John asked how his wife was, and Sergeant Sly responded that she appeared depressed and upset and that he was concerned for her welfare. He explained that the Mental Health Crisis Team were in attendance. John told Sergeant Sly that he thought Ricky was just attention seeking, that she would do this when she didn't get her own way. Her way being, according to John, to control both him and Alistaire. A check of police records against the Gollan Street address by Sergeant Sly showed there were eight calls made to Ricky and John's house over a 12-month period.

Once Ricky was alone, she ordered a pizza for dinner. She also phoned Steve and apologised for her behaviour and for all the trouble she felt she had caused him. To make amends, Ricky invited Steve over for dinner. She, most likely, would have enjoyed the company. Steve accepted her apology, though he declined the offer to share her pizza. The pizza delivery boy would be the last person to see Ricky Conway alive.

Ben Cartwright was on duty that day, Saturday, and had taken a meal break when he heard the radio call for the uniformed patrol to attend 'an attempted suicide at 35 Gollan Street'. In fact, Ben was with his colleague and boss, Detective Sergeant

Noel Lymbery. Noel was having a barbeque to celebrate moving into a new home. The two men got along well and Ben used his required respite to grab a bite and have a look around Noel's new place.

Ben waited for the uniformed officer to respond on arrival, knowing that if there was a deceased person, Ben would have to cut short his break and head over. It wasn't to be. Not then.

On Sunday 4 May, however, as Ben responded to his call out, he recalled the radio message the day before. Like the uniformed officers already in attendance, Ben presumed he was attending a suicide.

The scene at 35 Gollan Street was the same as the one that had greeted the uniformed police officers, only there was one significant person added to the group — Uniform Commander Denis McDermott. The Commander was standing with the Belconnen Duty Sergeant, John Collins. It isn't usual practice for a Commander to attend a death, but in this case, Ricky Conway was the wife of a fellow police officer, Constable John Conway. She had also worked for the AFP as a seamstress in the tailor's shop. Commander McDermott was there to give John whatever support he could.

John was an Australia Federal Police officer, attached to Traffic Operations, specifically Accident Investigation, at Weston Police Station. Officers working in Traffic perform the same duties as their State counterparts, except over the border in New South Wales they're known as the Highway Patrol. While John Conway would patrol the streets, undertake Random Breath Testing units, and perform other traffic duties, his primary job was as a draughtsman. He was employed to re-construct accident scenes in hard copy or as a computer model, to ascertain who was at fault if that was in question and present his findings in court. Ben Cartwright was a former Accident Investigation officer and had worked alongside John for four years before moving to Belconnen detectives. He knew John and Ricky well enough, as well as any colleague could know a fellow worker and his family.

Ben had a short conversation with the Commander and the Duty Sergeant. He was told John Conway had arrived earlier and identified Ricky's body. Phillip was too shaken and upset to perform the mandatory requirement. John had then gone to a neighbour's house where he waited to see if anyone wanted to talk with him.

When Ben stepped inside 35 Gollan Street he was surprised to see so many people, whatever their relationship to Ricky, milling around the lounge room. He had expected the whole house to be secured by the uniformed officers, not just the bedroom. No matter what the cause of death, Ben felt procedure needed to be observed.

The two uniformed constables who attended that day were Matthew Rippon and Phillipa Cottam. Constable Rippon led Ben to the bedroom. As Ben looked around, trying to find some evidence of how Ricky had died, he asked the constables why they thought it was a suicide. Their assumption was based on the radio call they received, stating they were to attend a 'suicide', plus the incidents of the day before. That wasn't good enough for Ben. He needed evidence, and there was none about. If it were a violent death, the evidence would be obvious. Likewise, if it were suicide, Ben would expect to find the means by which Ricky had killed herself. There was no rope, no empty bottle of sleeping pills, nothing to say how she died. It could be that Ricky just died in her sleep, though that seemed unlikely to Ben. What he knew of Ricky told him she was a healthy woman, and after all, she was only 42, not an age you'd expect someone to die in their sleep.

At that time, Ricky's death was a mystery to Ben and he wanted everyone out of the house. He requested Forensics be called to conduct a thorough inspection of the premises. The constables complied with his orders and began seeing Ricky's friends and relatives out. As the people filed past, Constable Cottam noticed a female protectively holding a book under her arm. It was a brownish coloured, hard cover exercise book. She stopped the woman, Gabby, Ricky's sister, and asked if the book came from the house. Gabby said it did, although hesitantly. Jacqui Dillon had made her aware of it. It was Ricky's diary. Constable Cottam explained that the book would have to remain, as forensics officers would need to examine it along with all of Ricky's other personal items. Gabby reluctantly gave up the book. She knew its importance, even though at that time the police did not.

As the uniformed officers were securing the house, Ben began his own careful inspection. Leaving Ricky's bedroom, Ben's attention was drawn to the toilet, which was in a room separate from the bathroom. The door was open and he stood just outside staring at it. There was something odd about it. The seat had been left up. Ben never knew a woman to leave the toilet seat up. He couldn't imagine why, if Ricky were alone in the house all weekend, the toilet seat would have been left as it was.

Ben enquired if either officer knew of anyone who had used the toilet. To the best of their knowledge, no one had. It could be that one of the Mental Health Crisis Team members from the previous evening had used the toilet, or even the person who delivered the pizza. If so, then it was likely that the toilet seat could give an estimate of the time Ricky died.

If it wasn't one of those persons, then who did use the toilet, and when?

Overall, Ricky's house was tidy and ordered. There was a place for everything and everything was in its place. In fact, through observation, you could almost say Ricky kept a fastidiously clean house.

Keys, other than Ricky's house keys, which had been left in the front door lock, were placed on a key holder near the door, along with a padlock and twined material. Decorative woollen rugs were laid out in almost every room. Ricky had furnished the lounge area with dark wooden wall units, each displaying an assortment of porcelain ornaments, vases, a crystal clock and other knick-knacks. The smoked glass coffee table still had the cards left by the two mental health professionals on it. Intricate lace doilies protected side tables, the top of a stereo speaker and the shelf area of the wall units. The three-seater lounge and its two accompanying chairs were covered in heavy plush, patterned fabric. Plain material had been folded and placed over the seats to protect them from wear. A small, red plastic child's chair sat beside, what appeared to be, the main chair. Prints of paintings and a collection of decorative plates adorned the walls. A sheepskin rug lay in front of the enclosed fireplace.

The dining area was small, but large enough to have a French-polished, extendable table with six matching chairs around it, along with a corner wall unit and separate chest of draws. A mounted wall display held more decorative plates, ornate beer steins and silver wine goblets. Coats and other outdoor apparel hung on a rack near the laundry. The light covers in both the lounge and dining rooms were made from material, with frills attached for extra effect.

Alistaire's room was incredibly neat and tidy for a seven-year-old. A dinosaur collection was all laid out on a table at the foot of his bed. There were two other tables in the room, one being home to all his soft toys, while the other, near the head of his bed, had action figures and other plastic toys. More soft toys, a toucan, bunny rabbit and teddy bear, among others, lined the top of a cupboard. Inside, was a collection of books and smaller toys in old ice-cream containers. Posters of Hollywood's *Toy Story*, dinosaurs and other things that had taken his interest were covering the walls and behind his door. Alistaire's clothes were either hanging or had been folded neatly in his wardrobe. There was nothing left lying around, except for one pair of shoes.

Even the two towels in the bathroom were folded carefully and placed over the railing. The only exception to Ricky's neatness could be found in the kitchen. The pizza carton sat on a bench with only half its contents consumed. There were unwashed cups and glasses in the sink, obviously from when she had played hostess to her unwanted guests, the police and the healthcare professionals.

As Ben made his way around the house and observed the order with which Ricky lived, down to the cleared cups and glasses, he wasn't convinced he was in the house of a person who had planned to commit suicide.

Once the house had been cleared, Ben instructed the officers to begin a search of all rooms. Everything and anything they found, however insignificant, was to be written down in their notebooks for the forensic investigators to photograph and examine. If Ricky had met with foul play, maybe the perpetrator had left behind a clue.

Phillipa Cottam began her search in the kitchen. She emptied the cupboards, eventually finding various over the counter and prescription medications. She lined them up on the bench, under the cupboard where they had been stored, for the medical officer to identify. She spent nearly half an hour in the kitchen before moving on to the rest of the house. Both officers searched the entire house, but found nothing to suggest how Ricky had died.

As the house was being searched, Ben walked outside and phoned Noel Lymbery on his mobile. Ben wasn't sure what he was dealing with, but he was sure Noel needed to take charge. He also contacted Operations and asked for them to send out a forensics team, Crime Scene officers. There was little for Ben to do but wait until forensics and the medical examiner had done their work.

It is actually rare for detectives to be treading around a crime scene before forensics officers have conducted their examinations. In some cases, the detectives may have to wait hours, or days before walking the scene. While waiting for Noel and the Crime Scene officers, Ben decided he'd visit John Conway at the neighbour's house, if only to give his sympathies.

John was seated at a table, slowly sipping on a cup of tea. Ben extended his condolences. John tried to talk, but periodically broke down. He'd bury his head in his hands and his body would shake with grief. Given the state John was in, Ben realised it was pointless asking any questions. He had John's assurance that he would call into Belconnen Police Station the following day to make a statement. Ben patted John on the back and suggested he go home; there was nothing he could achieve crying into his tea. John took Ben's advice and left.

During Ben's time as a police officer, particularly working in Accident Investigations, he had seen people grieve for the loss of a loved one. Not everyone cries; sometimes there's anger, denial, sometimes numbness and disbelief. Outside the house, people were grieving for Ricky in their own way, trying to accept the loss of a daughter, sister, mother and friend. John's behaviour just didn't ring true with Ben. In all the time Ben had worked with John, John never spoke positively about Ricky. He would always complain about her, and accused her of drinking too much and being too possessive. Ben had not been surprised to learn that John had moved out.

To Ben, John was acting like a man who was pretending to be grief-stricken. He didn't know why. Perhaps John was reacting the way he thought he should. Maybe it was guilt and not grief, given the way he usually spoke of Ricky. Perhaps John was hiding something. Whatever the reason, the only way he could describe his conversation with John was 'bizarre'. He used the exact word to Noel when they met up outside 35 Gollan Street.

Noel was briefed on all Ben knew and what had been done to date. Like Ben, Noel wasn't convinced they were dealing with a suicide. Noel's 20 years' experience as a police officer told him it was just all wrong. Noel couldn't see any reason for Ricky to die. Nothing that had been observed by any of the police made sense, if the suicide theory were to be accepted.

To better understand the situation, Noel spoke with Jacqui Dillon about the incident that occurred the day before. He wanted to know Ricky's state of mind, to find out if there was any substance in her wanting to take her own life. After hearing what had happened, Noel agreed Ricky was depressed, but her attempt at suicide, if it could be called an attempt, wasn't genuine. It seemed to Noel to be the actions of a lonely, confused person, who felt she didn't have control of her life.

Something had happened in Ricky's house within the past 24 hours that led to her death, but it wasn't clear what. That was the problem Noel and Ben had. What really happened to Ricky, when did it happen, and who was involved? They hoped the more detailed search by Crime Scene officers would give them some answers, or at least leads to finding the answers.

Forensics officers Robert 'Bob' Atkins and Phillip Turner began a detailed inspection of Ricky's bedroom, recording their findings and taking photographs. They were in the room with Dr Sanjiv Jain, the forensic pathologist. Meanwhile, Ben Cartwright checked the front and rear doors and windows in each of the rooms, and the manhole cover to the ceiling, trying to find any sign of forced entry. All the accesses to the house were secure. It didn't appear that anyone had broken in. So, if Ricky was murdered, or even a victim of misadventure, then she either knew her assailants, or they were able to talk their way in, or an opportunity existed for them to gain entry without causing any disturbance.

The bedside table, on the side where Ricky was lying, was of great interest to the forensics officers. On it were a packet of Horizon cigarettes, an ashtray with four butts in it and a tightly wrapped small piece of paper, a plastic fluid lighter and a jewellery box. Everything was photographed in situ, as it first appeared when the officers walked in. Then each item was examined closely, and photographs taken. The packet of Horizon was opened, revealing 18 cigarettes remaining. A tiny piece of jewellery, an earring stud, was found on the floor next to the bed, about a centimetre long, along with a piece of black fibre.

Dr Jain began examining Ricky's body, making preliminary observations at the scene. He and the forensics officers found vegetable matter, just below Ricky's ear, in the fold of the neck. A second piece of vegetable matter was found on the top sheet, when the doona was pulled back, on the opposite side to where Ricky lay. A very fine piece of hair, curled to form an arc, was located on Ricky's elbow. Each of the discovered items were bagged and labelled for further analysis at the forensic lab.

The officers continued their inspection, going to the laundry, where they found a rubbish bin. They placed the contents on the ground. The bin contained an empty spumante bottle, cask of wine, various foodstuffs and two popper-style juice containers. In the fireplace in the lounge room, they sifted through the ash and various unburnt and partially burnt objects were extracted. Amongst those objects was a folded piece of aluminium foil. When opened, the foil was measured to be ten centimetres by ten centimetres.

Ben's toilet seat, as it would be referred to later by Noel and the other detectives, was photographed. The bowl was examined. It could be that Ricky had lifted the toilet seat to then vomit into the bowl. Nothing was noticed to support that theory. The bowl was clean. Water from the bowl was taken for analysis.

The forensics officers had done all they could for that night. There was little point examining the exterior of the property till daylight the next day. The government contractor arrived and conveyed Ricky's body to Kingston Forensic Medical Centre. Even though the street had been sealed off earlier, Noel instructed an officer to remain on guard at the house as he and Ben made their way to their office at Belconnen Police Station.

Although it was late, Noel and Ben still had work to do. They discussed what needed to be done next, what priorities they would give to the various tasks, and who, out of the detectives' pool at Belconnen, would be given those tasks. Noel and Ben worked until just after two the following morning, giving themselves only a few hours' sleep before returning to continue their investigation.

CHAPTER THREE

Monday 5 May 1997

Persons of interest

John Conway arrived at Belconnen Police Station at around
10.30 on Monday 5 May. He was dishevelled. His world had
been taken from him. Ben Cartwright showed John to an
interview room and took down all he said in relation to his
marriage with Ricky and the events leading up to her death.
John couldn't help but sob while he gave his statement.

Giving the formalities of date of birth and address, 42-year-
old John told Ben he had moved out of Gollan Street the
previous March and was, at the time, living in a house in the
outer south-western suburb of Rivett. The house belonged to an
elderly couple who understood John's situation and had taken
him in after he left Ricky.

John began his statement saying he met Ricky in 1986, when
she was working at the Australian Federal Police tailor's shop,
located at the Weston Police Complex, with her mother and
father, Anna and Phillip Reiners. John and Ricky struck up a
relationship, and after only a few months, moved in together.

Alistaire was born in March 1990, and Ricky and John married in August 1991.

The relationship was good, according to John, in the earlier years, but things soured. John blamed Ricky's drinking. He admitted that both he and Ricky enjoyed a drink, but he felt Ricky had taken it too far and had begun drinking excessively. He even gave up the alcohol, hoping it would help Ricky, but she continued to indulge, becoming aggressive and demanding. Ricky had become dependent. She'd become an alcoholic. She would call John to find out where he was and what he was doing several times a day. Towards the end of their marriage, she told John she didn't trust him and didn't love him. John told Ben that he didn't believe Ricky really felt that way, that it was the alcohol speaking.

Over the years he and Ricky were together, John admitted that the police had been contacted a number of times to 'intervene in disputes'. Ricky and neighbours made the calls, and even Alistaire had called. John said he phoned the police once as well.

On 11 March, Ricky and John were having an argument, though John couldn't recall what it was about, and Ricky summoned the police. According to John, when police arrived, Ricky said she didn't want him in the house anymore and told him to leave. He did. He quickly packed a few of his clothes and left. He slept in his car for a couple of days and then was taken in by the elderly couple.

John returned to Gollan Street periodically over the next couple of weeks, mainly to see his son. During these visits, he stated he observed that Alistaire was having problems living with Ricky and arguments would erupt. The tension between mother and son also led to more arguments with John.

Alistaire stayed overnight at John's temporary accommodation on 1 April. Ricky didn't object. The next day, John and Alistaire went back to Gollan Street. John said he noticed Ricky was intoxicated and aggressive, so he decided to stay for a while and help get Alistaire's meal and ready him for bed. Then, when John was in his shed packing boxes he heard Alistaire and Ricky arguing. He walked back in the house and witnessed Ricky striking Alistaire. It was then that John decided to take his son away, as he felt Alistaire would be better off.

Concerned for his son's welfare, John went to the local court and took out a restraining order against Ricky on Alistaire's behalf. Ricky then made a formal complaint against John to the AFP Internal Investigations Department, accusing him of hitting her on the night of 2 April. Ricky, however, later withdrew her complaint.

The Family Court decided the issue of who would have custody of Alistaire on 23 April. The court ruled in favour of Ricky and gave John weekend visiting rights. John admitted to Ben the ruling upset him as he couldn't see Alistaire every day, but he acknowledged he appreciated the condition the court placed on Ricky, that she was to give up alcohol. John hoped she would. That evening, John returned Alistaire to his mother and stayed the night to help his son settle in, sleeping in his son's room.

Ricky invited John back the next night 24 April, to discuss future plans. Ricky wanted John back and even proposed they all move to Queensland together, to have a new start as a family. John had put in an application to transfer to the Queensland Police, a move he had been planing for some time. The night degenerated into an argument. John blamed Ricky's drinking as the contributing factor. Ricky ordered John out and told him she had called the police. John complied and waited outside. When the police arrived he told them what had happened and left.

The next day, Anzac Day, Ricky phoned John in the morning and he went around to Gollan Street. The situation was calmer and John spent the day with Ricky and Alistaire. He didn't see

Ricky again till Friday 2 May, though he had spoken to her on the phone during that time.

John detailed the events of the weekend, from Friday 2 to Sunday 4 May, when he picked up Alistaire from school and took him to his home for the weekend. Ricky apparently called several times during the Saturday to speak with both John and Alistaire, but, as stated by John, Alistaire didn't wish to speak with his mother. Late Saturday evening, Ricky called John again. She was angry and upset, though John couldn't tell if she had been drinking or was just very tired. Ricky told him about the Mental Health Crisis team and how the police had been called to Gollan Street because she had attempted suicide. John felt Ricky was blaming him for what had happened.

Ricky had attempted suicide in the past, and often spoke about taking her own life, according to John. He recalled two incidents. One time Ricky told him she had tried to hang herself with a necktie but it didn't work. The other was when she held a knife to her stomach and threatened to kill herself in front of him. John dismissed both incidents as just Ricky's way of seeking attention. He told Ben that he had saved Ricky's messages she had left on his mobile the Saturday afternoon, suggesting she would kill herself. John allowed Ben access to his mobile message bank to retrieve the messages. He also handed over a recent photo of Ricky for the police to use.

John signed his statement and left. Again, Ben gave his condolences. It was more a courtesy than an actual feeling that John deserved it. Ben couldn't believe everything John had said, and was particularly suspicious of his behaviour. His instincts told him that John was portraying himself too much as the victim within the relationship and that his grieving was too extreme.

During the time Ben worked in Traffic Operations, he never knew John to be overly emotional about anything. He was a 'cool customer', almost emotionally detached. The birth of Alistaire and even his marriage to Ricky seemed to come and go with very little fanfare or celebration from John on either occasion.

Ben and John did socialise, or rather share coffee and have the occasional meal break together at work. Ben was interested in John's work, how he applied his engineering skills to reconstruct an accident scene and thus be able to determine who was at fault. John wasn't one to socialise outside of working hours with the other male officers. In fact, Ben can't remember him ever having any 'mates' as such, male or female, though he did gravitate towards the females in the section.

The women in Traffic all thought of John as a gentlemen. He was polite and courteous. He was a quiet type, always sitting in the background. John wasn't what Ben describes as a 'blokey bloke'. He didn't follow sport or express any other interest that may have been shared by the others. He kept to himself. Although, there would be occasions, after speaking to Ricky on the phone, that John would become annoyed and tell whoever would listen about how hard it was to live with his wife. As in his statement, he told people how controlling and possessive Ricky was and that her drinking was becoming excessive.

Ben felt the John he had dealt with on Sunday and Monday was not the John he knew from their days together in Traffic Operations. While it is possible to feel the loss of someone you may not love, because of guilt or a realisation you do care for them, Ben wasn't convinced John was really feeling anything. But why the pretence? Why 'put it on' when Ben and other police knew better, knew what John really thought of Ricky? It didn't make sense. Nothing concerning Ricky's death made any sense.

Ben dialled John's message bank and recorded Ricky's messages. There were three messages left on Saturday afternoon at 3.28, 3.39 and 3.44, shortly after Ricky had gone to her next-door neighbour's looking for a piece of rope.

The first messages said, at 3.28: 'I know you never sort of um, answer your messages, but I hope to God you get this one. You've won him, you can have him, you and Kathy can have him, I'll be dead tomorrow. I've had enough. [Ricky crying] I've had enough, John, I'm not going to let you put me through this anymore. Bye. I love you.'

The second message at 3.39: 'John, I would've liked to have spoken to you in person. Unfortunately, it's impossible. I just want you to know [crying] even though all that you've done, I still love you, and always will, and I'll take that up to heaven with me. Thank you. Bye.'

The third message at 3.44 — 'Hi honey. I call you honey because it's the last time I'm talking to you. Um, I'm going to join Dad. I can't um, live like this anymore.'

The messages didn't prove Ricky had committed suicide. Ben believed it was Ricky's way of trying to get at John, although they certainly revealed Ricky's depressed state of mind at the time. It was well before the Mental Health Crisis Team had spoken with Ricky, when, as the two health professionals found, Ricky had overcome her depression and was looking forward to her future.

What also interested Ben was why did John save those messages? John had admitted Ricky called several times a day, particularly over that weekend. Surely, she had left other messages. Maybe? Maybe not? Either way, why save them?

While Ben was taking John Conway's statement, Noel Lymbery was briefing his bosses on Ricky's death and what action his detectives would take next. The enquiry into Ricky Conway's death was given the unofficial title of Operation Gollan, after the street where Ricky had lived.

Being the wife of a police officer, and also a former employee of the AFP, Ricky's death and any subsequent investigation was of interest to senior management. There wasn't much to report at this early stage as the cause of death still had to be decided. The autopsy was scheduled for later that afternoon. Noel did inform Commanders McDermott and Dau (Jon Dau being Detective Commander) and ACT Chief Police Officer Bill Stoll that he believed Ricky's death was suspicious. Both Commanders and the Chief of Police weren't allowing themselves to agree or disagree with Noel. They wanted to see more evidence.

It was the lack of any evidence indicating a suicide that Noel saw as suspicious. Even so, he accepted management's caution. The autopsy would hopefully decide the direction of the investigation.

Noel was known for speaking his mind, but never carelessly. He would give an opinion based on information available and his own experience. Whether others agreed or disagreed with Noel, they knew his judgment had merit. That's not to say Noel was stubborn. He valued other people's input and encouraged differing points of view. Some of Noel's colleagues described him as a 'red cordial' type of personality, hyperactive in the extreme, yet even-tempered and methodical in his approach to his team and the investigation.

Prior to being with Belconnen Detectives, Noel had spent eight years in what was then Special Operations, which evolved during the mid 80s into what is now known as Protection.

By the early 90s, Noel decided he wanted to get back to day-to-day policing. There were those in the AFP who didn't support Noel's transfer, believing he wasn't up to being a 'real copper'. Their reaction only spurred Noel on to prove them wrong.

In 1994 Noel arrived at Belconnen, after spending 18 months with Internal Investigations. As Noel puts it, 'getting a view of the Federal Police from the outside in'. It helped Noel understand the police environment better. After spending some time in the Belconnen's Burglary Task Force, Noel eventually moved into the detective sergeant's seat.

The reason why Noel went to see Mr Stoll wasn't only to brief him and the Commanders. It was to get their support for his detectives at Belconnen. Noel knew that if it was proven Ricky had been murdered the investigation would become high profile. This meant Internal Security and Audit (ISA) could be brought in to take over. ISA is a group of highly trained officers who are tasked to 'big jobs', such as frauds, extortions, drugs and homicides that involve the AFP.

Noel was concerned that his detectives would have done all the groundwork, only to end up handing the case over to ISA. He didn't want that happening and wanted assurances his team would remain on the investigation, irrespective of management's decision to bring in ISA or not. Noel respected his team and didn't want to see their hard work being overlooked. The Commanders and Mr Stoll agreed that Noel and his team would remain on the case, no matter what.

At the Kingston Forensic Medical Centre, Noel and Ben met up with Dr Jain to witness the autopsy on Ricky's body. Bob Atkins and Phil Turner also attended. If a cause of death could be found, even a likely cause suggested, then Noel would know where to start the investigation and the forensics officers would have a better idea of what to look for.

As the autopsy began a bruise was visible on Ricky's inner left elbow. The bruising was quite small, and at the centre was what Noel identified as a needle-stick injury. In fact, the size of the needle hole appeared larger than normal. Noel had seen enough track marks, needle marks, on drug addicts to know that Ricky's was oversized. It meant that Ricky had been injected with a large gauge needle, or, and it seemed incredible to Noel, that a needle had been placed in the same hole at least twice, thus spreading the hole wider.

The bruising was also an issue for Noel. He'd never seen any drug addict inject themselves in such a way as to produce the heavy, dark discolouration he saw with Ricky. To Noel, it was obvious the needle had gone through to the submembrane, causing a severe rupture. He didn't know any druggie that was stupid enough to cause such an injury.

Noel asked Dr Jain to cut around the needle mark to preserve it, so he could have it tested later.

What Noel wanted to do was see if he could locate anyone to examine the hole for tool marks, to determine if a large needle was used, or whether it was two or more smaller ones. He knew it was possible to get tool marks from hard surfaces, but he didn't know if it was possible to make the same tests on skin. Noel planned to find an expert somewhere that could help him, even if it meant calling overseas.

At this early stage of the investigation, there were two significant observations that gave Noel and Ben reason to believe Ricky's death was suspicious. Ben had his toilet seat, and Noel his needle mark. Both men would be known for launching a murder enquiry based on their individual observations, though this was not entirely true.

With no other trauma or obvious signs to indicate how Ricky died, the needle mark was the only significant injury, which led the detectives to believe they were dealing with a drug death. What they weren't sure of was whether Ricky had administered it herself, or if she had been experimenting with another person who accidentally overdosed her, panicked and left the scene. Again, both Noel and Ben had attended enough overdoses to know that they would have expected to find a needle with Ricky, had she injected herself, but there was none. It would be highly unlikely for Ricky to have overdosed and be conscious enough to clean up and get rid of the needle. Those who overdose pass out within seconds and are often found with the needle still inserted in their arm. So, the latter scenario had to be considered, that there was someone with her when she died.

The other theory was, again, that someone was with Ricky, but had deliberately injected her to kill her. Certainly, the bruising found on the left arm would not have occurred had an experienced drug user been helping Ricky to 'shoot up'. Noel felt whoever administered the needle to Ricky used force and had no consideration for her at all. It's the only way he could explain the bruising. As a policeman Noel knew how junkies shot-up. He also knew about needes from having been brought up on a farm, where he would treat animals using various gauge needles.

No other puncture marks were found on Ricky's body to indicate she had previously injected drugs. There were also no marks on her arms or anywhere on her body to show she'd been held down, or that any amount of force was used to subdue her.

Examining the organs, Dr Jain found all was normal, except the lungs and liver, which on closer examination, indicated heart failure. The lungs revealed a condition known as bilateral pulmonary oedema, that is, fluid on the lungs. When the liver was dissected, there was a pooling of blood around the veins, indicating acute central venous congestion. This is when the blood, instead of being sent up to the heart and distributed through the body, is suddenly stopped, creating a pooling effect. Both bilateral pulmonary oedema and acute central venous congestion are indicators of heart failure.

In short, Ricky died from heart failure, but what caused that heart failure was yet to be confirmed. It certainly seemed it was caused by the ingestion of a toxin. What toxin would be the responsibility of the Government Analytical Laboratories to determine. It would be weeks before the substance was identified. Till then, the police worked on an educated guess. Heroin.

With the cause of death being a suspected overdose, Noel and Ben visited Anna Reiners, Ricky's mother. Ricky called her affectionately, the 'old cheese'. Anna is a sweet, gentle woman, a loving mum who cares for her family. It was just over 40 years ago that Anna, her husband, Phillip, and two young daughters, Gabby and Ricky, immigrated to Australia from Germany. Even after all that time, Anna's heritage was obvious by her accent.

It was the day after Ricky's death and Anna was still in shock, still trying to understand what had happened. She was angry. She couldn't believe it. Not Ricky. Not so soon after Anna's husband had died. About seven months earlier Ricky's father had lost his battle against cancer. Now, Anna had to deal with the loss of her younger daughter.

When Noel and Ben told Anna they suspected Ricky had died from an overdose, she told them, 'I have no doubt John Conway murdered my daughter … you make sure you lock him up for murdering my daughter.' She explained Ricky would never have done such a thing to herself, because she had a phobia about needles and was anti-drugs.

Anna believed the motive was money. Her husband had changed his will before he died. Anna and her husband suspected John would harm Ricky, so the family home was left to Ricky. In her father's will she wasn't allowed to sell it, only to live in it. He was providing for her. In this way John could not benefit from Ricky's inheritance.

Gabby and Ricky's son, Phillip, supported Anna's allegation. Gabby had actually confronted John at the house on the night of Ricky's death telling him, 'Now you've achieved what you set out to do.' John just stared at her.

They explained to Noel and Ben that Ricky was under John's

spell. He had isolated her from her friends and family. He kept money from her so she couldn't go out. Gabby, who worked as a clerical assistant with the AFP, recalled the times John would see her and 'badmouth' Ricky to her. It was as though he was trying to turn her family against Ricky.

Phillip knew Ricky as a loving and caring mother, who was always smiling and laughing, even during the worst of times. Phillip was her son from a previous marriage. While being married to John, Ricky had changed. She'd lost her self-esteem and was at an all-time low. Phillip and John didn't get along. They had moments when they would confront each other, but they never came to blows. Phillip didn't like the control John had over his mother and his young brother. John undermined Ricky's authority and encouraged Alistaire to talk back to his mother. Phillip had tried to help his mother escape the relationship, but she wouldn't leave.

John had left Ricky in March to be with his girlfriend, Kathy McFie. Ricky's family told the detectives they always suspected John and Kathy were having an affair, and Ricky had learned the truth only about a month before her death. Kathy had been a friend of Ricky's.

Anna and Gabby explained John's manipulative character by telling Noel about the events surrounding Alistaire's last birthday. It was just after John had left home. Alistaire wanted to have his birthday at McDonald's, but Ricky couldn't afford to pay. John told her he would cover the cost and the party was booked. John was working the day of his son's birthday, but told Ricky that Kathy would turn up with the money. Kathy had a headache and couldn't attend. John then agreed to meet Ricky at McDonald's. The party was under way, but despite frantic phone calls from Ricky to John, he never showed. Ricky was forced to drive to Gabby's house in an attempt to borrow the money, but her sister wasn't at home. Ricky continued to call

John. Eventually, John arrived to pay the bill, well after the party had ended.

To Anna and Gabby, the birthday incident was just another attempt by John and Kathy to discredit and embarrass Ricky in front of Alistaire, his friends and their parents.

After the Family Court hearing, Gabby said she had been helping Ricky seek counselling and find a new home. Ricky was getting back on her feet and was looking forward to her future with her young son. She didn't know of any reason why Ricky would want to kill herself. It must have been John. It couldn't be anyone else.

It was a very serious allegation, though Ben and Noel weren't surprised the family felt the way they did. If what they said was true, it was easy to think John could be responsible for Ricky's death. It would explain his poor acting and why there were no signs of forced entry found at the house. Even though Ricky had kicked John out, it was likely he still possessed a key.

The allegation put enormous pressure on the two detectives and how they ran the investigation. John Conway was a police officer, and if he did kill Ricky, and the investigation failed to prove it, then Noel and Ben could be accused of protecting one of their own. The Reiners family would be the first to complain.

Even worse for them was if they didn't solve the case and an internal audit of the investigation revealed they'd missed a vital piece of evidence. How do you explain that to a grieving family? They want results, and the police have to deliver.

Investigating a fellow officer meant everything Noel and Ben did would come under close scrutiny, during and after the enquiry. Scrutiny would come from Ricky's family, AFP management and the media. In Ben's words, 'We knew we'd have to cross our T's and dot our I's ... as is the case in any investigation, but more so when your suspect is a police officer.'

Carefully broaching the subject, Noel asked Anna if she had noticed anything to indicate, or knew if Ricky had used drugs. Anna gave an emphatic 'no'. She'd already told them that Ricky was anti-drugs and would never take them. Noel would have liked to accept Anna's trust in her daughter, but experience told him that most mothers think the best of their children. He and Ben would have to talk to friends and associates, and do their background checks to make sure.

Before seeing Anna Reiners, Noel had made some phone calls organising as many police as he could to meet at 35 Gollan Street. He wanted to have the place searched top to bottom for any possible drug paraphernalia. Noel even enlisted the help of two very experienced AFP drug squad detectives, Darren Rath and Dave Harrison. Their knowledge would be invaluable in identifying any common household item that might be used to administer or process drugs. They would also help in being accustomed to the hiding places which druggies use to stash their gear. If there were any drugs, a syringe or any other item used for drugs in the house, Noel was determined to find it.

A total of eight detectives assembled at Gollan Street. The two forensics specialists, the drug squad officers, Noel and Ben, and two other detectives from Belconnen, Constables Patriza Costa and David Quilty. Bob Atkins and Phillip Turner, the forensics officers, picked up where they had left off from the night before, examining Ricky's bedroom. The others searched the remainder of the house, the garage and a shed.

The ashtray sitting on Ricky's bedside table took the forensics investigators' interest, particularly the tightly scrunched up piece of paper. The paper was removed and carefully unfolded. It had red writing on it and was identified as packaging for an alcohol swab, the type used to sterilise the skin before administering a needle. On further examination, swabs were also found scrunched up and discarded in the ashtray, not obvious at first glance. This discovery raised more questions than answers. After all, if Ricky had been injected forcibly, why bother sterilising the skin?

Finding the swabs might show Ricky had taken the drug willingly, and that it had all gone horribly wrong. Whatever their hypothesis, the detectives knew the answer would be with whoever gave Ricky the drug.

There was nothing else found in the house, other than the piece of foil found in the fireplace the night before that could be linked to Ricky having drugs, or drugs having been on the premises. The garage, however, was a different story. Sifting through the clutter, which greatly contrasted with the tidiness of the house, the detectives came across a number of syringes located in a drawer of an old cupboard. There were around 14 syringes all in different sizes. Some were still in their packaging and some had the needle attached. They were dusty and a few were discoloured.

Noel wasn't convinced any of the syringes would be what they were looking for, but he was curious why John had so many. If John had killed Ricky, he would have ditched the syringe, not put it back where the police would find it. John was cleverer than that. Then again, it could be that John didn't actually do the killing, but employed someone to do it.

While Noel didn't know John as well as Ben, he knew him by reputation. 'Killer' Conway was his nickname. Not because he had ever killed anyone, but because as a Traffic officer John never issued cautions to motorists, only tickets. Most patrol officers ended their shift having written out five or six tickets and probably cautioned the same number. John would return to the station with a fistload, more than doubling his colleagues' efforts. John booked everyone for everything, however minor the infringement.

Noel saw John's zeal as arrogance, and evidence of his own need to have a sense of power and superiority over others. If

Noel was right about John's personality, and John did kill Ricky, then Noel knew they would have to look hard to find any link. It wasn't going to be easy. Noel and Ben agreed to have a half-kilometre sweep of the area around Gollan Street conducted the next day.

Although John Conway appeared to be the prime suspect in Ricky's death, Noel and Ben still kept an open mind. They didn't want to be accused of being blinkered. With any investigation, police adopt a broad approach. They then make enquiries about all the information they receive to narrow their focus and eventually uncover the truth.

Noel and Ben had another person of interest to investigate. He'd come to their attention through interviews with family, friends and neighbours of Ricky's. Mark (not his real name) was seen visiting Ricky on several occasions well before the weekend of her death. It was also established that Mark sold and used marijuana, and possibly speed. He'd been known to inject speed. He knew Ricky through her son, Phillip, and had been a family friend for years. Mark even baby-sat and did odd jobs around the house for Ricky in his younger days.

Mark, therefore, became someone who could 'help police with their enquiries'.

It was 2.30 Tuesday morning when Noel and Ben finished their work. They would have gone on, but fatigue had caught up with them. As for Mark, Noel decided he could wait till later in the day.

CHAPTER FOUR

Ulrike Conway née Reiners

Ricky, as she was commonly known, was born Ulrike Reiners in Germany on 17 March 1955. She was the younger of two daughters of Anna and Phillip Reiners. Her sister, Gabriele, was born six years earlier.

Ricky was a gregarious, happy-go-lucky child with a sweet tooth, a mischievous sense of humour she inherited from her father, and a love of the outdoors. Perhaps knowing her mother wished for a boy the second time around, Ricky became the neighbourhood tomboy, preferring the rough and tumble games to dolls and tea parties. Although six years younger, Ricky would always look out for Gabby and never hesitated taking on any kid, boy or girl, who teased or upset her. She even embarrassed Gabby by playing cupid, inviting boys home to meet her older sister. Ricky and Gabby were each other's best friend, having had a nomadic start to life, as their parents moved continents in search of a better life.

Ricky's parents had lived through one war, seen their country divided into east and west, and heard of fellow countrymen dying on barbed wire as they tried to escape across the Berlin Wall. The year after Ricky's birth there was even more turmoil threatening the stability of Europe and the world. In 1956 an uprising in Hungary, part of Eastern Europe, saw the Russian military respond with force. Around the same time, Britain, France and Israel joined in a military intervention to prevent Egyptian President General Nasser from nationalising the Suez Canal. Although they were living in the 'free' West Germany, the Reiners believed Europe was a powder keg, just waiting for another reason to go to war. They didn't think it was a safe place to bring up children and decided to immigrate somewhere far from trouble. It was decided they would apply to the United Sates of America and Australia. They had no preference. They would go to whichever country first accepted them. Australia granted the Reiners residence, but in 1956 Phillip and Anna weren't ready to leave Germany and declined.

In April of 1957 the Reiners were in Cologne and visited the Australian Embassy. It was an impulsive decision. Anna and Phillip were interviewed at length, and at the end the official asked when they would like to travel. The question took both by surprise; they weren't expecting to be accepted so quickly. In a jocular tone, Phillip replied, 'Yesterday would be good.'

Neither Anna nor Phillip thought anymore about it, till they arrived home that afternoon. They discovered Phillip's mother sitting and crying in the house. When they enquired what was upsetting her, she replied, 'You're going to Australia ... the papers are on your desk.'

The Australian Embassy official had taken Phillip seriously and delivered the final paperwork to the Reiners' home soon after speaking with them. The Embassy even advised they travel by plane, as the official thought the boat trip would have been too hard on the young parents and the two girls. In June that same year, the Reiners arrived in Australia, settling in Bonegilla, a government migrant centre in the Wodonga district of Victoria near the border of New South Wales.

Soon after setting foot in Australia Phillip began looking for work to support his family. His search took him to Canberra where he secured a position at a menswear store, relocating his family to, first Yarralumla, then Deakin, both southern suburbs of Canberra.

While the locations were close to where Phillip worked, the living arrangements weren't ideal. The Reiners were sharing with other families. It was the domestic discord of their housemates that forced the Reiners to eventually move east, just over the border of the Australian Capital Territory to Queanbeyan in New South Wales. In 1958, the Reiners had also started their own business, a tailor's shop in Civic, Canberra's city centre.

Initially, Anna and Phillip would catch the bus to work, that was, when Phillip was allowed to board. A bus driver once refused Phillip passage saying he wasn't a 'worker', just because he wore a tailored suit and not overalls. It is still a mystery why the bus driver would have displayed such prejudice towards Phillip. The incident with the bus, plus the fact that the Reiners' business demanded they work ridiculously long hours, forced the family to leave Queanbeyan and take up residence on the floor of their shop.

Ricky and Gabby's back yard became the retail shops, businesses and eateries in central Canberra. When Ricky wasn't getting under her parents' feet, lost in the off-cuts of fabric, she'd be found window shopping, hand in hand with Gabby. That was, until Ricky's hunger drove her to seek out food. Slipping away from her older sister, Ricky would go to one of her favourite places, Seven Seas, a fish restaurant that sold takeaway fish'n'chips. Ricky would stand at the counter of the Seven Seas and plead for some hot chips, saying she was hungry and that her parents didn't feed her. The vendors knew better, but they fell for the chubby little girl's big brown eyes and gave in to her demand. Ricky loved food, especially palmares, pastries sprinkled with 'hundreds and thousands' which her mother would have ready for her in the afternoons.

Although Ricky was an active child, she couldn't help but put on weight. Despite Anna's best efforts to control Ricky's eating habits, Ricky would always find food, even if her mother had hidden all the treats. For Anna, getting young Ricky on a diet and keeping her on it was a losing battle.

By 1962, the Reiners finally found their family home in the north Canberra suburb of Downer, after having spent a couple of years in a unit at the simplistic cubiform style Northbourne Flats, considered a prestigious address at the time. The house in Downer was new, part of the then expanding urban sprawl of the city as the population began to grow, numbering just over 50,000. The house was so new that Gabby decided to look out at the view from the lounge room window and fell through the unfinished flooring. The builders had left a drop cloth covering the hole. It wasn't quite ready to be inhabited.

Once it was finished and they had moved into in a 'real' home, Ricky soon made friends with the neighbourhood kids, particularly the boys. They would lean over the fence and yell for Ricky to join them on one of their suburban adventures. She was a popular member of the gang. In Anna's words Ricky was 'robust' and could mix it with any of the boys, climbing trees, rummaging through a building site and playing tag. Ricky would often return home in the afternoon, her clothes covered in dirt, sporting the odd cut and bruise, trophies of her neighbourhood escapades.

In 1968 Anna and Phillip sold their tailoring business and Phillip took employment with a company selling stainless steel cookware door to door. The cookware company asked Phillip if he would set up a dealership in Germany. The opportunity to return to their homeland was too great and the Reiners boarded the boat, renting out their home in Downer. They weren't sure how long they would be away. The company suggested it would take a minimum of five years to establish the business. Anna thought the move would be permanent. Unfortunately, Phillip wasn't given the support from the company he had hoped for and after two years they returned to Australia.

During the time in Germany, Ricky had blossomed from a tomboy into an attractive young woman. She shed her 'baby fat', as well as her desire to climb trees and wrestle with the boys. Her appearance — clothes, hair, and even make-up — became important to her. She was no different to any other teenage girl.

The change in Ricky was noticed by her neighbourhood friends. When Ricky returned to Downer, the kids were excited to have their mate back. One by one they craned their necks over the back fence to greet her. 'Ricky's back, Ricky's back,' Anna could hear the boys calling to each other from the veranda. But as each boy saw Ricky for the first time, they fell speechless. Ricky was no longer just 'one of the guys', and the boys now lined up to ask her for a date.

At 16, Ricky left school, secured a position with ICL, a computer business, and enrolled in a secretarial course at TAFE. In 1973, Ricky's parents had started a business located in The Boulevard, off Arkuna Street in the city's centre, selling imported carpets, antique furniture, porcelain, crystal ware, Meissen figurines and other knick-knacks. Ricky asked her parents if she could work for them. They naturally agreed and so started a long working relationship.

After a time at The Boulevard, the Reiners moved their business to Belconnen, in western Canberra. They ceased importing carpets, but added other items to their inventory, such as dinner sets and other home accessories. The business didn't go so well, as it soon became evident that the items were too pricey for the area.

Eventually the Reiners sold the business, or at least the fittings to the shop, and Phillip picked up a job with a landscaping company. It wasn't to last too long, not after Phillip went to clear away what he perceived was a stick and turned out to be a black snake. At the time Phillip was cleaning up around the new Police Complex in Weston and he enquired if they needed a tailor. One year later Phillip, Anna and Ricky began altering uniforms and sewing on badges for the Australian Federal Police.

In 1973 when Ricky was 18, she married a German she met through her parents. He was pleasant, served in the Army Reserves, had his own auto electrician business and seemed to be what Ricky was looking for. Anna and Phillip were happy for their daughter. Gabby and her husband, Hans, would share many weekends together with the younger couple fishing and camping. Ricky and her husband lived with her parents for some time, as Gabby and Hans had done earlier. Eventually they found a place of their own.

Four years after the marriage Ricky gave birth to her first son, Phillip, christened after her father. The Reiners thought Ricky's marital home was happy and caring. The truth was quite the opposite. Ricky had kept from her family the difficulties that had developed. She was always cheery, never letting her home life affect her time with her parents and sister. Initially, Ricky learned to live with the problems, but after Phillip was born the situation is believed to have become untenable. According to Anna and Gabby, Ricky's first husband was demanding and put his own needs and wants before his wife or his son. His behaviour, again, as stated by Ricky's mother and sister, brought about the loss of his business.

Once they'd learned of the situation, Ricky's family banded together. Her mother and father, and Gabby and Hans, all gave what practical and emotional support they could to help Ricky and her son.

The marriage soon ended and Ricky found herself another beau. Anna remembered seeing Ricky's new man at a distance and thinking to herself, 'couldn't you find someone better'. The Reiners weren't happy with Ricky's choice. They felt it was too soon for Ricky to start a new relationship, but they nevertheless accepted her decision. After all, it was her life. Ricky married for the second time in 1983. The relationship soon turned violent, and Ricky became a victim of abuse. As before, Anna and Phillip Reiners knew nothing about it until it had grown to the point where Ricky couldn't take anymore.

Ricky's son, Phillip, remembered his mother always shielding him from her pain and suffering. She would take him to his room and play with him. She would get him to draw and paint, get his mind occupied, anything to distract him from the violence that awaited her in the adjoining room. Ricky wanted Phillip to think life was fun, and not the angry world she was experiencing. To Phillip, Ricky was more than a mother, she was a friend. His best friend.

No matter how bad things became, Phillip remembered his mother always made sure he was bathed, fed and ready for bed at the same time each night. He had routines and Ricky made sure he kept to them. If other children were in the house, Ricky would see to them all. She had a natural affinity with children. She'd have them follow the same routine as Phillip and buy them a video to watch as the adults relaxed.

In 1986 Ricky and her second husband separated. He didn't take it well and phoned Anna, threatening to burn Ricky's house down. Anna called Ricky and told her to contact the police in case her ex-husband carried out his threat. Two general duties officers from the Belconnen Police Station attended. One of the officers was John Conway.

It's not clear, but it could be that John remembered Ricky from the AFP tailor's shop from when he was a recruit. In any case, soon after the call to Ricky's house, John became a regular visitor to the shop and they started their relationship. It wasn't long after that John moved in with Ricky.

Anna recalled being told by Ricky's ex-husband that on the night he made his threat, John Conway turned up to where he was staying. The ex-husband had been drinking and had passed out on his bed. He blamed the alcohol for why he made the call to Anna. He alleged he woke up to find John holding a gun to his head and warning him never to bother Ricky again.

Although they still worked together, Anna noticed that Ricky didn't call around to their house as often as she used to. She stopped meeting Gabby for coffee. Ricky was a popular person and had developed friendships with lots of different people. She was a very social person who loved to dance and she loved company. Anna also noticed that Ricky didn't mention her friends as much, and didn't appear to have kept in contact with them. This sudden isolation came after John Conway had moved in. Ricky's parents could see that John was stopping Ricky from living her own life. Other than on birthdays, Christmas and other special occasions, they rarely saw her away from work. When they did, it was more often than not without John. Ricky would visit when John was on duty.

Ricky was an avid gardener and she had a garden that was the envy of the street. It was her pastime, her solace and an escape from the burdens of life. John decided the garage was his. That was to be his refuge, somewhere he could go to escape Ricky. He put his own lock on the garage door, which then prevented Ricky from getting to her gardening tools. The garden quickly became overgrown and Ricky was denied one of her pleasures.

Ricky's son, Phillip, had his own problems with this new man in his mother's life. Like the rest of Ricky's family, Phillip just wanted to see his mum happy. Even though he was still quite young, he understood what she had been through. He cared for and loved his mother greatly. He accepted John. There was no reason not to. In time, however, John would antagonise young Phillip, telling him he was no longer the man of the house. He would accuse him of being jealous and speak down to the young boy. John would try to get Ricky to act differently towards her son, to discipline him his way, attempting to drive a wedge through their close relationship.

There were times no doubt when Ricky thought the two were bonding, like when John took Phillip for a drive in his police vehicle. John drove down a back street, hit the accelerator and raced along the road turning on the lights and siren. Phillip would try and talk to John, but John only ever gave monosyllabic answers. He wasn't big on having a conversation with young Phillip. John never offered Phillip any affection, unless he was posing for a family photo, and even then, it was a lot to ask John to stand next to Phillip.

In 1990 Ricky gave birth to Alistaire. The next year, John and Ricky were married. Anna said she and her husband didn't know about the marriage until after it had happened. Ricky called her to let her know. Apparently it was John's idea to keep it small and keep it secret. Ricky's parents felt they had got to know John quite well, just from what they saw and heard from Ricky. Though they didn't know it all. They never knew the extent of the physical and psychological torture John inflicted upon their daughter. They knew enough though, that Ricky's father would on occasions comment to Anna 'one day we'll hear he's shot them all'.

As Phillip grew older, he could see more clearly what John was doing to his mother. He knew her as an outgoing and confident person, even during the rough times in her previous marriage, but with John she had become a shell. He had worn her down. She was alone and she was lonely. John had put Ricky in a situation where she felt she had no one to turn to but him. It hurt Phillip to see his mother like that.

At 16 Phillip moved out. He begged Ricky to leave with him and to bring Alistaire. The two brothers had formed a close and secretive friendship. Alistaire once said to Phillip in a conspiratorial tone that he knew his father wouldn't approve of their relationship, but he loved his older brother and they would always be friends. Despite Ricky's suffering, she wouldn't leave John.

In October 1996, Ricky's father was hospitalised with cancer. Ricky could only visit him twice because, as Anna learned later, John refused to give his wife the money for petrol. Phillip Reiners died later that month.

Just before he passed away Ricky's father changed his will. Originally the Reiners' family home would go to Gabby and Ricky, and they could do with it as they saw fit. John had expressed an interest in buying Gabby out, to take on full ownership of the house.

Ricky's father now changed that. After consulting with Gabby, Phillip decreed that when Anna died, the house would go to Ricky only. She could live in it, but she could never sell it. When Ricky died, the house would go to her elder son.

Basically, Ricky's father was making sure his daughter and her sons had somewhere they could always call home. He wasn't allowing John Conway to turn the house into capital. Anna's relationship with John was never what could be called close, but when he learned of the change of will, the relationship between son and mother-in-law became more distant.

It was for this reason that Anna was surprised by John's phone call to her on Sunday 4 May. He greeted Anna with a 'Hi Mum'.

Anna was lucky if she got a 'Hi' before that time. Anna suspected something was wrong, but never guessed that the sunshine of her life was lying in her house, murdered.

The day before Ricky had called her mother and told her that she was happy she had won custody of Alistaire, but that she still loved John. Anna was more pragmatic, asking how her daughter could love someone who had abused her and manipulated and controlled her for his own purposes. Ricky admitted she would get over losing John, but she couldn't help loving him.

Ricky was looking forward to her future. She'd made appointments with counsellors and clinics to deal with her drinking. Giving her sister moral support, Gabby had even accompanied Ricky to a meeting. They looked at rental properties together, should John force Ricky to sell the house. Slowly but surely, Ricky was trying to regain her self-esteem and be the person she used to be.

To Anna and Gabby, Ricky was their sunshine. She was a very special person to all the Reiners. She was the person they always knew to have a smile and give an infectious laugh. Ricky was a daughter, a sister, a mother, a best friend, and generally a sincere and honest person.

All Ricky wanted was what she dreamt of as a child. She wanted a loving husband who would be a good father, and for them to raise a family in a secure and caring environment. The type of environment she and her sister had while growing up. Sadly, the reality was different. The Reiners admit that Ricky was no angel and she had her faults, as anyone does. Her biggest fault, however, was her choice in men.

CHAPTER FIVE

Tuesday 6 May 1997
Enquiries, the diary and a jacket potato

Noel was at his desk by five o'clock in the morning. Ben and the rest of the team commenced duty at seven the next morning. Noel had had no sleep. He just took the time to shower and get into fresh clothes. Ben, at least, had three hours' sleep. In fact, that would be the average amount of sleep they would get each night over the next three to four weeks.

Ben recalled a time, when, at three in the morning, he was in bed staring at the ceiling and going over the investigation in his mind. He decided there was no point in trying to sleep. His mind was too busy. He decided he might as well go to work. When he walked in the door he saw Noel poring over statements.

'What are you doing here?' Ben asked.

'Same as you … couldn't sleep,' came Noel's reply.

Ben organised the half-kilometre sweep of the area surrounding 35 Gollan Street, recruiting uniform police and other detectives.

Noel felt more had to be done during the sweep. He wanted the stormwater and sewage drains to be checked in case any evidence had been flushed down the toilet or dropped in the gutter. He contacted the Australian Capital Territory Electricity and Water Corporation (ACTEW), requesting they supply a crew to search the drains.

Once gathered, Ben gave the assembled group their directions. It was simple. Gollan Street would be the start point and everyone would fan out from there. The street was lined with police vehicles as officers, heads down, began a painstaking search of every front yard, back yard, garden shed, roadway and gutter for half a kilometre from No. 35. A yellow-vested maintenance crew from ACTEW opened up the manholes to access the underground pipes. They dug up the yard and checked the sewage lines.

The police search came up empty-handed. Despite the exhaustive search they found nothing that could be linked to Ricky's death: no syringe or anything else that may have been discarded by a fleeing felon, or a panicked friend. The crew from ACTEW did find something, a decomposing potato in the drain leading from the house to the street drainage system. Their discovery caused some laughter amongst the police.

Ben could see the funny side as well, but the potato did have significance. The potato had blocked the drains. How it got there was a mystery. There was a lot of rubbish trapped behind it, which had been sifted for the sake of the search, but there was nothing to be found. To Ben, this meant that had anyone discarded anything down the drain, like a syringe or the needle, then it would have collected behind the potato. So, the potato actually proved that there was no needle to be found. If someone had injected Ricky they had taken the syringe and needle with them.

Noel's superiors weren't happy when the ACTEW invoiced the AFP $7,000 for their work on the day. A very expensive potato. A very expensive exercise, but one that had to be done. Noel was not going to give any opportunity for anyone to criticise the investigation or his team for not being thorough.

Search warrants were executed on Mark's premises. He was the friend of the family who was known to have visited Ricky. From what the police had been told by those who knew Mark, Noel expected to find cannabis and speed hidden away at his house. It was clean. The only evidence of drug use was a syringe cover found in a box in Mark's bedroom. Mark claimed it wasn't his and that it belonged to his girlfriend. The box had remained unpacked from when they both returned from Bathurst, in central western New South Wales.

In his interview with police, Mark admitted he used marijuana and had experimented with speed. He also admitted that the syringe cover was probably his, from when he injected Panadol six or seven months earlier. He had processed the over the counter cold remedy into liquid and then filled a syringe. He'd only done it once.

It had been nearly ten years since Mark last saw Ricky, when she phoned him in late 1996. It was out of the blue. Ricky knew of Mark's drug habit, and asked if he could purchase some cannabis for her. Ricky wanted the drug for her father who was dying of cancer. She'd heard that marijuana helps ease pain and she wanted to ease her father's suffering as much as she could. Sadly, it was all too late and Ricky's father died soon afterwards. Mark wasn't able to get her the drug in time.

Mark saw Ricky about three weeks before her death, in April. She had called him again. This time she was upset and wanted someone to talk to. Mark caught a taxi and went around. Ricky spoke about her relationship with John, how he had taken

Alistaire away and that she had to appear at the Family Court. Mark stayed with Ricky for two nights and one day, just helping around the house. He even took an old microwave to Cash Converters for her. He was paid $15 for the whitegoods. When he went to give the money to Ricky, she told him to keep it. The microwave was only rubbish cluttering up the house. She was glad it was gone and she knew Mark needed the money.

When Mark stayed at Ricky's she allowed him to smoke his dope, providing he did it outside. She didn't like the smell and, in fact, Mark knew she was anti-drugs. She didn't like people using drugs, but she made an exception for Mark. He was a family friend.

It wasn't marijuana Ricky objected to as much as hard drugs — cocaine, heroin, amphetamines and the like. As with any mother, Ricky prayed her sons would never use them. Apart from the time she wanted marijuana for her father, Ricky never requested or purchased any drugs from Mark.

Mark's statement supported what Ricky's mother, Anna, had told Noel and Ben earlier. As for Mark, he had an alibi for the night of Ricky's death and he denied any knowledge of it. There was no reason for police not to accept Mark's innocence. He was no longer a suspect, and he was released without charge.

To be sure though, Noel tasked Constable Oren Kulawiec to conduct enquiries into Mark's statement. Constable Kulawiec would check the taxi company, Cash Converters and speak with a number of Mark's friends and associates to verify his story.

There's an adage in Homicide that states the first 24 to 48 hours of the investigation are the most crucial. It's the initial observations and study of a crime scene, the collection and preservation of evidence that will later lead police to finding the answers. However insignificant something may be at the beginning, that something might prove to be the offender's undoing later.

The enquiry into Ricky's death had now been running for two days. A cause of death still had to be determined. Despite the educated guesses, the syringe was missing, and both a motive and suspect were left open for argument and speculation. There was nothing in all the evidence taken from the house that stood out to say who had killed Ricky Conway or why. That was, until Noel and Ben started reading Ricky's diary that had been collected by Constable Phillipa Cottam on the night Ricky's body was discovered. The actual diary was being examined for fingerprints, but copies had been made for the investigating team.

Incidents referred to in the diary were supported by anecdotal evidence from neighbours and friends, and by police reports.

On 11 March, the time when John had stated to Ben Ricky told him to leave, police had also been called. On arrival, Ricky accused John of assaulting her. She alleged John had kicked and punched her before she ran to a neighbour's house for help. According to the statement taken by police, John had attempted to force Ricky out of the house. Ricky told the police that John pushed her towards the front door and pinned her against it by her arms and shoulder. He had said to her, 'You should get out, I'm not getting out.'

Ricky raised her arms to prevent being pushed out. John pulled her away, opened the door, and then shoved her out. He followed, pushing her down the three steps leading from the veranda. For whatever reason, Ricky said she didn't want to lay charges and the officers remained while John collected his things and left.

John hadn't mentioned the assault in his statement.

The day that John took Alistaire from the house, John said he did it for Alistaire's sake. He was in the garage and heard Alistaire and Ricky arguing. He saw Ricky physically abuse the child and John intervened, fearing for Alistaire's safety. Ricky had written in her diary and told friends a very different version.

On that night, 2 April, John arrived at Ricky's after spending the day with Alistaire and told her he was taking their son away, whether she liked it or not. Ricky tried to stop him, but John ignored her and began collecting some of Alistaire's clothes. Ricky attempted to grab John to prevent him from leaving with Alistaire. John turned and punched Ricky to the ground and kicked her.

John Conway took out a restraining order against his wife, on behalf of his son, the next day. Ricky decided she wasn't allowing John to control her anymore. She made a complaint against John to the AFP Internal Investigations Department, telling them of the assault. She had sustained a number of injuries — laceration of her lower lip, bruising to her right upper arm, bruises to her right chin, and pain in her lower jaw. Ricky had a doctor's report to support her allegation. John was furious.

At that time John had applied to transfer to the Queensland Police, but no transfer would be accepted while John had an internal investigation over his head. Also, if he were found guilty of assault, he could be sacked from the AFP.

According to Ricky's diary John convinced Ricky to withdraw her complaint. He made a deal with her. He promised he would drop the restraining order and give their marriage another try if she withdrew her complaint. He never kept his end of the bargain.

Noel made enquiries at the Family Court, which revealed the battle John and Ricky had been through and why the court chose Ricky over John.

It was learned that John's portrayal of Ricky to the Family Court was in stark contrast to what he had told Noel and Ben. There were also other issues and evidence presented that raised their suspicions of John still being 'in love' with Ricky. Despite

John's best efforts, the truth was revealed in the Family Court and Ricky was granted custody of Alistaire. Reading the court order, Ben found no mention of or conditions regarding Ricky's drinking. It seemed John had made that part up.

John told Ben he was upset by the court's decision, but what he would tell his supervising sergeant showed he was more than upset. While working a Random Breath Test unit, Sergeant Larry Andrews asked John how the custody hearing turned out.

'I'm upset,' John told him. 'I think I lost because I was a police officer and I work shift work. I told the judge that I could change my shifts … but it wasn't good enough.'

John expressed his hatred for Ricky and that he was concerned for Alistaire's welfare. He believed the court had got it wrong. He added, '… it's easy to see how people could kill family court judges and their ex-wives'.

Noel and Ben were particularly interested in an entry in Ricky's diary for 25 April, Anzac Day, two days after John had returned Alistaire on the orders of the court. Ricky wrote, '*I rang John at 6.30am & asked John to come over for coffee. He came over just after 7am. I made coffee. We sat in the lounge room. I went out to get a tissue, then came back & had 2 mouthfuls of coffee. Said I was feeling drowsy. Tipped coffee out & saw froth inside cup. Said to John, you drugged me, he said no, go & lie down. So I did. Brought me in glass of water, had mouthful, tasted bitter like coffee. Felt pocket of his jacket. Felt a small bottle. Asked him to show me bottle. Finally showed me. Was a small brown bottle with dropper. Said was nose drops. Eventually admitted putting it in drinks. Wanted me to calm down so we could talk.*'

What had John given Ricky and why?

Certainly, all the evidence available to the police suggested the likelihood of John killing his wife, and there was a documented history of violence against Ricky. But would he kill her? As for the incident on 25 April, it could have been that John wanted to calm Ricky as he told her. There may not have been anything sinister in his actions. After all, Ricky and John's relationship was volatile and maybe John was attempting to avoid another conflict.

Noel and Ben had read Ricky's versions of events, but what would John say?

CHAPTER SIX

Wednesday 7 May 1997
Shaking the tree

Noel Lymbery had been with Belconnen detectives for only three years. He admitted that his experience as a detective was limited at that time, so he relied on the support of his team, which included Ben Cartwright.

Ben started at Belconnen the year before Noel and he'd already worked on a couple of homicides. Ben and Noel became friends and mixed socially, sharing the same laconic sense of humour and, more importantly for Noel, they shared the same work ethic. Ben may not have the hyperactive or stubborn personality of Noel, but they do share a thoroughness, an eye for detail, and the determination to achieve their goals. They complemented each other well, being each other's sounding board and devil's advocate when deciding what action to take next, particularly with the investigation into Ricky Conway's death.

There was a lot of discussion and debate in the detectives' office on the morning of Wednesday 7 May. The issue was what to do with John Conway.

Questions had been raised by Ricky's diary, statements taken from friends and neighbours, and the reports from police who had been called to Gollan Street. There was conflicting information on various incidents leading up to Ricky's death. John had watered down his version of events, and had neglected to volunteer other pieces of information when giving his statement to Ben, the Monday after Ricky's death.

Ben wanted to question John. He wanted him across the table in a formal record of interview. It was a risky move. There was certainly enough evidence to warrant speaking with John. There wasn't enough evidence to arrest or charge him. Questioning John now would alert him that police saw him as a possible suspect, therefore putting in jeopardy any possible evidence that hadn't yet been found that might link John to his wife's death.

Every team member had an opinion. Some agreed with Ben, others didn't, preferring to wait till they had more evidence. There were even those who thought John just couldn't have murdered his wife. They told Ben and Noel very plainly that they were wrong. It had to be someone else. A police officer would never commit such a heinous crime.

Noel quietly thought it was naive to think an officer wouldn't commit murder. After all, an officer is only human and subject to weaknesses like anyone else. Noel had experienced enough as a policeman to know what people were capable of, regardless of their standing in the community. Even so, he encouraged his team to have their opinions.

Having people believe John was innocent could work for Noel. He felt he could use them as a barometer, to gauge if the evidence they were assembling proved John's guilt. If the evidence convinced John's supporters of his guilt, then a jury might well accept it too.

Noel wondered whether it was too soon to bring John in.

In normal circumstances, a brief of evidence is put together before interrogating the suspect. That way, if the suspect refuses to talk, at least they can be arrested and the evidence should speak for itself. In this instance, it was more 'gut feeling' than hard evidence.

Noel thought that what they had, which was little, and talking to John just might 'shake the tree'. For Noel, it was a case of 'getting to know your enemy'. Noel wanted to get to know John — how he would react and what lies he was willing to tell. While Noel didn't think John would ever confess, he saw the interview as an opportunity to assess his prime suspect. Knowing John's character might help the team later in the investigation. In any case, at this stage they had nothing to lose. Noel decided to go along with Ben's plan.

Ben called John and asked him to attend Belconnen for a taped record of interview. John agreed. Ben stressed that he didn't have to, that he could refuse the request, reminding John he would be under caution. John told Ben he had nothing to hide and was more than happy to help. A time was arranged for around 2.30 that afternoon.

By now, the detectives' office had become a major incident room, with a whiteboard set up displaying photos and scribblings on butcher's paper related to the investigation — names of witnesses and their relationship to Ricky, tasks completed, tasks to be done, and such like. The last thing Ben wanted was John walking in and seeing the whiteboard. They didn't want him knowing they were investigating a possible murder. Ben called down to the front desk and gave them instructions. They were to phone ahead when John Conway arrived so he could be taken straight to the interview room.

The forensics officers had gathered some 36 items for examination by the Government Analytical Laboratory. The items included the two alcohol swabs and packaging, the manchester from Ricky's bed, her night clothes, an earring she was wearing and the stud and bar found on the floor near the bed, samples of her hair, fingernails and the vegetable matter discovered near her ear and on the sheet, the hair fibre found on her person, the hard-covered diary, liquids from the kitchen and laundry drain pipes, the liquid inside the toilet, the glasses and cups in the sink, the empty casks of wine and bottle of spumante, and the drawer of syringes to name a few.

Noel Lymbery attended the laboratory that afternoon. He wanted to go through what had been collected and discuss with the analysts and the forensics officers, Phil Turner and Bob Atkins, which items he wanted tested, and what he wanted them tested for. There was no knowing what relevance, if any, these items would have for the investigators. It was just a matter of collecting everything and seeing what turned up.

The first step was to examine some of the items for fingerprints and then check those prints against Ricky's and the database of offenders. Federal Agent David Reece, a specialist in fingerprinting, examined the alcohol swabs, hoping to be able to extract enough of a print to be able to put it through the system for a match. Despite his best efforts, Agent Reece was unable to find any identifiable fingerprints on the swabs. He did find latent prints on the diary, which were matched to Ricky. Latent prints are a partial finger or palm print that has enough identifiable characteristics for comparison. The remainder of the items scrutinised did not reveal any identifiable prints, other than those of Ricky's.

Simon Christen, an analyst with the Government Analytical Laboratories, conducted tests on the liquids found in the kitchen, bathroom, laundry, and on the contents of the casks and bottle of wine. The purpose of the testing was to identify any drugs that might be present. Simon was specifically testing for morphine, monoacetylmorphine (MAM), and for ethanol and benzodiazepine-based drugs. In layperson's terms, heroin and alcohol. No traces, however, were found. Ethanol, as would be expected, was discovered in varying degrees in the wine casks and wine bottle.

While the results of the testing were not extraordinary, it did tell Noel and the team that whoever injected Ricky didn't dispose of any drugs on the premises. Most likely, they didn't mull the lethal cocktail there either, but arrived with the syringe ready to go.

Mulling is the name given to the process of preparing heroin for injection, adding water, applying heat and mixing it together, usually in a spoon or small dish. Each addict, however, will mull their own way, adding whatever substances they prefer to the mix. Had that been done at Ricky's, then traces might have been found in the pipes if the implement had been rinsed or washed. Also, the Drug Squad detectives who searched the house on the Monday would have easily identified the spoon or dish, as the underside of the utensil would have been scorched.

Although the detectives suspected Ricky had died from a heroin overdose, the results from the toxicology examination were yet to be known. It could take weeks, depending on how many other tests the lab had listed.

During this time Noel began his enquiries into whether the Scientific Unit could determine if a large gauge needle, or more than one needle, had pierced Ricky's skin. The unit accepted the challenge and started making calls to their counterparts interstate and overseas to see if there had been any such tests conducted before. Noel and his team just had to be patient and wait.

Ben Cartwright was doing some paperwork at his desk when, out of the corner of his eye, he noticed a figure standing in the centre of the detectives' office staring at the whiteboard. The figure wasn't familiar and he looked up to see who it was. Ben reacted quickly, distracting the visitor's attention. It was John Conway.

The time was 2.45 pm. John had arrived at Belconnen Police Station at a time when one shift was ending and another about to start duty. The duty sergeant from the earlier shift had not yet passed on Ben's request to his relief. John Conway strode in and was directed straight up to the detectives' room. John would've only been staring at the whiteboard for less than a minute before Ben steered him away.

It's unlikely John knew the importance of what he was staring at. Certainly he wouldn't have had the time to fathom the meaning of all the photos and scribble. John had gone from serving in general duties to Traffic Operations. He had never been involved in any major investigation run by detectives, let alone a homicide enquiry.

The mood was relaxed as Ben and Noel took their seats across the table from John. The time was 2.58 pm. John was cordial and polite. Noel and Ben had with them documentation, a computer log on the number of times police visited Gollan Street, Ricky's statements to police, the Family Court order and Ricky's diary. John was given the mandatory caution, that anything he said might be used in evidence. Ben offered him the opportunity to contact a friend or solicitor, but he declined.

John gave an account of when he met Ricky in 1986. He said he'd first noticed her when he went to the tailor's shop at the Police Centre in Weston. Some time after that, while working as a general duties officer, he attended a call to a domestic disturbance. The caller was Ricky. Ricky's second husband, whom she had separated from, had threatened to burn her house down. John met Ricky again at the tailor's shop and their relationship developed.

John said he supported Ricky through her separation, as he had just separated from his first wife. According to John, he had returned home from work one afternoon and was informed by a neighbour that his wife and child had gone. She had another neighbour drive her and her daughter to the airport, where they caught a plane to Queensland to be with her parents. John was devastated to lose both his wife and child. It was after this that he had begun dating Ricky.

Within a couple of months of seeing each other, John moved in with Ricky. Their son, Alistaire, was born in 1990, and they married the year after. John was in love with Ricky. He told Ben and Noel that he loved Ricky before they even lived together. He still loved Ricky.

Ben allowed John to give his answers, to give his version of events, without any challenge. Then, Ben asked about 11 March, the date John moved out of the house. The affidavit Ricky gave police on what happened that night contradicted John's version. Even though there was a medical report to prove Ricky had been assaulted, John denied laying a hand on her. In the past, John had wrestled a knife out of Ricky's hand, the knife she threatened to kill herself with, holding it against her stomach. There were also times when he had to physically separate Ricky and Alistaire during their arguments, but he never struck her.

John said, that while he had left the house, he always intended to get back with Ricky. The move was temporary, to give Ricky time to sort out her drinking problem. That was what was destroying their marriage. If Ricky had given up the alcohol then John would have moved back and they would have been one big happy family. John went further and said, regardless of Ricky's drinking, he had every intention of returning to her, because he loved her.

There was discussion of the incident on 2 April, the day John took Alistaire away. Ricky, again, said he had beaten her. John strenuously denied the assertion. Ben put it to John that Ricky not only wrote about the assault in her diary, but also produced a medical report and told several other people. John still denied it. Did that mean John was saying Ricky was a liar? John didn't like to use the word, not against Ricky, but then he didn't disagree.

John denied ever promising Ricky that he would drop the restraining order if Ricky retracted her complaint to the Internal Investigations Department. He said Ricky had made that proposal; but he didn't care about the IID complaint and he wouldn't drop the restraining order or the application for custody. His thoughts were for Alistaire's welfare. He only dropped the order after advice from his solicitor before the Family Court proceedings.

Asked, if at this point, he still considered there was a chance he and Ricky would get back together, John replied 'yes'.

The cost to John for fighting for his son's custody amounted to $5,000. Why then, if John thought he and Ricky could salvage their marriage, did he continue to seek custody?

John thought it would help with Ricky's problems. She would have to get help and reduce the amount she drank. He said he hoped they would get back together and put it all behind them.

After John lost the battle in the Family Court, Ricky wrote that John said to her, 'We're finished.' John denied it.

John had said, 'The fight is over ... it's finished.' He clarified that he was referring to the court battle and that he wouldn't pursue it any more. Yet, only a couple of questions later, and John admitted he'd spoken to his lawyer about overturning the court's decision. He hadn't thought of doing so until he'd read the orders, and that they hadn't placed any restrictions on, or made reference to, Ricky's drinking. He wasn't contesting the custody, only making sure that Ricky was ordered to control her drinking, for Alistaire's sake.

John wasn't known for his lavish spending; in fact, he was known as being frugal. Ben was curious how John could afford the legal costs, thinking he may be taking the money from savings he had accumulated. John admitted he would use his overdraft to pay the solicitor and that he didn't have that amount saved. He also told Ben that he and Ricky had separate banking accounts, though he didn't explain why.

Ben was particularly keen to ask John what he remembered happened on 25 April, the day Ricky detailed in her diary that she thought John had drugged her. John said he had been called by Ricky in the morning and went around to see her. She made coffee for the both of them, but his tasted sour. While Ricky was in the toilet, he poured his coffee down the sink and made himself another, which tasted normal. Ben wondered what John thought had been put in the coffee. He said that Ricky might have put salt, instead of sugar, into the coffee. A common mistake.

Ben knew John well enough to ask, 'But you don't have sugar, do you?'

John replied, 'No, I don't.' John explained that both Ricky and her mother would always add sugar to his coffee, no matter how many times he told them he didn't take it.

While John was making a fresh cup of coffee in the kitchen, he noticed two pieces of foil sitting on the window ledge, one partially opened and the other tightly wrapped. He unfolded the partially open one and noticed a white powder. It seemed strange to him. He had never noticed foils in the house before. He folded it back up and put them both in his coat pocket, returning to the lounge room.

When Ricky walked back in to the room, John noticed she was unsteady on her feet. He presumed she was intoxicated. Ricky said to John as she entered, 'I'm as high as a kite.'

John had only heard Ricky use that expression once before, many years ago. John wasn't sure what Ricky meant by it. The time before John had returned home from work to find Ricky in the back yard smoking a roll-your-own cigarette. Ricky apparently told John, on this occasion, that it wasn't normal tobacco and that she'd been cultivating some plants. John couldn't remember the name Ricky used to describe the plants, but he did remember they weren't normal garden plants. He and Ricky argued and he ripped the plants out of the ground.

The day after the coffee incident, John handed over the two foils to the Drug Registry. He did so because he was curious to know what the white powder might be.

Ben was amazed. Why didn't John just ask Ricky? After all, he was so concerned about Ricky's drinking affecting the welfare of his son, why wouldn't her behaviour and finding two silver foils spark his concern even more?

John said he didn't know it was an illicit drug. He wanted to know what the powder was before saying anything. Although John had been a police officer for over ten years, he had had very little exposure to drugs because he was a Traffic Operations officer, so wasn't sure what was in the foils.

Ben held his composure. Being a detective, it's expected the suspect will lie, but Ben knew John. They had worked together for four years and Ben felt John was treating him as fool.

In Ben's words, 'If I took a silver foil with white powder on to the street, a ten-year-old kid would tell me it was heroin ... and here was a police officer claiming to have no idea of what it could be.'

During one of the breaks to collect more audiotapes, Ben marched down the corridor. Adrenalin filled his body. He recalled John's responses in the interview and began planning his next line of questioning. A colleague, Sergeant Anton Major, just happened to be passing and greeted Ben, unaware of his mood. Ben violently shook his finger at the unsuspecting Anton. 'He did it ... he fuckin' did it ... mark my words, he did it!'

Ben was 'pumped'. Whenever Anton saw Ben after that day, Anton would point his finger at Ben and repeat his words, displaying the same fervour Ben had shown. It became a running joke. Anton had never seen Ben so fiery.

Despite Ben's outburst, he calmed down and reminded himself that he had to keep an open mind. It was early in the investigation, and he couldn't afford to have tunnel vision. John might have looked like being the most likely suspect, but the police hadn't yet found out everything about Ricky.

There are rules police must adhere to when interviewing a suspect. The rules apply across Australia. The officers conducting the interview can only put the facts, as they know them, to the suspect. The suspect can then refuse to comment, deny, or accept what is being said, without challenge. This is why it is important for police to have a strong brief of evidence against a person before interviewing them. The brief is what the prosecutors use to take the matter to court. It's the evidence that is vital, more so than any interview, unless of course the offender makes admissions.

Five hours into the taped record of interview, Ben and Noel took a break. Ben was still agitated by John's blatant lying. Noel advised him that he wasn't going to get a confession out of John. John wasn't going to give it up if he was guilty. That being the case, they decided to go in hard, to put pleasantries aside and suggest to John what they thought his involvement was in Ricky's death. They weren't going to accept his answers anymore without a challenge. John wasn't going to get away with lying to them.

If John were guilty, to question him in this manner was a risk. It is a tactic used in court, but not allowed in police interrogations. They ran the danger that the whole interview could be inadmissible in a court of law. The pressure was on.

The interview resumed and both Noel and Ben took John back over the earlier questions, applying their new strategy. John remained defiant. He loved Ricky and would not have done anything to hurt her. He became distraught, breaking down in tears when speaking of his love for Ricky.

John admitted the elderly couple who had taken him in were in fact Kathy McFie's parents. He was adamant Kathy McFie was only a babysitter and that there was nothing sexual between them. He had not considered ever having a sexual relationship with her.

Noel and Ben thought Kathy sounded wonderful, considering she had looked after Alistaire and was allowing John to stay at her place without taking any money. Kathy was on a disability pension. John agreed she was a good person, and he would assist with the groceries on occasions, but they were not in a relationship.

They confronted him with Ricky's allegation that he was having an affair with Kathy. John responded by saying that Ricky thought he was having an affair with any female he spoke to.

Getting back to the foils John found in the kitchen at Gollan Street, Noel and Ben decided to share their thoughts on the matter. They didn't believe John at all. In fact, they believed that John didn't find the drugs as he described, but that it was he who had purchased or found them elsewhere. He had done this so the police would think Ricky was a heroin addict. John denied it.

They asked if John had ever taken alcohol to the house. The question was based on information Ricky's mother, Anna, had given them. Ricky spoke to her mother after John and Kathy had visited her for her birthday on 17 March, six days after he had left. Ricky complained to her mother that John had brought a bottle of spirits to the house and was trying to get her drunk. Ricky refused to drink.

John explained the purchasing of spirits on Ricky's birthday was a tradition, and he was only doing what he had done since they'd been together. Ben found it strange. One moment John was saying he wanted Ricky to give up alcohol, and the next he was taking a bottle of spirits to her house. John, again, said it was customary, but Ben wasn't letting him off easily. How could

John, someone who had described Ricky as an alcoholic, a wino, an unfit mother, take alcohol to the house? It didn't make sense.

John agreed in hindsight that it wasn't the right thing to do. His only defence was that 'it was tradition'.

John had an answer for everything, even if it didn't convince Ben and Noel.

Noel was concerned about Alistaire's behaviour towards Ricky. Alistaire had sworn at his mother and hit her with a chrome bar and cricket stump on separate occasions. Noel asked if John had influenced Alistaire to behave the way he did.

John denied it. He said his son was sometimes 'a handful', but he could control him, whereas Ricky couldn't.

Police had already learned from their initial enquiries that Alistaire idolised his father and would do anything for him. It was also suggested to them that John manipulated his young son almost to the point of being brainwashed. Noel felt the way Alistaire treated his mother was following John's example, that the young boy had seen John hit Ricky. John continually denied the allegation. He claimed, despite the medical records, that someone must have hit Ricky, but it wasn't him. According to John, Ricky would also fall down on occasions and injure herself.

As for the needles in the garage, John had forgotten about them. He bought them ages ago, and used them to fuel small engines, the type used in model aeroplanes.

Ben had had enough. He decided to put the question directly, '… why did you kill her, John?'

'I didn't kill her.'

'Why did you organise her death?'

'I did not organise her death.'

Ben told John he thought Ricky's death was incredibly convenient for him, because now he could head off to Queensland with Alistaire and Kathy. It was all too convenient.

Throughout the remainder of the interview, Noel and Ben let their suspicions be known. They told John they believed, as he had told them Ricky was a heavy sleeper, he entered the house at night and injected her with heroin. Or he employed someone to do the deed. They asked where he got the drugs from, had he stolen them from the police lock-up, and who did he involve in the killing?

John denied everything, repeating he loved Ricky more than he loved his son. Though, when pressed by Ben and Noel, he wasn't sure which one he loved more.

The interview concluded at 9.09 in the evening. It had lasted just over six hours. When they finished, Noel and Ben were expecting John to be irate, to express his anger at having been subjected to the intense questioning.

The tapes were turned off and John sat back in his chair, 'Gee, glad that's over … how about another cup of coffee?'

As the interview was taking place three search warrants were written up and signed by a magistrate. Two were for specific dwellings in the southern suburbs of Rivett and Griffith. A third warrant was for John's car, a white Nissan Patrol four-wheel drive.

Noel sent detectives to execute the warrants on the two homes. Ben led John to the garage of the police station where his vehicle had been moved for the search. John watched, casually chatting to Noel and Ben as other police pored over the four-wheel drive. Nothing incriminating was found. The car was clean.

John was allowed to leave. He boarded his Nissan and drove off. When he reached Belconnen Way, heading east to meet up with Northbourne Avenue, he put his foot down, speeding along the road. Noel had assigned an unmarked police car to tail John. If he was guilty, it was possible that John might go and visit the people he had contracted to kill Ricky. The surveillance vehicle did its best to keep up with John without being noticed, but John reportedly drove 'like a bat out of hell'.

On Belconnen Way, they noticed John pull over to the side of the road. He alighted from the vehicle, went around to the passenger side, opened the door and appeared to be leaning under the seat or dashboard. After a short time he returned to the driver's seat and drove off. He continued to drive at high speed, losing the surveillance.

When Noel and Ben heard about John pulling over and checking the passenger side, they knew they'd missed something. There was something to be found in the car, but they hadn't noticed it. Noel and Ben were not happy. It could have been vital evidence. Then again, it may have been nothing. The police could have dislodged something in the vehicle that had irritated John and that he'd stopped to fix. Noel and Ben wondered if they'd ever find out what caused John to stop.

Stuart Flats is a Housing Commission project in Griffith, a south-eastern suburb of Canberra. The estate provides those on welfare and low incomes subsidised rent. The address on the warrant was the home of Kathy McFie, Alistaire's babysitter. Detective Constable Susan Ball, who had only started with the investigation the day before, arrived at Stuart Flats to execute the warrant.

Constable Ball asked if Kathy would allow her and the other police who accompanied her to search her unit. Kathy agreed. Constable Ball didn't need to serve the warrant because Kathy had given her consent.

As police looked for any evidence that might relate to Ricky's death, Constable Ball took Kathy's statement.

Kathy was driving home one day around July 1996 when she was pulled over by an AFP Traffic Operations officer. That officer was John Conway. He had detained Kathy because smoke was billowing from her exhaust. She explained she needed a replacement motor and had lined one up. Instead of issuing Kathy with a defect notice, John gave her his card and told her that before she collected her new motor he would check its mechanical condition and make enquiries to learn if it was stolen or not. A couple of days after that, Kathy called him about the replacement motor. He invited her for coffee and, from there, a friendship developed.

Six months after that meeting, John told Kathy about his wife and child. A couple of months later that, Kathy went to Gollan Street and met them. Kathy had spoken to Ricky on the phone a number of times before that, so Ricky invited Kathy over. Kathy became friends with Ricky and was a regular visitor to the house. She observed that John and Ricky's relationship was unstable.

Ricky apparently told Kathy that she had a drinking problem. Kathy said Ricky was consuming half to a full four-litre cask of wine a night. Ricky had asked Kathy for help and she offered to go to Alcoholics Anonymous with her, but Ricky declined. They would talk about Ricky's marriage problems, her arguments with Alistaire, and the effects her drinking were having. Kathy stated that Ricky would call her during the arguments and Kathy could hear John, Ricky and Alistaire all yelling at each other. When she was at Gollan Street, Kathy said she had to physically intervene between Ricky and Alistaire on occasions.

Kathy told Constable Ball that John had taken Alistaire to her parents' place at Rivett on the night of 1 April. John and Alistaire stayed there for three weeks, till Alistaire was taken back to Ricky after the Family Court hearings. According to Kathy, John was most upset at losing because he knew how frightened Alistaire was of Ricky. John was seriously concerned for Alistaire's safety.

Kathy admitted that John was living with her. He had moved into the unit a week ago, but they weren't sleeping together.

John and Alistaire slept in the bedroom, while Kathy slept on a mattress on the lounge room floor. The unit had two bedrooms, but there was only one bed.

To account for John's movements on the night prior to Sunday 4 May, Kathy made a point of saying that where she slept on the floor was near the door to the bedroom. Should anyone leave the bedroom they would have to step over her, making her aware of their presence.

On the Saturday John left for work at 1.30 in the afternoon, returning a little after midnight the following morning, still dressed in his uniform. John told Kathy about Ricky's attempted suicide and the visit by the Mental Health Crisis Team. John went to bed at one o'clock, while she stayed up reading till three.

In relation to John picking up Alistaire the Friday before, Kathy told Constable Ball that John said he didn't find Alistaire at school as arranged, but had to drive to Gollan Street where he met both Ricky and Alistaire. Why there was this discrepancy, when John had told police he met Alistaire at the school, is unknown. But that was what Kathy had said.

Kathy added that Ricky had spoken to her about her use of marijuana, that she'd smoked it in the past. She also mentioned the time Ricky purchased cannabis for her dying father in October 1996, but wasn't sure if Ricky used any of it for herself.

John had spoken to Kathy about his transfer to Queensland Police, saying that he and Ricky would go if he were to get the posting. John apparently wanted Ricky to go, but Ricky had told Kathy that she wouldn't leave Canberra. John was not surprised. John wanted Ricky to give up the alcohol to save their marriage, but she wouldn't do that either. John regretted he and Ricky couldn't reconcile their differences.

Kathy was devastated when she heard that Ricky had died. John had told her after talking on the phone to an ambulance officer who was at Gollan Street on Sunday night. She didn't know what to say to John. Kathy did make the comment that she wouldn't have been surprised to hear Ricky had died in a car accident while she was drinking.

The search of the premises didn't come up with anything of interest. An AFP notebook and diary were found on a table in the kitchen area. Constable Ball did find an alcohol swab in the medicine cabinet in the bathroom, which she took into her possession.

The search of Kathy's parents' house in Rivett didn't yield anything either. Noel and Ben reviewed their decisions. Was it right to have brought John in? What were they hoping to find with the warrants? Had they missed something in their search of his Nissan Patrol?

If they had the time over, Noel and Ben couldn't think of what else they would have done differently. They did what they did and the future would tell if their decision was right or not.

Midnight on Wednesday 7 May, Noel and Ben wearily tidied their desks. It had been a long and exhausting day.

CHAPTER SEVEN

Thursday 8 May to Friday 23 May 1997

Door knocks, toxicology, and a breakthrough

For the next three weeks, every detective on the investigation team, and others brought in to help with the workload, pounded the pavements around Gollan Street in Evatt and Stuart Flats in Griffith. They knocked on doors and questioned every resident who was at home. It's the most mundane part of any investigation. It can also be the most vital. People's recollections of seemingly insignificant events might help police put together a picture of what happened to Ricky, and possibly help identify who was responsible.

When Operation Gollan began, Mr Stoll and the Commanders, Dau and McDermott, offered Noel the resources of experienced detectives. Noel declined. He had his way of approaching the investigation, and he knew who would be best suited to perform the tasks. Noel was to prove to his superiors there was a method in what they considered was his madness.

After all, what team leader would refuse the assistance of an experienced officer?

Noel knew his colleagues well enough, through experience rather than personally, that the more seasoned detectives, while excellent at reviewing the evidence and assessing its worth, weren't always as impassioned at doing the hard slog to pound the pavement and knock on everyone's door. Noel preferred to enlist the help of young officers, both uniformed and newly promoted detectives. It didn't matter to Noel if they had never worked on a large-scale investigation. He didn't want them for their experience, he wanted them for their zeal, enthusiasm and willingness to follow directions to the nth degree.

Some of the officers that would work with Noel gathering evidence had only been in general duties for as little as six months. The situation became a quid pro quo. Noel had a team of eager officers who would carry out their orders to the letter, and the officers gained invaluable experience that would help in their careers. It worked well.

While statements were taken from most people living in Gollan Street and the surrounding area, the door knock didn't offer the investigators any new information. They did chase up what were, at the time, considered to be possible leads. Some local kids told police they had seen a needle in a nearby park about four months earlier, and a couple of neighbours remembered being woken on the Sunday morning of Ricky's death at around two by a barking dog.

Police checked to see if there was any likely connection to Ricky's death, but there wasn't. Or at least, the information didn't appear to have any relevance.

The investigation team focused on Stuart Flats, seeking any information they could on John Conway and Kathy McFie. Kathy seemed to know most of the people in the complex. She knew them well enough to acknowledge, while there were others she had become more familiar with and with whom she would enter into conversation. John, however, seemed to keep to himself. He was seen in Kathy's company, but few of the neighbours had actually met him. There was little any of the neighbours could tell police that would corroborate their suspicions.

During the door knock of Stuart Flats, Detective Andrew Gomsi made a note about seeing Kathy McFie speaking with a Danny Williams. Danny was known to police. He had drug and theft related charges against him and a police record that dated back to his juvenile days. In fact, Danny was serving weekend detention for drug possession at the time. Detective Gomsi didn't think there was anything untoward going on between Kathy and Danny, but he thought he'd pass his observations on, just in case anything came of their association in the future.

Police continued gathering background on John Conway, Ricky Conway, and 42-year-old Kathy McFie. They spoke to friends, associates and family. The investigating team wanted to know more about each of the persons, as individuals and their relationship to one another. A lot of what they found out during the three weeks confirmed what they already knew. John's first wife, however, gave police a very different story about their separation than he had.

Ben Cartwright tracked down John Conway's first wife, Rosalie, who was living in Queensland. Ben flew interstate and took a statement from her at her local police station.

John's first marriage lasted around 12 years. Unlike the version John gave in his taped record of interview, Rosalie left Canberra because of health reasons. She had become intolerant of the cold, which affected her circulation. Her doctor suggested she move to a warmer climate, so she returned to Queensland with her daughter. Rosalie had discussed the move with John and he said he would be applying for a transfer to Brisbane, but instead, their marriage dissolved.

In Ben's words, 'He [John] put his wife and kid on a bus, waved goodbye and never saw them again … what sort of guy does that? *How* can you do that?'

Whether Rosalie and her daughter flew to Queensland, or caught the bus, is inconsequential. The point for Ben was that John knew his wife was leaving and had discussed moving north with her, but that was all he did. Rosalie's trip to Queensland was not unexpected. John waited till she had gone before ending the relationship. From Ben's perspective, it showed John to be incredibly detached and a coward.

Another interesting piece of information for Ben was that Rosalie, prior to leaving Canberra, had suspected John of having an affair with Ricky. Again, another contradiction to what John had said in his interview. He wasn't separated from his wife when he met Ricky, as he had told Ben and Noel, but was still very much married. In fact, what finally ended the marriage was when Rosalie phoned John from Queensland one evening to discuss future plans and a woman answered. It was Ricky. John spoke to Rosalie and tried to explain, but it was too late.

John's wife described him as being arrogant and wanting his own way. John, as he had confessed, didn't have many friends. He was a loner. Of the friends he did have, they tended to be women. He never attempted to contest the custody of his daughter although he did keep in contact. He would call her for her birthday, at Christmas, and the like.

Before joining the police, John had been with the Royal Australian Air Force. He studied engineering and wanted to become a navigator. He was knocked back, and then left in 1985, a year before he met Ricky.

* * *

The two weeks after Noel and Ben's record of interview with John Conway, he would call the office for Operation Gollan about every other day requesting an update. His manner was polite, friendly, but occasionally his emotions got the better of him. John would always ask for Ben, as he knew him better. When Ben wasn't available Noel would take the call.

Neither Noel nor Ben would give John any information. They wouldn't be evasive. They were cordial and sympathetic to John's situation. They'd just tell him they were still following leads, letting him believe they were going through the motions, rather than running an investigation. He would ask when the inquest would be, and Ben and Noel would tell him the same thing, 'Later in the year.'

John was anxious for the coronial inquest to be over. With any suspicious death, the coroner is presented with evidence from the police and the pathologist's report. From that the coroner holds an inquest to determine the cause of death, who may be responsible and whether there is enough evidence to pursue the matter legally. John would have hoped that the coroner would find Ricky had committed suicide.

Given Noel and Ben's grilling and their admission that Ricky had died suspiciously, it's doubtful even John thought his hopes would be realised.

It was possible the coroner would find Ricky died from misadventure, in that she experimented taking the heroin with a person or persons unknown. The coroner could also make an open finding, meaning Ricky's death and who was responsible was still unknown, but the police could continue their investigations. With an open finding, the coroner can still make submissions as to who is most likely responsible. Either way, once the case gets to a coronial inquest, it usually means the police have run out of leads and don't have enough evidence to pursue any suspect.

If anything, Noel and Ben did have time on their side. They could continue to stall John, or in Noel's words 'play' him. An inquest is usually held six months after the death. This gives police time to gather whatever evidence they can.

If John was guilty, Noel believed he would have felt safe. He'd gotten away with it. The only reason he called Ben was because he thought he had to. It was part of his role-playing. He was trying to convince everyone he loved Ricky and couldn't have killed her.

John would have known that had Noel and Ben had any real evidence they would have just arrested him. He had been able to walk away after the six-hour interview. Noel knew John thought he was free. Any trace of evidence against him would have been cleaned up. 'They tried, but they couldn't get me' is what Noel assumed was going through John's mind.

Noel and Ben knew a little, probably more than they realised at the time, but couldn't prove anything. Their bosses wanted results. Results drive all investigations. It's very well to have theories, but the Commanders and the Chief of Police wanted practical progress. Even some of their colleagues thought that Operation Gollan had exhausted all the avenues open to it.

After making enquiries, literally, around the world, the AFP Forensic Scientific Unit finally got back to Noel on the testing of the puncture hole. It wouldn't be easy, but they were willing to give it a try. Unlike a knife wound where the size of a blade can be determined by the depth of the cut, or the type of blade by the smoothness or tearing of the wound, a needle-stick injury is very fine and smooth. It would be a first if the AFP Forensic Scientific Unit could determine whether one large gauge, or two or more smaller gauge needles penetrated Ricky's arm.

Despite some uncertainty as to the success of the testing, Noel had excited the scientific officers at the prospect. They were willing to accept the challenge and ready to go.

Noel phoned Dr Jain and requested the section of skin and membrane that he'd asked the pathologist to keep. Dr Jain had some bad news. Unfortunately, to determine to what extent the heroin had penetrated the membrane, Dr Jain had to cut into the section, destroying the sample.

Noel was disappointed. He knew now he couldn't prove his theory, and he'd have to pass on the bad news to the AFP Forensic Scientific Unit.

The toxicology results became known about the same time. They confirmed the earlier suspicions that Ricky had died from an overdose of heroin. In fact, the concentration of heroin, or morphine as it is clinically referred to, was 3.3 milligrams per litre in the blood, 0.61 milligrams per litre in the urine, 36 milligrams per litre in the bile, and two milligrams per kilogram in the stomach.

The fact there were lesser quantities in the urine indicated that Ricky had died at least 15 minutes after being injected, before her body could properly process the drug — not that that would have been possible, as the amount in her blood was the highest ever found in a human body within the ACT, or for that matter, Australia. It equated to ten times the amount normally found in people who had died as a result of a heroin overdose.

With the heroin found in the stomach, Dr Jain believed that the only way it could be there was if it had been ingested. Ricky must have taken the drug orally. Noel asked if the drug could have leached through the walls of the stomach from the blood vessels surrounding it. Dr Jain admitted the process of osmosis had been considered, but he couldn't be sure. Dr Jain recommended Noel send samples to Professor Olaf Drummer, Associate Professor in Forensic Medicine at Monash University in Victoria. Dr Jain knew Professor Drummer as an expert in drug related deaths. If anyone would know, Professor Drummer would.

Noel and Ben thought, given the coffee incident recorded in Ricky's diary and John's discovery of the foils, he had attempted to introduce heroin into Ricky's body. He could have been trying to fill her body with enough traces of the drug to have an analyst believe there was past use of the drug before the overdose.

One test for long-term drug use is to examine the hair. It absorbs drugs, like any other tissue, through the blood. Hair grows approximately one centimetre per month and the length of drug use will correspond with the length of hair. Meaning, traces found in one centimetre or less of hair indicates the person has only used the drug in the last month. Five centimetres or more and the person has been using for up to or over five months.

If Ricky had never used heroin, and the overdose was the first introduction of the drug to her body, then no trace should be found in her hair. Rather, the drug would only be present on the follicle, which is bathed by blood. Ricky's hair, however, contained traces of morphine close to the scalp, within a centimetre. This would mean Ricky had been taking heroin in the last month.

There was another explanation, however. Hair is incredibly absorbent, able to soak up traces of whatever it comes into contact with. It was possible that the traces of morphine found on Ricky's hair could have come from blood contamination during the autopsy. This would contradict any evidence the defence might try and introduce saying Ricky had a history, if only recent, of heroin use.

It was very likely Ricky's hair had been contaminated. That meant John hadn't had sufficient time to deceive Ricky into taking the heroin unknowingly.

Yet, there was the heroin in the stomach. After studying the samples and reading the report from Dr Jain, Professor Drummer agreed that the process of osmosis seemed to be the most likely cause for traces of heroin being in Ricky's stomach. He did, however, also admit that he couldn't categorically rule out the likelihood that Ricky had previously ingested the drug.

Security of Operation Gollan was of concern to Noel. John Conway had worked at Belconnen Police Station and still knew a number of officers. The day he waltzed into the detectives' room unannounced was evidence of his familiarity. While the enquiry continued to be based at Belconnen, Noel was worried that John might find out more than Noel wanted him to know. Noel didn't think any officer within the station would deliberately pass on information, but it was likely that they would overhear team members talking in the corridor. If John were to then be speaking casually with an officer from Belconnen, that officer could let something slip, even if the officer were unaware of the significance of his information.

On the evidence to date, it was quite clear to Noel's bosses that if Ricky was murdered, the prime suspect had to be her husband, John Conway. While the logic was obvious, it didn't mean they didn't have doubts.

Police officers are part of the law enforcement fraternity. It is very hard for them to believe anyone in their ranks could commit murder.

Commanders Dau and McDermott, and ACT Chief Police Officer Stoll, understood the dilemma Noel faced if he continued to run the operation from Belconnen. Whether they fully agreed with Noel's suspicions of John Conway or not, they agreed that remaining at the station could compromise the investigation. They allowed Noel to move his team to the Winchester Centre, the operational headquarters of ACT Policing.

Operation Gollan didn't have to move far, as the Winchester Centre is only around the corner from Belconnen Police Station. It did give the team more room and better security. Noel could now plan his investigation, set up a proper incident room, and know that John Conway couldn't just walk in off the street.

Noel also requested that, given John was the prime suspect, Internal Investigations be brought in on the case. After all, murder is the most serious crime anyone, especially a police officer who is entrusted to serve and protect, could commit. The allegation alone should require the input of Internal Investigations. Mr Stoll contacted Internal Investigations. They considered the request, but thought the matter was being handled well enough and they didn't feel there was a reason for them to become involved.

With the move to the Winchester Centre came the secondment of another officer to the team, Constable Corey Heldon. Corey Heldon was brought onto the investigation as an intelligence coordinator to assist Constable Oren Kulawiec with the growing workload. Basically, all statements, interviews, officers' notes and any other pieces of information would be given to Corey and Oren to analyse and enter into a database. It would be their job to categorise the information, cross-check names and descriptions looking for common links or threads, and make recommendations to Noel as to the information's relevance to the operation.

All major operations have an Intel officer. It is difficult for a team leader, or any other officer, to be able to keep up with the number of enquiries being conducted all at the same time. An officer's workload is too great, and they must be focused solely on their task. They can't be fully aware of the progress in every enquiry. By passing all the information through a central point, the Intel officer, he or she can then begin 'joining the dots' and keep the whole team abreast of where the investigation is going.

As an example, one officer might find out from a neighbour that an unfamiliar car was seen in the street the night Ricky died. The officer might become suspicious and decide to investigate the car further. Another officer, however, speaking to a separate neighbour, finds out that the car belonged to a relative or friend visiting for the weekend. An Intel officer, having seen both statements, would then advise no further action on the vehicle, providing it is proved to be the same vehicle. The Intel officer would advise action, if say, it wasn't someone visiting in the street, and the second officer's neighbour gave more information, like a description of the occupant.

Investigations can be like jigsaws. You know what it is meant to look like, but you're not sure you have all the pieces. Sometimes, however, the one piece you're looking for can be in a place you never thought to look.

In time, Oren moved from the intelligence role to other duties within the investigation, leaving Corey to handle all the incoming information. In Noel's words Corey became the 'hub' of the investigation. Noel saw Corey's role as being pivotal in the investigation. He knew there would be a number of different lines of enquiries being conducted looking into Ricky and John's background, and he relied on Corey's assessment of the information to decide what or who needed further investigating.

Noel had another job for Corey. He gave her the record of interview he and Ben conducted with John. Noel asked Corey to check John's recollections against information they had gathered from associates, neighbours and friends. Corey made a chronological list of events and incidents John referred to in his interview. Against the list, Corey used other people's statements to verify what John had said. Not everything John had told Ben and Noel matched. There were too many inconsistencies. Corey even picked up that John said he had been to a shopping mall with Alistaire on Anzac Day, the day of the coffee incident, yet the mall was closed that day. While it could be argued John had a poor and confused memory, Corey's analysis of John's interview only strengthened Noel and Ben's suspicions.

Corey took a copy of a photo of Ricky and placed it on a wall in the office, well away from the link charts bearing pictures of friends, relatives and suspects. She wanted to remind herself and the others why they had been brought together. The team appreciated the gesture and Ricky's photo remained a focus for all.

John Conway phoned the investigation unit in the early morning of Friday 23 May, just before 10.00 am. He asked to speak to Ben, but Ben was unavailable, so Noel took the call. John had recently retuned to work, after having been on bereavement leave since Ricky's death. He felt his colleagues treated him quite well. They had expressed to him their sympathies and condolences. Naturally, John wanted to know what was happening with the investigation, if there was anything more Noel and Ben knew about Ricky's death. Noel only said that the investigation was still progressing. There wasn't much more for Noel to say.

Noel took the opportunity to talk casually with John, to sound him out on how his life was going. He asked John about the house and what his plans were. John said he was thinking of renting it out, providing his transfer to Queensland was accepted. John still wanted to join the Queensland Police and hoped the investigation wouldn't interfere with the process. Noel suggested John, Kathy and Alistaire call in for an interview, to tidy a few matters up. Kathy had still to sign her statement she'd given to Susan Ball on 7 May. John agreed and made a tentative arrangement for the following week. Noel replaced the receiver. It was frustrating for Noel. There was so much he wanted to say to John, if only to gag the smugness in his voice. But he couldn't.

On that Friday, Noel was being pressured to show some progress on the investigation. Almost three full weeks had passed. Noel and Ben had their suspicions, but there was little evidence coming forward to support their theory. Their superiors were starting to make noises, suggesting that if nothing new were forthcoming, the operation would be wound down and the team split up and posted back to their original duties.

Noel, Ben and the rest of the team had worked too hard to see it all end without a result. They knew what had happened. They knew John Conway was involved in the murder of his wife, Ricky. They just needed more time to prove it. There was a feeling that there was some piece of evidence out there. It could be, which they hoped it wasn't, something they had missed or not realised in their earlier investigations. It could be, also, something or someone yet to be known to the team.

A phone rang in the incident room. Ben picked up the receiver, a reflex action. The caller identified himself as a detective from Woden Police. He had a person in custody who wanted to talk about the Conway murder. The prisoner said she knew who killed 'the copper's wife'. Ben looked at his watch. He felt this was the break they were waiting for and he wanted to note the time: 11.17 am. Ben would never forget it.

At Woden Police Station, Detective Constable Joanne van der Son introduced Noel and Ben to Karen, who had been arrested earlier that morning for possession. Before speaking to Karen about what she knew, Noel and Ben were curious why, after almost three weeks, she had decided to pass on her information. Karen admitted she was both scared and troubled by what she knew. In fact she still wasn't sure she was safe.

Karen surprised Noel and Ben by saying she wasn't scared of who killed Ricky, but of the police.

In March, Karen met a man named Barry Steer through her de facto husband, George (not his real name). George and Barry both dealt drugs, but George had been arrested and was serving time at Goulburn Correctional Centre in southern New South Wales. With George in gaol, Barry became a regular visitor to Karen's address. Karen was quick to add that she was never unfaithful to her husband and that Barry was only a friend. Barry was just looking out for her.

A couple of weeks ago, Barry was at Karen's unit. He said he needed to talk to her, to tell her about something that had happened. Karen wasn't sure why Barry wanted to speak to her. He didn't seem agitated or concerned, he just talked.

Barry told Karen that he and a mate had killed a woman. They had given her a hot shot. A hot shot is a mix of heroin and battery acid. That didn't fit with the autopsy report, but it wouldn't be the first time a felon had elaborated to impress.

'What woman?' Karen enquired, not sure whether to believe her visitor or not.

'A copper's wife.' Barry then detailed what had happened, 'We had a key ... went running in ... we seen her and grabbed her. I held her down and Danny gave her the shot ... I was on top of her and I said, "I've got to tell you a story."'

Barry said he and his mate were being paid $55,000 for the job, and that it was easy. His justification for doing the job was because he'd been told Ricky was a child basher and in his mind she deserved to die.

Barry mentioned the names Kathy and John, though Karen was a little confused over who was McFie and who was Conway. Barry added that he didn't care if the police questioned him, because there would be no investigation

'The copper and his mates in the police force would look after things,' Barry assured Karen.

Karen didn't accept what Barry had told her. It seemed too far-fetched. She hadn't known Barry for long, but he didn't fit the stereotypical contract killer. He was a malnourished drug pusher, not an assassin. A day later, Karen was in a taxi when she heard the news report. Her body chilled at the news. Police were after anyone with any information in the mysterious death of Ricky Conway, wife of police constable

John Conway. It was too bizarre to have been a coincidence. Karen now believed Barry.

Only the day before Woden detectives arrested Karen, she was walking through a public car park and noticed Barry. He attempted to sell her some heroin, but she declined. They began to talk and Barry shrugged towards a skinny male not far from where they were standing.

'That's Danny,' Barry told Karen. 'He's the one I did it with … that's him … that's Danny.'

Barry never gave Danny's last name and Karen hadn't seen him before that day, so she couldn't help police any further.

Karen was burdened with what she knew. It affected her sleep and she was afraid to call the police, for fear Barry was right about the police covering up the murder. She thought she'd be killed if she said anything, either by Barry or the police. Karen had a drugs record and she imagined police, the Special Operations Team, would raid her place and execute her, saying she had resisted.

After being arrested, Karen felt she had nothing to lose. She needed to tell someone. Noel and Ben assured her there was no conspiracy. Cop or no cop, if John Conway had committed murder, they were out to get him.

Karen's statement supported Noel and Ben's theory on how Ricky had died. It connected 29-year-old Barry Steer to Kathy McFie and John Conway, and there was a fourth person, Danny, yet to be identified. The only description Karen could give of Danny was that he was 'skinny'. Noel and Ben planned to visit Goulburn Correctional Centre the next day to see if Karen's husband, George, could give more information on Danny.

Even though Karen's statement was damning to all the parties, there still wasn't enough evidence to go and arrest everyone. Noel and his team needed more. They needed conclusive evidence linking all the players, and ideally, for one or more to admit to the whole conspiracy. Even without confessions, a strong brief of evidence needed to be put together. Noel knew he would have to rely on surveillance and electronic listening devices, hoping to catch incriminating discussions if the targets became careless and talked about the murder amongst themselves.

Noel and Ben immediately gave Commander John Dau and the Executive Committee of the AFP a briefing on Karen's information. It was a bombshell. Karen knew too many details, details that had been kept from the media, for it to be a hoax. There was only one way she could have known what happened, other than being involved herself and that was hearing it from the killer.

Noel requested electronic surveillance be placed on all the targets — John, Kathy, Barry and Danny, once they learnt his identity. The team would need to have more officers to conduct visual surveillance of the homes. Noel needed resources, and he got them. The Executive Committee gave their full support.

Noel warned the Committee it would cost money. Mr Stoll assured Noel, 'It's not the money that matters, it is justice.'

Operation Gollan was officially renamed Operation Aquatic. Noel and his team were now formally working on a murder investigation. The Executive Committee gave Operation Aquatic the highest priority within the Federal Police. Whatever Noel wanted from this point on, he got. He just had to ask and show good cause.

CHAPTER EIGHT

Game on

Reading through Karen's record of interview, it became apparent to Ben where his toilet seat fitted in. Obviously Barry Steer, or his mate, Danny, had used the toilet during their time in the house. While they might have used it, it didn't give Ben an indication as to how long the two men stayed in the house. It could have been minutes, or it could have been hours.

The matter of the needle mark, however, was still not resolved. Barry Steer hadn't mentioned anything other than the fact Danny had injected Ricky. They might have, as Noel thought, injected her more than once in the same hole. Given the amount of heroin found in her body, they had either done exactly that, or used a whopping big syringe and needle. It would have to remain an unanswered question for the moment.

Another oddity were the alcohol swabs. Why would anyone, commissioned to kill a person by injecting them with heroin, bother to sterilise the skin before doing so?

It didn't seem to make sense. It could be they were attempting to make it look like Ricky had injected herself. Yet, they didn't leave the needle and didn't bother to try and locate a vein. They just plunged the needle in without any consideration for Ricky, causing uncharacteristic bruising for a drug user. Then again, as far as Ben knew, these two guys were drug addicts, and the use of the swabs was nothing more than habit.

On the morning of Saturday 24 May, Noel, Ben and Karen drove from Canberra to Goulburn, just over an hour's drive along the Federal and Hume Highways. They were visiting George, Karen's de facto, to find out what he knew of Barry and Danny, specifically Danny's last name.

Any prisoner known to give information to the police, however vital that information may be in the eyes of most people, is known as a 'dog'. Suffice to say that if the inmates find out he or she has 'dogged' another, retribution can be hard and swift. A distorted code of honour amongst thieves. One of the rules for survival inside gaol is to just keep your mouth shut.

Before Noel and Ben could speak with George, Karen spoke to him alone. They allowed her to enter the Correctional Complex unaccompanied, while they waited for her return. Noel and Ben were relying on Karen to assure George that they were only after simple information on Barry and Danny. They weren't out to make George's life difficult. They weren't interested in whatever dealings he had with the other two, and they weren't announcing their visit to the world.

If anything, Noel and Ben had to keep an especially low profile. It was possible Barry and Danny had other associates in the gaol, and they didn't want to risk having anything getting back to their suspects.

Karen had been spooked by Barry's admission. She had suffered mentally and emotionally. If George felt anything for Karen, then hopefully he'd be angry at the anguish Barry had put his de facto through, angry enough to speak to the police. After more than an hour, Karen emerged and said that George would speak with the two detectives.

As it turned out, George had been worried about Karen. She had visited him after Barry told her what he'd done. George had already decided, only the day before, the same day Karen had been arrested, that he needed to tell police about what he and his wife knew. He wasn't happy about Barry visiting his wife and upsetting her.

George had met Barry Steer at Campbelltown Detention Centre in late 1996. They met up again by accident when they both happened to be in Woden a couple of months later. George didn't keep in contact, but Barry did drop by his and Karen's unit a couple of times. George never went to Barry's place and didn't know where he lived. After he was imprisoned again in March, George had heard that Barry had been hanging around his wife. He wasn't impressed, especially after Karen told him about Barry killing the copper's wife.

George didn't know who Danny was and admitted he didn't know Barry well enough to be of any help. He did promise Noel and Ben that he wouldn't be making any contact with Barry, or anyone else, about what they'd discussed.

The visit didn't really help the investigation, but it was one of those things that had to be done. As for Karen, she agreed to help police. Noel and Ben hoped Barry might visit her again and give more detail to tie in John and Kathy.

Karen was still anxious though. She worried what would happen to her if Barry found out she'd spoken with police. Noel and Ben gave her their contact phone numbers. She could call them at any time. They were there to protect her.

Operation Aquatic was under way. Arrangements were made for experienced AFP officers from other States to join the team and assist with the visual surveillance of the suspects. Noel didn't want to run the risk of John recognising anyone.

Sergeant Richard 'Dick' Thrift coordinated the surveillance on all the suspects. He recommended that ACT policing officers track John, while those from interstate observed Stuart Flats. Although some of the ACT officers had worked with John and ran the risk of being noticed, they had the advantage of knowing Canberra and could keep themselves at a safe distance and would not be compromised.

As he had done before, Noel also recruited from the uniformed ranks, as well as officers he'd worked with in Special Operations who he knew would be dedicated to the team. Their job, amongst other things, was to man the listening devices.

The officer would have to listen to the conversations and then record what was relevant to the investigation. They had the advantage of being able to radio straight to the team with any news or developments, so that appropriate action could be taken. For a lot of the officers manning the listening posts, it would be their first experience in a large-scale investigation.

Manning a listening post can be a tiring, thankless and boring task. In a week's worth of conversations there might be five minutes of dialogue that would be worth anything to the investigation. If they were lucky. In other cases there might be nothing.

To keep those officers working at the listening posts motivated and feeling a valued member of the team, Noel would, each night of the investigation, visit every post and brief them on the day's developments. Noel would meet surveillance teams at a park, where the temperature was below zero. Many of the surveillance officers had only three hours' sleep a day on average for the duration of the investigation and survived on a diet of hot dogs and strong black coffee. Such is the life for those working on surveillance. They are the unseen and unsung heroes of investigations. They work covertly, provide enormous assistance to the investigators and their work is conducted, at times, under very trying conditions. On this occasion they were tasked to observe a fellow police officer, an accident squad member, while that officer was at work and in his off duty time. It was autumn, turning to winter. The weather conditions were harsh, sub-zero temperatures every night and some days. Resources were short and members worked ridiculously long hours, but the surveillance team had the same attitude to the task as the rest of the Operation Aquatic team. This was the investigation of one of their own who had crossed the line. The investigation had to be done effectively and what it took to do it correctly would be done.

When Noel and Ben asked how things were going, the Surveillance Team Leader would respond, 'Fucking minus 27 degrees, how do you think things are going?' It was said in good humour and that humour and esprit de corps lasted the entire investigation.

With the start of Operation Aquatic, as well as the officers running surveillance and manning the listening posts, Mr Stoll assigned Detective Sergeant Brian McDonald.

Brian McDonald was one of the AFP's most experienced investigators, having worked on a number of homicides and other serious crime operations. In fact, his reputation as a detective was unparalleled within the AFP. Brian, however, was coy about such claims. Despite his reputation, Brian never took credit for any of the results attributed to him by others. He always said it was a group effort and that his team did all the work.

Noel was unsure of Brian McDonald's inclusion in the operation. He was concerned that, maybe, management had positioned Brian to subtly replace Noel as the team leader. Now that the enquiry had become a high priority, it didn't surprise Noel that someone more experienced would take control.

Noel's concerns were quickly put to rest when, on his arrival at the operation's office, Brian McDonald explained his brief. Brian had been instructed to assist Noel in any way he could, particularly with the application for listening devices and telephone intercepts. Brian had become a self-made expert in the area of electronic surveillance, or more importantly, the application for, and wording on, the warrants to approve the installation of the devices. He would also be a Team Leader, responsible for the officers manning the listening posts.

A warrant basically sets out the parameters within which the police must work, as well as identifying the type of evidence they wished to gather pertaining to a particular line of enquiry. In other words, if the warrant being served by a police officer states they are to search a silver car belonging to a particular person for the reason of ascertaining whether a body had been concealed or carried in the vehicle, the police can't search a black car owned by the same person. Police the world over must adhere to what is written on the warrant, however narrow the focus. That, however, doesn't mean police can't act on anything illegal they observe during the execution of the warrant.

From the moment Brian McDonald joined the Aquatic team, his experience, composure and direction greatly added to the investigation. Noel briefed Brian on what he hoped they would get from the listening devices. It was decided to intercept John Conway's home phone, the phone at Weston Police Station Traffic Operations used by John, Barry Steer's home phone, and to place listening devices in both John's and Barry's homes.

At this time, John and Kathy had left the Stuart Flats complex and moved into 35 Gollan Street, as John told Ben, 'For Alistaire's sake.'

Detective Constable Susan Ball, who had taken Kathy McFie's statement, was given the task of writing the affidavits for the telephone intercepts. The affidavits are documents the judge considers, which outline the police evidence to support the application for the intercepts.

Susan Ball was one of the officers who couldn't believe John Conway could have murdered his wife. She had worked with John in Traffic Operations. It's human nature. Most people wouldn't ever consider a person they knew was capable of murder, let along a fellow police officer.

As Susan typed out the affidavits, reading through the evidence that had been compiled by the rest of the team, including the statement from Karen, she broke down and cried. It was too much for her. Her faith in a once trusted colleague had been shattered. Noel actually thought of taking Susan off the case at that time, but he thought better of it. Had Noel requested Susan leave Aquatic, he felt she would have seen it as a failure of duty on her part. Noel didn't believe she had failed him. She had an opinion, but the evidence proved her wrong.

If anything, Susan Ball became a great help to Noel, particularly as he used her later to run the enquiry on heroin, everything from the effects of the drug on the human body through injection, smoking, ingestion or other means. Susan carried out the task, seeking assistance from Professor Olaf Drummer and other local and international experts. Through her detailed enquiries, there was little, if anything, Susan didn't know about the effects of heroin.

Noel and Ben weren't sure what they would really get from installing the electronic surveillance. John had been a 'pretty cool customer', Kathy would follow John's lead, and Barry was a typical druggie with a big mouth. Danny was an unknown and still had to be identified. If anything, Noel and Ben were hoping to learn weaknesses of those under surveillance and what they thought of each other. It might be that Noel and Ben could use the information to their advantage. Maybe create a rift between them somehow.

The amount of money Barry had said John and Kathy were paying him and his mate created some discussion amongst the team. After all, $55,000 was a lot of money for an invalid pensioner and a uniformed police officer to pay. It was more than John earned in a year at his base salary.

It was likely Barry and Danny hadn't yet been paid. That appeared obvious from Karen's statement that she bumped into Barry only a day or two before selling drugs in a car park. He'd hardly continue selling drugs when he had enough money to leave the Territory and head for the Gold Coast. He would have definitely afforded himself a decent holiday if he'd been paid.

Ben knew John to be a miser. When they worked in Traffic together, John always arrived to work with a cut lunch. The most he would ever buy from the canteen was a cup of coffee. Ben couldn't recall ever seeing John put his hand in his pocket for anything more. As it was, John had admitted he would be applying for an overdraft to pay the $5,000 legal fee for his custody challenge. Then why would he promise so much money to Barry and his mate?

Understandably, the incentive would have to be great to convince someone to kill his wife. Barry, however, was living off welfare and had a drug habit, being addicted to cannabis. He sold dope and, on occasion, heroin to make ends meet. In Ben's experience it was conceivable that just a couple of thousand would have seemed like a fortune to Barry.

As Barry was still dealing it could mean there was a problem with the money. John wouldn't or couldn't pay the full amount, and that could be his undoing. Then again, Barry and his mate might have to wait for Ricky's will to be finalised. John might be using the money he would inherit from Ricky's superannuation. John was the sole benefactor in Ricky's will. Noel ordered a complete audit of all of John's accounts to see if they could find any paper trail.

*   *   *

With the warrants for the listening devices and telephone intercepts approved by ACT Chief Police Officer Stoll and Commander Dau, and signed by a Federal Court judge, it was now time to get them active. The warrants were passed on to Telstra to activate the taps on the phones. Ben went with the AFP technicians to have the listening devices installed at the Stuart Flats complex and 35 Gollan Street.

Listening devices would be installed in John and Kathy's motor vehicles as well. To the best of their knowledge, Barry didn't have a car.

Within a day or two of Karen's statement the surveillance team identified Barry Steer's 'skinny mate' as being 21-year-old Danny Williams, the same Danny Williams Detective Constable Andrew Gomsi had observed speaking with Kathy McFie during the earlier door knock of the complex.

Corey Heldon immediately ran a check on Danny. To her dismay, she found out that Danny had been serving periodic detention the weekend of Ricky's death. He could not have taken part in Ricky's murder if he was locked away. This information also put into question the reliability of Karen's account. Had Karen heard correctly, or did Barry lie to her?

Needing to know more, Corey made enquiries at the Detention Centre at Red Hill. She was very careful not to let on why she was asking about Danny Williams. Corey received some surprising news. Danny had been released early on Saturday 3 May. He had not served a full weekend, corroborating Karen's statement. Corey passed the information onto the team and Danny's home and phone were included on the warrants.

By 6 June all electronic surveillance equipment and listening posts were in place. Operation Aquatic was ready.

Interestingly, the mood amongst the original team members had changed from when they were operating under Gollan. During Gollan there was some doubt as to John Conway's involvement. Now, working under Aquatic and with the information supplied by Karen, the team were focused on gathering all the evidence they could against John.

They were angry that a police officer would abuse his trust, and deceive his colleagues by committing the ultimate of crimes. John was not going to get away with murder if they could help it.

Listening to an average day in the life of Barry Steer and Danny Williams was not an exciting or glamorous task. Ben Cartwright describes Barry and Danny's day as being, '[they] get out of bed sometime between 10.00 am and midday … put on telly, sit on couch and fail to move till around three or four … get up and go into town … score drugs … come home … sit on couch … use drugs … watch telly … go to bed about midnight'.

That was the routine day in and day out, seven days a week. Their conversations weren't much better with the main topic revolving around drugs, the purchase of drugs, using drugs and getting the money to buy more drugs. Occasionally they would also discuss their favourite television programs, *Jerry Springer* and *Ricky Lake*.

To the relief of those officers manning the listening posts and to the investigation as a whole, Barry and Danny would discuss Ricky's murder.

It was Barry who did most of the talking. Barry was the 'mouth', as Danny said very little, or was not given the opportunity to do so. The conversation between Barry and Danny about Ricky's murder was recorded on Monday 9 Junc, three days after the electronic surveillance had begun.

Danny had called to see Barry and they began discussing their need for money. Both had bills to pay and were promised money, but the payment was late. Apparently they had been promised they would be paid in four weeks, but it was past that and they were becoming anxious. Barry is heard saying, 'Wish this fuckin' bitch would come over. I need some money. At least find out when we're gonna get some fuckin' money ...'

Barry later says, 'They're just not fucking, they ... they don't give a fuck, Danny. Honestly, they don't give a fuck. The job's been done. They don't give a fuck about us. What are we gonna do? Run to the police and say they owe us money? ... she come home, knocked on my door and said "I've been away, I'll come and see you next week, I'll have your money for you next week" ... she's really startin' to shit me ... she can go and get fucked. I'll go up to John because it was his fuckin' wife so he's the person responsible for the money and I'll tell the cunt, "You don't give me my money in seven days, cunt, and I'll have you in gaol." Simple as that.'

As the days went on, Barry made several verbal threats to physically harm John if he didn't pay them their money, though he only expressed his anger to Danny.

When they weren't discussing the lack of money, Barry and Danny would casually reminisce about their part in Ricky's murder, as most people would recall a night out with friends. The conversations were disturbing and chilling to those listening. Danny couldn't remember the night in much detail, but Barry did, and would go through the events of the night in minute detail. He even reminded Danny how they drank two 'poppers', fruit juices, from Ricky's fridge.

Hearing Barry say that they drank poppers was important to the investigators. Two empty popper juices were found in Ricky's bin when police conducted their search. While it didn't seem unusual at the time, it now played an important part in verifying that Barry and Danny were in Ricky's house the night she died.

Police never doubted Karen's evidence, or what they'd heard from Barry and Danny, but knowing about the poppers gave them corroborative evidence in linking the two men to the murder. Police could now be sure Barry and Danny were in the house on the night Ricky was murdered.

Barry went on and even suggested they should have searched Ricky's house for any money, or taken what they thought they could sell. When discussing Ricky and how they held her down and injected her, they would laugh. Neither Barry nor Danny showed any remorse, or any feelings of guilt at taking her life. They didn't consider Ricky a person, as someone's mother, or as someone's daughter. She was just a means to earning money.

John and Kathy were much smarter. There weren't any incriminating conversations coming from their home, work or vehicles. It's likely John suspected his phone and house were bugged, or at least decided to play it safe in case they were.

Police did notice that whenever John and Kathy wanted to talk about something in more detail, they would retreat to the back yard, or take a drive to a local park and walk around the field. Whatever John and Kathy spoke about would remain with them. All the surveillance teams could do was photograph the clandestine meetings.

There was contact between Kathy and Barry. Kathy would call Barry from a public telephone booth. She never phoned Barry from the Gollan Street home, and it appeared that Barry and Danny were told never to phone her or John. Even so, police had Barry's phone tapped and recorded the conversations.

Kathy met with Barry in his unit at the Stuart Flats complex. The discussions between Barry and Kathy centred on money, supposedly the money owed to Barry and Danny. The recordings weren't always clear. Kathy would give excuses why she couldn't pay them, which they seemed to accept, despite expressing their anger and anxiety in her absence.

Police, like Barry and Danny, were wondering if any money would ever change hands. That was until Wednesday 18 June when Kathy phoned Barry and told him she had the money. She referred to a note being left for her. She also made the point that she had to borrow the money.

Barry became all excited and raced to Danny's place, telling him to get his shoes on as they had 'got the call we've been waiting for'. It had been arranged for them all to meet up at a service station at Dickson, midway between Evatt and Griffith.

A surveillance team sat off the service station to video Kathy with Barry and Danny. The video operator got as close to the meeting point as he could without being detected. He lay on the frosty ground, the moisture seeping through his jacket making him even colder. He fought the chill, holding the camera steady, poking the lens through the thin cover of bush shielding his position.

Unfortunately, there was no audio, as the Holden Commodore Barry and Danny used had not been fitted with any listening device. Police were unaware of Barry having access to a vehicle. Still, the meeting was an important one and having vision of all three persons, plus the earlier recordings organising the get-together was incriminating for the threesome.

When Barry and Danny arrived back home, they complained at the amount they'd been given. Again, Kathy made excuses and she had promised to pay them more later. Barry and Danny were not happy.

When Kathy arrived home to John, they spoke about the weather. John didn't even ask where Kathy had been or what she'd been doing. It was just another day in the Conway-McFie household.

Wednesday 18 June was quite an important day for the detectives working on Operation Aquatic. Not only had they heard Kathy making arrangements to pay Barry and Danny and caught them all on video, but an earlier phone call between John and Kathy took their interest as well.

John had phoned Kathy from work earlier that afternoon. The conversation began normally with each exchanging pleasantries and John enquiring after Alistaire's health. The young boy seemed to have been running a fever that day, but had recovered. John then tells Kathy about an accident he attended, where a Mercedes and a van collided. The van had rolled onto its roof. It was a major accident with ambulance and rescue services attending, and received the attention of a local television news broadcaster, Capital Ten.

What was of interest to the team was the following conversation where John is telling Kathy of someone he met at the scene. 'Without mentioning any name, ah, guess who I saw, ah, at the prang?'

Kathy knew immediately, 'Of course'.

'Yeah.'

'Hm ... did you speak to him?'

'Hm ... as if I didn't know him.'

'Yeah, fair enough.'

'Have to ...'

'Of course ...'

'Ah, two other ... two other connies were there and, ah, so was my sergeant.'

'And he came and spoke to you?'

'Ah, not directly. He just made a comment about the quality of the, ah, Merc.'

'Oh okay ... huh, God, if he had half a brain he'd be dangerous.'

'That's about right.'

John and Kathy then went on to discuss domestic issues.

There was nothing more for the detectives to work on, but they had enough. A call was made to Capital Ten news and the investigators were able to get a hold of the camera tapes from the accident. The camera tapes are the unedited filming. A news crew will film a lot more than they actually broadcast.

Viewing the tapes, John Conway was seen standing near the Mercedes with another man. As the image was enhanced it became clearer who the man was. It was Danny Williams. Thanks to that footage and the telephone intercept, John could never deny knowing Danny. Slowly but surely the team on Aquatic were connecting all the dots.

As police kept monitoring the listening devices, Noel visited Anna Reiners to finalise her statement. During Noel's visit, Anna remembered some things with regard to John and Ricky. Anna recalled Ricky finding a coffee mug with a card from Kathy to John. Kathy had given John the mug as a gift and signed the card with her love. To the best of Anna's recollection it was in 1996. It was then that Ricky phoned Kathy to confront her, and Kathy said she was under the impression John was separated. Kathy apologised and added, had she known John was still married she would have 'backed right away'.

A little time after the phone call, Ricky unaccountably invited Kathy to Gollan Street and Kathy then befriended Ricky.

Without knowing the details of the investigation, Anna was suspicious of Kathy and her relationship with John. She believed Ricky had confided in Kathy, as Ricky had a very trusting nature, but Kathy would pass on whatever was discussed to John. As far as Anna could see, John and Kathy had conspired against Ricky.

During the Christmas of 1996, Anna had arranged with Ricky to care for Alistaire, to help Ricky and John save some money. John stepped in and told Ricky that Kathy would be looking after Alistaire. Ricky didn't like it, but went along with the arrangement for John's sake.

Anna told Noel that John's gun had been taken away from him. It was when he and Ricky first met. She couldn't recall any details, but she distinctly remembered it had something to do with the breakdown of his first marriage.

Anna produced a superannuation policy Ricky had with the Duntroon Military College where she had a casual position as a seamstress. The policy included a death cover of $35,240. Ricky had cashed in her superannuation with the Australian Federal Police when she left. The only money owing to Ricky was from Duntroon.

Anna added that she had had no contact with either John or Alistaire since Ricky's funeral. In fact, she remarked that at the funeral, John Conway had brought Kathy with him. Anna was disgusted.

Noel promised he'd speak with John and try and get him to call to arrange visits with Alistaire. Before Noel left, Anna stated Ricky had told her, after the custody hearing, that John would visit Alistaire's school twice a day, during the morning recess and at lunch, in contravention of the court order.

John continued to call the offices of Operation Aquatic. He particularly wanted to know if Ben had been told anything about his application to Queensland. Ben hadn't heard from them, and John, again, hoped there would be no problems. He was looking forward to taking Alistaire to Queensland and putting everything that had happened behind him. John added, since being back at Gollan Street, he'd noticed some jewellery and ornaments had gone missing. He suggested to Ben that Ricky might have sold the items to fund her drug habit. He also spoke about Ricky's account, which had almost totally been withdrawn, and couldn't understand what she had done with all her money in the weeks leading up to her death.

Based on John's information, police visited various pawnbrokers around Canberra, asking to check their records for any purchases that may appear against Ricky's name. Before a pawnbroker can make a purchase they must ask for some form of identification from the seller and record the details in a ledger. Ricky's name did not appear in any of the purchase documentation. Police, however, did find the names of Barry Steer and Danny Williams. Each had sold various items during the early part of 1997.

Police continued their door knocking of Gollan Street and the surrounding area, contacting people who were unavailable during the first visit. In an adjoining street to Gollan Street they came across a couple who were woken by dogs barking in the early hours of Sunday 4 May. The investigating team had already heard from people recalling dogs barking at that time, but that was all they had. This time, the couple were able to give more information. When they woke up they also heard a male voice speaking to someone else and saying, 'Get out of here.'

In Gollan Street police found the owner of a dog. The barking on Sunday 4 May had also woken the owner. The owner stated that the dog never barked at cars, only at people who walked past the house. The time was 2.16 in the morning. The owner went to see what was disturbing the dog and noticed the security lights illuminated on the house across the street. The lights were motion sensitive. Again, she heard male voices, more than one, moving along the street.

If those voices were Barry's and Danny's, as the police suspected, then this information helped the investigators with a possible time of death. Ricky either died just before two or just after that time, depending on whether the disturbance was caused by Barry and Danny's arrival or them leaving the scene.

Noel and Corey Heldon visited Jacqui Dillon. Jacqui was devastated to find out that Ricky had died of a heroin overdose. She didn't believe her friend would ever take hard drugs. It wasn't Ricky. Jacqui gave more details regarding the coffee incident on 27 April. She saw Ricky in the afternoon. Ricky looked terrible and Jacqui asked if she had been 'on the grog'. Ricky denied it and said John had given her something in her coffee to relax her, but she'd been 'off her face' for hours.

Jacqui warned her friend not to see John again, and to sever the relationship. Later that day, Ricky phoned Jacqui saying she had confronted John and accused him of poisoning her, adding that she could never trust him again. According to Jacqui, Ricky said that John responded to the poisoning allegation by saying, 'I wouldn't do that to you because they'd know it was me that done it [sic].'

Jacqui thought it unusual that John wasn't seen at the Gollan Street house after that day. She'd heard that John was visiting Alistaire at school during recess and at lunch.

Ricky had also gained access to John's sanctuary, the garage, where he kept all his tools and other belongings. John would occasionally hire his engineering and handyman services out building sheds and other small constructions for people around the area. Jacqui suggested to Ricky that she should sell some of his tools to help pay the bills. Soon after that, John began removing his possessions.

Noel spoke with another neighbour, who admitted to having had a relationship with John while he was married to Ricky. She described John as being an intelligent and controlling sort of person who displayed very little emotion. Their affair was brief, and lacked any form of romance.

On 11 June, John Conway, Kathy McFie and Alistaire attended the Winchester Centre as earlier requested. Detective Constable Susan Ball took Kathy to read over and sign her statement that she'd made on 7 May, while Ben spoke with Alistaire in the company of the police psychologist, Sonia Jacobs. Sonia was employed by the AFP to provide counselling and support to officers. She had been dealing with John Conway since the night Ricky's body was discovered.

With Kathy and Alistaire being looked after, Noel sat down with John. John was relaxed and comfortable. He was naturally curious about the investigation. Noel explained that, while a lot of work had been done, the police would still have to re-interview a lot of people. He justified the process by explaining that the first statements were taken hurriedly, and now more detail was sought, especially for the coronial inquest. Noel also said that the inquest had been pushed back until early the next year.

John accepted the situation as unavoidable, but was unhappy at the invasion of his privacy the investigation created. He'd had to deal with dodging the media since day one, and now the Queensland Police had put his application on hold. He wanted the coronial inquest to be over so he could resume his life. Noel told John that the team couldn't find any evidence to suggest Ricky had previously used heroin. John referred to Ricky's purchase of cannabis and asked if police were following that lead. Noel said they were, but couldn't give John any more details.

Noel deliberately began talking about Ricky, particularly in the context of being a mother and that, for Alistaire, she would be difficult to replace. Noel noticed John was uncomfortable talking about Ricky as a mother. Noel pushed the point, subtly asking how Kathy was fitting in and how she was feeling living in the house after Ricky's death. All Noel remembered John saying was 'Fine'.

John didn't want to get into a discussion. He didn't want Noel in his head. He changed the subject, talking about how some of his work colleagues had changed since his return. Some had totally ignored him. Noel was sympathetic, as much as could be under the circumstances. Their conversation was interrupted with the arrival of Alistaire, who'd just finished speaking with Ben.

Ben has three children of his own. He's a doting father and was the best choice for speaking to Alistaire. The discussion was casual, and there was nothing that came from it to help the investigation. Ben was more curious about how Alistaire was holding up with all that had happened. He seemed to be coping. For Ben, that was the main thing; though he knew, one day soon, Alistaire would lose his father.

Ben felt for the young boy. None of it was his fault, yet he would suffer for his father's actions.

CHAPTER NINE

Covert operations

On the weekend of 21 to 22 June 1997, police pulled over a Holden Commodore in the southern Canberra suburb of Calwell. The female driver was unable to give a sufficient sample for breath testing. She suffered from asthma. Police took her back to Woden Police Station to test her in a more controlled environment. They also told her they suspected her vehicle was used for the purposes of dealing illicit drugs. The driver's name was Joan (not her real name) and police knew her as the sister of Barry Steer.

Joan's car was of interest to Operation Aquatic, being the car Barry had used to meet with Kathy on 18 June. Surveillance kept a close watch on the vehicle, knowing Barry would occasionally borrow the car, or have his sister ferry him around.

Police had discussed placing a listening device in the car, but the topic would become academic.

Having satisfied the police she was not over the limit, Joan left the station. The experience, however, was not a welcome one for Joan. She knew her brother had used her car to sell drugs and she didn't want any part of it. She sold the car the following day. On a visit to her brother's a couple of days later, Joan would confront Barry over the incident and the police allegation, but he denied it all. Joan was not convinced.

The listening devices and telephone taps had extracted a lot of useful information. Noel met with Ken Archer and Kerry Hempenstall, solicitors with the Director of Public Prosecutions office. Ken and Kerry felt, based on what the electronic surveillance had produced, that Operation Aquatic had collected sufficient evidence to charge Barry Steer, Danny Williams and Kathy McFie.

Unfortunately, Ken didn't think there was enough to charge John. Not for murder, anyway. This was because John had kept himself well away from any meetings with either Barry or Danny, and never discussed anything with Kathy while in the house or on the phone. While there was evidence to say John knew Danny, and he could be linked to Barry through association, there was no evidence to say he knew what Barry and Danny had done. More importantly, there was no evidence to say John had actually organised the murder. It had always been Kathy meeting with the boys.

There was also the lack of a money trail. Police had only ever seen Kathy withdraw money to give to Barry and Danny. There was nothing in John's accounts to indicate he'd paid any money to either man. Operation Aquatic needed to gather further evidence if they were to charge all four with the same offence, the murder of Ricky Conway.

There were also discussions on the admissibility of earlier evidence gathered by the team, particularly Ricky's diary. Noel and Ben were concerned by the possibility of any defence challenge to the diary. After all, the events documented by the memoir clearly showed the type of emotional and physical abuse

Ricky suffered during the relationship, contradicting what John had earlier stated to police. Even more importantly, it was Ricky who was giving the account. It was Ricky's voice, and Noel and Ben knew that the diary would carry great weight when arguing against John's version of events.

Ken examined the issues surrounding the diary, whether part or all of the journal could be admitted as evidence. He assured Noel and Ben that the diary would be accepted. He couldn't find any reason for the document to be excluded, either by its discovery, having been acquired by Constable Phillipa Cottam from Ricky's sister on the night of Ricky's death, or because of its content. The diary should get in.

Noel wanted to know more about John Conway. He needed to understand what motivated the man and, when the time came, what interview techniques he should employ to get John talking.

Noel contacted Dr Rod Milton, a forensic psychiatrist who had worked for many years providing police with offender profiles on violent crimes, and assisting police on how best to interview a suspect.

Armed with various statements, interview tapes and notes on everything Operation Aquatic knew of John Conway, Noel drove to Sydney to personally brief Dr Milton. Dr Milton gave Noel his initial response to all the material he read and viewed.

Based on that information, Dr Milton believed John Conway was not able to form close personal attachments or, for that matter, long-term relationships. As Noel had deduced for himself, Dr Milton agreed that John was a 'control-oriented person' who needed to be in control of those around him, and to know that they were doing his bidding.

During the search for needles at the Gollan Street house the day after Ricky's death, police noticed a lot of AFP paraphernalia hoarded in the garage. There were pens, pads, diaries, audio-cassettes, even badges. It wasn't a situation where John may have bought home one or two. There appeared to be boxloads of booty. Police didn't take a lot of notice of the items as they were specifically searching for anything relating to drugs, but they did make a note. Anna Reiners confirmed John's collection of AFP items, particularly cloth badges, which he had acquired without Anna's or her husband's knowledge when they worked in the tailor's shop. According to what Ricky had told her, John would swap the badges with other law enforcement officers around the world through the Internet — a kind of cyber swap meet for like-minded collectors.

Dr Milton was particularly interested in the hoarding. He quoted eminent psychologist Erich Fromm (1900-1980) who, inspired by Sigmund Freud and Karl Marx, developed personality theories. In Fromm's theory, people hoard to feel secure, but are often cold and aloof, can even be destructive, and their action is a way of 'withdrawing from the family'. To Dr Milton, hoarding is a classic behavioural trait of those seeking control. He believed John had a rather obsessional, controlling nature, and could do harm to himself or his young son if put in a pressure situation.

If Noel and Dr Milton were correct about John being a control-type personality, the interview strategy was fairly simple.

Basically, Noel was told the best way to manage John was to make him feel comfortable, secure and in control. Then, to take that control away from him. John would hopefully be confused and feel antagonised enough to act out of character and make mistakes. What this meant was that Noel would have to sympathise with John about his circumstances, make him feel secure, then tell him something that would 'pull the rug out from under him'.

114

Interestingly, Noel had already begun using the technique instinctively, though he hadn't yet said anything to John to really upset him. Noel believed John thought he was being upfront with him during the investigation to this point. Noel had resisted saying what he really wanted to.

Shortly after speaking with Dr Milton, Noel visited John at his office in Weston Police Station. Noel had been through a divorce. Noel reckoned he had some things in common with John, at least enough for John to think they shared mutual feelings.

John appreciated Noel's situation. The two men talked about relationships and the difficulties associated in keeping it all together, with Noel giving a sympathetic ear. Then Noel delivered his blow. While he said he understood John's predicament with Ricky and accepting John believed she was controlling, he told him, 'At least I never killed my wife.'

John didn't respond. He sat staring at Noel, emotionless. Their time together was over and Noel left.

Noel wasn't provoking John to get an admission; he knew better. What Noel hoped would happen was John would call Kathy and maybe, just maybe, say something that might incriminate him in Ricky's death. John didn't. He didn't call Kathy and he didn't speak to Kathy about the meeting when they were alone in the house either. They would go to the park or the very back of their yard and talk about things, which the police couldn't hear.

At no time did John ever mention his meeting with Noel. That in itself seemed strange to the investigators. Certainly, for Ken Archer and Kerry Hempenstall; they believed John's actions would be seen as being suspicious to a jury, but they still wanted more.

Noel didn't just try this technique once. He returned to see John a couple of times. John would enquire about the coronial inquest, which had now been re-scheduled for September, and mention how his neighbours in Gollan Street were giving him a wide berth. With regard to the inquest, Noel suggested John should get himself legal representation, explaining he would receive a hard time over the 'coffee incident'.

John shrugged off the suggestion. He would appear for himself. He had nothing to hide. Noel then told him Kathy would most likely have to appear, as she was considered to be the other woman. John defended his position, repeating that Kathy was only a babysitter and that was where their relationship ended. He justified it further by saying that Ricky had suggested Kathy move in as a babysitter some time before her death.

Noel tried to push the point another time when he told John about some ripped pieces of paper he found in Ricky's handbag. Ricky had written words on each piece of paper, 'love', 'commitment' and 'betrayal', and then torn them up. Noel believed it was Ricky's way of telling John he had betrayed her with Kathy.

After each visit everyone would wait to see if John would phone or speak to Kathy about the meetings. He didn't. As much as Noel tried to stir John up, John never said anything to Kathy. At least, not while the police were listening in.

Throughout the investigation Noel had issued a number of press releases generally calling for information, which did yield results. The most important information came from Karen and another from an anonymous caller to Crime Stoppers also identified Barry and Danny as the two who had killed Ricky. The identity of that caller remained unknown as much as Noel tried to discover it. During this time Noel and Commander Dau fielded calls from journalists wanting to know more. The police officers never gave a categorical statement as to whether Ricky's death was a suicide or murder. At best, they would agree her death was suspicious.

In every investigation some information is forthcoming from police while other information isn't, as was the case with Noel not releasing the toxicology results. They would be used to confirm Barry and Danny's involvement because only they would know how much drug they had injected.

Still requiring more information, Noel, Ben and the rest of team discussed the likelihood of using the media to solicit a reaction from the main players. Surveillance revealed that Barry and Danny religiously watched *Australia's Most Wanted* (*AMW*), a weekly television program detailing as yet unsolved crimes across the country and requesting the public's help for information.

The idea would be to have John, Anna and Ricky's son, Phillip, appear on the program. Police would then listen to what Barry and Danny had to say after seeing John playing the bereaved husband. Noel was curious how John would react being asked to go on the show.

Noel phoned John at home to ask him and to his surprise, John agreed. He seemed relaxed and very receptive to the idea, according to Noel. As their conversation went on, Noel decided to purposely let slip some information on the investigation. He told John that the amount of heroin in Ricky's body was ten times the amount found in other overdose cases. He also told John that his team were treating Ricky's death as a murder. Noel waited for a reaction, but John kept his cool.

After the phone call the police at the listening posts waited to hear what John would say to Kathy about being asked to appear on *AMW*. He didn't say a word. John didn't tell Kathy anything about the phone call from Noel. Nothing was said about the amount of heroin or the investigation. It was also noted that Kathy never asked. After a little while, however, John suggested to Kathy they go for a walk.

Noel contacted the producers of *AMW*. They informed Noel they couldn't put the segment to air till August, almost a month away. Noel discussed the option with Commander Dau, but the delay was too great as Noel's superiors were hoping for a result before then.

Commander Dau was annoyed that Noel had told John they were investigating a murder, whatever the reason he had for doing so. Mr Dau's concern was that the enquiry might have been compromised. John could be destroying evidence. Noel didn't agree. John had been careful from the start, whether he believed he was a suspect or not. If there had been any evidence, John would have already disposed of it.

When Noel phoned John with the news that Commander Dau had not given his approval for the *AMW* segment, John seemed relieved. He told Noel he was relieved for Alistaire's sake. Seeing the segment going to air would have been traumatic for his son.

Although the idea of using *AMW* was canned, Noel and Ben knew that all the parties watched the local evening news. There was still a possibility they could get what they were after by holding a press conference. Still, they had to think about when would be the best time, and just what exactly they were going to say. There was no point in holding a conference if all they were going to do was repeat what had already been published and broadcast about the investigation. They needed a new angle to get the media excited and to 'stir the pot'.

Life in Gollan Street seemed to be running along normally for John and Kathy during the first few weeks of July. If John was concerned about the investigation, he wasn't sharing it with any of the police manning the listening posts.

John and Kathy did discuss celebrating their one-year anniversary. They decided to toast the day they first met when

John pulled Kathy over for having a smoky exhaust. They spoke about their finances and the prospect of buying a house.

If John's transfer to Queensland were successful, John and Kathy would rent out both the house in Gollan Street and the new house they intended to buy and move north. If not, then they'd rent out Gollan Street and live in the other house. John apparently wanted to be far away from Ricky's family and friends.

Police recorded a number of conversations where John was making enquiries about his various bank accounts, wanting to withdraw money to use as a home deposit. He even arranged to access money from his parents and was given approval on a bank home loan.

John and Kathy found a house for sale in the southern Canberra suburb of Rivett, the same suburb where Kathy's parents lived. John made an offer and it was accepted. With a deposit put down, the contracts would be exchanged in August.

As John and Kathy were investing in real estate, Barry and Danny were becoming even more anxious about their money, and Barry was particularly worried about his sister's car having been pulled over by police.

Kathy caught up with Barry at Stuart Flats, telling him she didn't have any money and that she and John were nearly broke. They even had to pay over $500 on a phone bill that was in Ricky's name.

Barry sympathised and suggested to Kathy, 'Dig her up and have her pay 'em … that's what I say … dig her up and have her pay 'em.' He then laughed, finding what he'd said to be very funny.

Instead of becoming angry with Kathy at not having been paid, Barry told her he was happy to wait. He would rather she gave him and Danny a large amount, preferably the balance, than the dribs and drabs which they'd been receiving to date. He calculated that it would take Kathy probably ten weeks to save up a substantial amount of money. How Barry worked that out was never made clear. He assured Kathy that Danny would agree to the arrangement after he talked with him.

Barry also asked for Kathy's help, or rather John's. He wanted John to find out what he could about why Joan was pulled over by police. It appeared, despite Barry's plea of innocence, his sister still blamed him for being harassed by the cops.

Hearing Barry's request was of great interest to the members of Operation Aquatic. This meant that Barry felt John was indebted to him for a reason. Barry believed John owed him a favour and he was calling it in. It was another piece of information to tie John to Barry and the murder.

Kathy wrote the details down on a slip of paper and said she'd get back to him if there was anything John could find out.

Barry was on a roll and continued asking for favours. He even asked Kathy if he could swap flats. After all, her flat was predominantly vacant since she'd moved in with John and there was every chance she'd be off to Queensland once the coronial inquest had concluded.

The reason for the swap was because Barry suffered from back pain and had to climb up stairs to access his unit, which aggravated his condition. Kathy's unit was on the lower floor, just above the car park area — a better proposition for Barry and his back. Again, Kathy said she'd get back to him when she was sure about what was happening with John and her.

Barry was happy with the meeting, but when he met up with Danny later, Danny let him know he was not. Danny wanted money. He had bills to pay, as did Barry, but Danny wasn't as easygoing. Even so, he realised there was little he could do if Kathy and John had no money. They both had to wait for however long it took. It was the only option they had.

* * *

As more and more evidence was gathered from the electronic surveillance, Noel, Ben and Brian McDonald would meet with Ken Archer and Kerry Hempenstall to review the tapes. They discussed who they thought, of the four, was the weakest link. Who would roll over on John?

Kathy was unlikely, given her relationship with John. Barry, although he softened on the issue of the money, still came across as a tough guy. He sounded like he wouldn't give up without a fight and certainly wouldn't 'dog' on anyone, despite his empty threats towards John. Danny Williams seemed to be the best option.

Even before the murder, Danny was serving periodic, or weekend, detention. The thought amongst the team was to visit Danny one weekend and try and turn him into being an informant. They would then wire Danny up and get him to contact John, drawing him into conversation about the murder and getting his admission that he organised the killing.

It was a daring plan. In fact, if it didn't work, it would be their last chance at getting anything on John. They'd have to arrest everyone and go with what they had. There'd be no turning back and no more time. It was a big gamble.

When the plan was presented to Commander Dau, he accepted that it was risky, but agreed it could work. Again, everyone from the Chief Police Officer down wanted a quick resolution to the investigation. Mr Dau thought using Danny would speed things along. Noel, Ben, Brian McDonald and the rest of the team began putting together plan A.

There were logistics and legalities that had to be worked through before Noel and his team could approach Danny. Danny was in custody, albeit weekend detention, and he would have to be bailed into Operation Aquatic's custody if they were to talk with him.

While Noel was waiting on advice from the Director of Public Prosecutions, it was decided to go ahead with a press conference to stir the pot. Commander Dau would be the spokesperson.

It was agreed to take the gloves off and formally state that police were treating Ricky's death as a murder, citing the amount of heroin in her body as the main reason. The conference would, hopefully, get all the parties talking, particularly Barry and Danny. Based on the boys' reaction to the conference, Noel and his team would have a better understanding of how to approach Danny to get him to cooperate.

Up until this point, Barry and Danny were under the impression that they would get away with the murder because John was a cop and, with his connections, the whole matter would be swept under the carpet. By announcing that police were investigating a murder, police hoped Barry and Danny would be spooked, and that their sense of security would be shaken enough to cause them to act irrationally. They might contact John directly, rather than going through Kathy, and make demands for their money to skip town. Police weren't sure what reaction they'd get from either of them, but they thought the conference would definitely yield some benefit.

The press conference was planned for Monday 21 July. All local print and electronic media outlets would be invited, with a media release sent to them prior to the actual conference.

Once the press conference was held, Noel and Ben knew it would only be a matter of days before they'd have to arrest Barry, Danny, Kathy and John. The arrests would have to be executed regardless of how Barry and Danny reacted and however the operation's plans unfolded. The investigation would then have run its course and the team knew there would be little gained after that point.

A number of arrest options had to be arranged. Did police arrest everyone at the same time, or was there an advantage in, say, arresting Barry and Danny separately without alerting Kathy and John? Was that a better option than bailing Danny and working on him alone?

Noel, Ben, Brian and the others would spend the time leading up to the conference debating the pros and cons of when, where, who and how to arrest the foursome.

CHAPTER TEN

Icing on the cake

Knowing the arrests of Barry Steer, Danny Williams, Kathy McFie and John Conway were looming, the team on Operation Aquatic assessed how best to contain their targets. Police knew enough of the individuals to know when they would have the advantage, minimising any risk to the arresting officers.

There was, however, a concern involving John Conway that had to be dealt with. John was a police officer, and as such, was issued with a Smith and Wesson six-shot service revolver. Noel and Ben knew, from speaking with Anna Reiners, that John would occasionally take his revolver home and keep it in the bedroom. Whether John was arrested at work or at home, he would have access to the gun. Not an ideal situation for the arresting police.

There were a number of reasons why the revolver had to be removed from John. No one could say how John would react when confronted with being arrested and charged with Ricky's murder. There's no knowing how anyone will behave in the circumstances until it happens. John might, simply, allow police to arrest him and take his fight to court. Then again, if he knew police were about to pounce, he might take his own life or even Kathy and Alistaire's as well. He could also decide to go out in a gun battle with police.

While the scenarios might seem extreme it must be stated again that police had no way of knowing how John would react and, as part of standard procedure, they needed to relieve him of his revolver, thereby removing any risk to himself and others.

Commander Dau spoke with John's superior, Superintendent Barratt. When John arrived for duty on Saturday 19 July, the Superintendent called on him and explained he would have to hand over his service pistol. The excuse given to John was that investigators on Operation Aquatic had a suspect in Ricky's death, and they were concerned John would take the law into his own hands if he knew the suspect's identity.

John complied with the command, although he wasn't happy. By giving up his revolver, it meant he was unable to patrol the roads, making him desk bound. In Australia and in most countries where police are issued sidearms, an officer cannot perform public duties unarmed. They are issued with a firearm for their protection and the protection of the community. So, John Conway stayed at his desk, filing and basically just filling in time.

Meanwhile, Noel, Ben, Brian McDonald and Commander Dau prepared for the press conference on Monday. Noel had briefed his team, including those officers manning the listening posts. It was decided not to inform John. Again, they hoped to put him and Kathy off guard. Monday was promising to be an interesting day for the investigation.

Commander Jon Dau, with support from Noel Lymbery and Brian McDonald, addressed the waiting media in the morning of Monday 21 July. The morning was chosen to get the story out in time for the early edition news services.

Commander Dau cut to the chase, telling the journalists that Ricky Conway had died from 'a massive overdose of heroin'. This was despite earlier reports that the toxicology results were inconclusive as to how Ricky had died.

Commander Dau went on to say, 'The circumstances surrounding her death are highly suspicious ... it certainly raises some substantial questions that need to be asked, and certainly it does suggest it may have been foul play.'

Mr Dau called for any witnesses to contact Crime Stoppers. He explained that whoever had killed Ricky, '... obviously entered the house and left the house and moved through Gollan Street and the area around that house over the weekend, and they may have been seen, they may have been heard'.

Commander Dau finished the conference by adding, 'Police are pursuing several lines of enquiry that look promising.' He wouldn't be drawn on giving any further details.

While the conference was in progress, a representative from the coroner's office phoned John and told him that the inquest was being put back again. There was no confirmation on a new date. All John was told was that the inquest wasn't likely to be held until the beginning of the next year (1998).

As John and Kathy readied themselves to leave the house, they noticed television cameras being set up across the road. Alistaire had already been dropped at school. John and Kathy knew something was happening, but didn't know what. They waited as the journalists did their stand-ups with the house as their backdrop. Eventually, John and Kathy were able to leave and made their way out of Gollan Street.

A surveillance team followed John's Nissan Patrol from Evatt to near Stuart Flats in Griffith. He was dropping Kathy off. John didn't go into the complex, but rather stopped at a street nearby. Kathy made her way to the flats as John drove off.

Kathy met up with Barry in his unit. Barry had seen the news, but didn't appear perturbed by what he had heard. He still felt he was safe and he and Kathy discussed money as they had many times before. Barry was still waiting for Kathy to save up the large amount owing to him and Danny.

While Barry was unaffected by the news conference, Danny was totally unaware. According to Ben Cartwright, who'd been waiting anxiously for reports from the listening posts, Danny was too stoned to even know what day it was.

After some time, John returned to Griffith, parking in Easts football club's car park, adjacent to Stuart Flats. Kathy walked to the Nissan Patrol and they headed away. Not a word was said as John drove. He brought the vehicle to a stop at a nearby park, and John and Kathy then went for one of their walks.

The plan seemed to have fallen flat. None of the targets had reacted how the police had hoped. The press conference did not solicit the results expected, but it did result in something surprising.

On the Monday evening, after the press conference had been aired on the local news services, Crime Stoppers received a call. The caller claimed to have information about the murder of Ricky Conway, stating that two people were involved in her death, Barry Steer and Danny Williams. The operator who took the call contacted Operation Aquatic immediately. The caller had given police her name and contact number. The caller was Joan, Barry's sister.

Knowing Barry as they did, the team always suspected he would have discussed the killing with his sister. Apart from his young son and Danny, Joan was the only other person who frequently visited Barry, and was close enough to share his confidence. While nothing was mentioned about the murder when they were together in Barry's unit, it didn't mean he hadn't spoken to her about it sometime earlier.

Now, Noel, Ben and the rest of team were anxious to know exactly how much Joan knew and whether she could help put John in the picture.

Noel phoned Joan and she agreed to meet with him that night. It seemed from the phone call that she had plenty to say. Noel, Ben and Corey Heldon collected Joan from her house and drove her to the Winchester Centre. Ben and Corey began to interview Joan.

Joan was aware of Barry's involvement in the murder five weeks earlier when Barry, as he had done with Karen, said he needed to talk to her about something. Joan first thought he wanted to talk about his son, but then he told her he and Danny had killed a woman. They had injected her with an overdose of heroin. Joan's memory was that Barry had injected Ricky while Danny restrained her. This was the opposite of what Barry had told Karen.

Barry also told Joan that they had called around and sat drinking coffee with Ricky. Then they grabbed her from behind, put her in a headlock and forced the needle into her.

The more he told Joan about what happened during the early hours of Sunday 4 May, the more she began to believe him. Even Barry couldn't have made up such details. He spoke about how Ricky seemed to accept her fate. How he told Ricky, as she was standing in the darkened hallway, to go back to her bed and lie down. Ricky made no attempt to fight them. Not a scream.

Barry and Danny had killed the 'lady' because she was a child beater and she 'deserved to die'. Barry said he had no remorse for what he had done and that he'd do it again, 'easy'.

Interestingly, Barry told Joan he and Danny were only getting $5,500 each for the job, a lot less than the amount he told Karen, but a more believable fee when considering John and Kathy's financial situation.

Barry detailed John Conway's role in the murder to his sister, how John initially recruited Danny and then Danny recruited Barry, and that John had supplied them with the heroin. Joan also said Barry had told her, should he or Danny get into any trouble, they could rely on John to fix things and keep them safe. All they had to do was call him.

The impression Barry left with Joan was that nothing would ever come from any investigation into Ricky's death. Barry had literally got away with murder.

If Joan knew all this five weeks earlier, why wait till now to tell police?

The answer was simple and not that different to Karen's reasons. Joan believed her brother when he told her Ricky's murder would be covered up. She'd heard news reports, but nothing to suggest to her police were investigating a murder. While she was horrified about what Barry had done, she didn't feel she could tell the police because they were the same people protecting Barry. She didn't think they'd pay her any attention. It wasn't till she saw the press conference that evening on television that she started to think maybe the police were after whoever killed Ricky. After all, why would the police announce that Ricky's death was a homicide if they were trying to sweep the matter under the carpet?

Joan decided to relieve her conscience and called Crime Stoppers. Despite Barry being her brother, she couldn't allow him to go unpunished. It wasn't right.

Ben saw Joan's statement as the icing on the cake. She'd told Ben and Corey what they already knew, but added some more information to deliver, for them, a complete package.

They hadn't finished with Joan just yet. Noel, Ben and Corey discussed how best to utilise Joan's knowledge and her closeness with her brother. It was a big ask, but Ben and Corey put it to Joan that they'd like to place a listening device in her car to record her and Barry. She was under no obligation to do so. The two detectives explained the purpose of the listening device and how police would use the recordings.

Should Joan agree, they would like her to initiate a conversation with Barry about the murder, to extract as much information as possible. Joan thought for a minute and agreed. She was happy to help the police in whatever way she could.

As it turned out, Barry had asked Joan to drive him to Queanbeyan, east of Canberra, on the Wednesday and Thursday. Barry was serving a community service order at Queanbeyan Police Station for having been convicted of break, enter and steal the January before. Joan would also drive him to collect his four-year-old son on the Friday. Barry had custody of his son every other weekend. There would be plenty of opportunity for Joan to talk to her brother about the murder.

After spending most of the evening at the Winchester Centre, police drove Joan home. Noel had arranged to meet with her the next day and have the police technicians fit the listening device to her car.

Even though police had sufficient evidence against Barry and Danny, most of which had come from their own mouths during various conversations, police still needed more on John. The last thing Noel and his team wanted was any chance John could escape conviction through a lack of evidence. Joan was their opportunity to have Barry give up John, without him being aware.

Joan had become a valuable witness, but that didn't mean she wouldn't change her mind at the last minute. There was a lot riding on Joan's cooperation and Noel, Ben and Corey wanted to be sure Joan was ready to handle the responsibility.

Noel and Corey decided to talk with Joan again before fitting the listening device into her car. She'd had a night to sleep on the request and the police wanted to be sure she understood

The Victim

Ulrike "Ricky" Conway,
born 17 March 1955, died 3 May 1997

*Ricky was a sweet-toothed 'tomboy' as a child, who grew to become an
attractive and outgoing woman during her adolescence, and a devoted and
caring mother in adulthood. According to her family, all Ricky ever
wanted in life was to give her children what she had had as a child —
a secure and loving environment.*

(photos courtesy of the Reiners family)

Above: *Ricky's father,
Phillip, holding her on his
hip with Gabby standing by
his side. The photo was
taken in Deakin soon after
the family arrived in
Australia from Germany.*

Above: *Ricky, the
mother, cuddling her
younger son, Alistaire*

Right: *Ricky relaxing
here, photographed just
a few years before her
untimely death.*

The Crime Scene

These photos of 35 Gollan Street were taken by police on the night, and the morning after, Ricky's body was discovered. They reveal Ricky's taste for heavy woods and plush fabrics. More importantly, they show a well-kept house, particularly Alistaire's bedroom. While all appears normal, the photos contradict John Conway's allegations that Ricky was unstable and unable to manage as a mother or wife. (photos courtesy of Australian Federal Police)

Top: *Exterior of 35 Gollan Street. Danny Williams claimed he climbed between the garage and the neighbour's house to reach the back yard.*

Above: *Ricky's lounge room on the night her body was discovered. On the coffee table are the cards left by the Area Mental Health Services team. There is also Alistaire's little red chair.*

Above: *The lounge room again, looking out to the entrance. In both photos, Ricky laid material down to protect the plush lounge and chairs.*

Right: *Alistaire's room. Other than a pair of shoes lying on the floor, everything has a place and everything is in its place.*

All photos show an ordered and neat domestic home. This is at odds with John Conway's portrayal of Ricky as an alcoholic, a bad mother and wife.

The Suspects

On 1 July 1996, John Conway, then an ACT Traffic Officer, pulled over a driver for having a smoky and noisy muffler. That driver was Kathy McFie. John, uncharacteristically, let Kathy drive away without a ticket – but he did give her his mobile phone number. Soon after, Kathy and John began a relationship. Kathy also befriended Ricky, John's wife. This triangle would have a fatal consequence, and draw into the picture two petty criminals, Danny Williams and Barry Steer. (photos courtesy of Australian Federal Police)

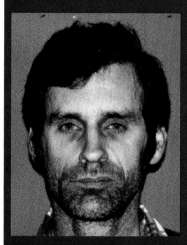

John Terence Conway, Ricky's husband

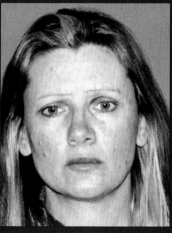

Kathy Marie McFie, began a relationship with John and befriended Ricky. John told police Kathy was no more than just a babysitter.

Daniel Scott Williams knew Kathy and said he was recruited by John and Kathy to find someone to kill Ricky.

Barry Steer, friend of Danny's, agreed to help his mate commit murder because he believed Ricky 'deserved it'.

Ricky, a couple of months before her murder.

The Evidence

Some homicide investigations are straightforward, with the victim having been stabbed or shot – then there are others that rely on the observation and skills of the detectives handling the case, where the cause of death isn't immediately obvious. (photos courtesy of Australian Federal Police)

Left: *A toilet seat left up mightn't mean much to most people, but it caught the attention of Ben Cartwright; it made him ask, 'If Ricky was home alone all weekend, why was the seat up? Who was the last person to use it?' It would be enough to start raising suspicions about Ricky's death.*

Below: *The wrappers for the alcohol swabs — an unusual thing to find where the deceased has committed suicide by overdose. The swabs are scrunched up tightly and lie under the ashes.*

The drain on National Circuit in Barton where Danny Williams disposed of his and Barry's gloves and balaclavas after murdering Ricky

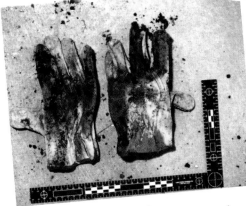

Only one pair of gloves were retrieved by police during the search of the drain on the National Circuit.

Right: *They did, however, find both balaclavas.*

The Trial

*Newspaper coverage of the trial —
one simple word summed up John
and Kathy's complex involvement
in Ricky's murder — GUILTY.
It'll be near 20 years before either
will be able to resume their lives
within society.* (clippings courtesy of
The Canberra Times)

what she was doing for them. They explained to Joan what evidence they needed. Basically, what questions they wanted Joan to ask her brother. They needed clarification of some of the evidence they'd already gathered against Barry, and they also needed to know more of John's involvement.

Noel made sure Joan understood what the repercussions could be. After all, she was asking her brother about the murder he committed, and he could become aggressive thinking she was setting him up. Joan could be taking a big risk, despite the fact that police would be following her. There was also the point that she was turning on her blood brother, and she could isolate herself from other members of her family. Noel reminded her she'd still have to appear in court, most likely at both the committal and the trial, each time with her brother in the dock staring back at her.

Noel wasn't meaning to scare her, he just wanted Joan to be sure. She was steadfast. Barry had committed the most grievous of crimes and she believed he should pay.

Corey explained, despite the device being fitted, if Joan had any second thoughts, even up to the minute Barry sat in her car, she could call it off. Joan was under no obligation to the police to complete the task. Her agreement was purely voluntary. Corey assured her that Noel and everyone would understand and respect her decision.

Joan understood and appreciated the option of backing out, but she guaranteed Noel and Corey she would keep her promise.

The listening device was fitted to Joan's car. She was ready to go, and on the morning of Wednesday 23 July she picked her brother up at Stuart Flats and drove him to Queanbeyan. An unmarked police car followed at a distance, listening to every word during the 15-minute drive.

Barry didn't seem fazed by Joan's sudden interest in his role in Ricky Conway's murder. Then again, Joan was clever enough to use the excuse of seeing Monday night's news to broach the subject.

Just as Karen and Joan both described, Barry spoke about his involvement very nonchalantly. He conceded police knew it was a murder by the amount of heroin injected into Ricky's body, and the fact no needle was found. This also seemed to be a sore point between him, Danny and John. In Barry's words, Danny had 'fucked up' putting two needles into Ricky. John apparently had said to Barry on one occasion soon after the murder that he expected it 'to look like an overdose'. John wasn't happy, which is the reason Barry gave his sister for not yet having been paid the full amount. Had police accepted Ricky's death as a suicide or overdose, then the coroner's inquest would have been held and John would have settled the payment. As it was, John and Kathy were waiting for everything to calm down. Kathy had told Barry that John's finances were frozen.

While Barry acknowledged police were investigating a murder, he didn't think they had anything else to go on. He felt he and Danny were safe, explaining that they'd kept their distance from John and only ever spoke to Kathy about the money. This was done in case the police were keeping John under surveillance. The fact police had only ever interviewed Barry once, during their initial door knock of Stuart Flats, and that they hadn't returned, had him believe that the police were looking elsewhere for suspects. Possibly, among Ricky's friends and family. Barry had nothing to fear and was looking forward to getting the money he was owed.

But why would he do it in the first place?

Barry's answer was brief. Danny asked him and he needed the money. Plus, John and Kathy told Barry Ricky was a child beater. Barry was under the impression from John that Ricky was a former heroin user and had hepatitis C. That was why he and Danny thought police would believe she had overdosed.

Barry did clarify that John didn't actually buy the heroin. Barry and Danny did, but they used John's money.

When asked why Barry was so certain he'd get away with the murder, Barry replied that all the evidence pointed to John, or someone who knew Ricky, because there was no forced entry. He and Danny had used a key they got from John. They even used Kathy's car to drive to the house. No one saw them. It all went perfectly. The only complaint Barry had was about the fee.

According to Barry, Danny had agreed to too little. Barry wouldn't have done the job for under $25,000, but he went along with the offer because the deal had been done.

Joan was concerned that if Danny spoke to the police, Barry would be put away for life. What would happen to his son? Barry might never see him again.

Barry reassured his little sister that it wouldn't happen. Danny would never talk, as Danny was the one who injected Ricky and killed her. Whatever Joan had thought he'd told her earlier, it was Danny who held the needle while Barry did the restraining.

Barry informed Joan he'd only get five years for being an accessory. Joan insisted even five years was a long time away from his son. Barry didn't think it was an issue, as police didn't know what they were doing and Danny would never dog on him or the others.

The police listening in were taken aback when Barry callously detailed how he would deal with Danny if he ever spilled his guts. He would simply take him out. Likewise, if John ever betrayed him and Danny, or forfeited on the money, Barry would deal with him as well, sending a message to Kathy. Barry even stated he knew where Kathy's son lived, suggesting he'd threaten Kathy with her son's life if there were any problems.

Joan continued to play chauffeur to Barry on the next two days, Thursday and Friday. Again, she would think of a reason to talk to her brother about the murder, mainly saying she was worried for herself as she knew too much and police could suspect her of being involved. Barry didn't really say anything new, going over the same things and trying to ease his sister's concerns. He did suggest the idea to kill Ricky had come from Kathy, and John had just gone along with it because he had had enough of his wife and there was no alternative.

On Friday, however, Barry began to reflect on what he'd done. Not in a remorseful way, but rather revelling in the moment. He'd always seen himself as a hitman because, making a joke, he'd been hit as a child enough times. It made him tough. Nothing hurt him, so it wouldn't hurt him to kill someone. He admitted he could kill again. He'd have no hesitation. Killing Ricky was easy, and he'd do the same to any other mother who mistreated her child, as he believed Ricky had mistreated Alistaire. He would even kill his de facto wife if he ever found out she had abused *their* son.

Barry stated he'd kill the Prime Minister, John Howard, for a million dollars, and he'd never get caught because he wasn't a known assassin.

Joan definitely delivered on her promise. For the first time police had Barry Steer giving details of the murder and implicating John in the soliciting of the crime. Operation Aquatic had exhausted all the avenues for gaining more information, barring an arrest and hoping one of the four might talk. It was decided, after reviewing all the tapes and other evidence, that the next step was to plan an arrest.

They ditched the idea to bail Danny and try and get him to sell the others out. There was enough evidence to put Barry and Danny away, while the brief against John and Kathy was circumstantial. Even without anyone rolling over, Noel and his team believed they had a strong brief of evidence to present to court. It was now just a matter of working out when and how to take out the targets.

CHAPTER ELEVEN

Sunday 27 July 1997
... they're all goin' down

At seven in the morning on Sunday 27 July, members of Operation Aquatic began their duty. Scientific and video officers would join them later in the day to discuss the details of the arrest.

Being Sunday, police knew that Barry was at home with his son and Danny was in weekend detention. That afternoon, Barry's son would be picked up and Danny would return to his flat. Then, simultaneously, two separate teams would execute the arrests warrants on the men.

Barry and Danny would be transported to the Winchester Centre where they would be interviewed separately. Noel and his team still hoped to get one or both to give evidence against John. The next morning, Monday, police would arrest Kathy after she dropped Alistaire at school. Being isolated from John and hearing what the police knew of her involvement in Ricky's murder, Kathy might agree to help. If all went to plan, police would then arrest John at his office and he'd be charged with the murder of his wife.

The plan enabled police to take advantage of each of the suspects, to have time with them and to try and get them to talk. Ben saw it as being a cunning plan, meticulously detailed, with every contingency accounted for. They'd even arranged with the Care and Protection Services to collect Alistaire from school and place him in foster care. The police were ready. All they had to do now was wait.

In planning the arrests, Barry Steer was identified by police as someone to approach with extreme caution. Given what Barry had told Karen and what police heard him tell Joan, it appeared he could put up a fight. After all, Operation Aquatic had information he'd sold knives to a local pawnbrokers. There was a possibility he could have other knives in his house for his protection.

Noel is the type of team leader who leads by example. He wouldn't ask anything of his officers that he wasn't prepared to do himself. Therefore, when it came time to pick the arrest teams, Noel put himself with the officers assigned to arrest Barry Steer. Brian McDonald would lead the group to take Danny Williams.

The day was spent revising, over and over, how best to contain Barry and Danny to minimise any risks, and what interview strategies would be used to extract as much information as they could. Everything was in place. It was just a matter of time. The listening post and surveillance teams kept a watch over the suspects, monitoring every move.

All appeared normal for a Sunday at the Gollan Street house, Barry was enjoying the company of his son, and Danny was tucked up at the Youth Detention Centre at Red Hill, a suburb near Griffith. All was going to plan.

That was, till Danny fell ill and was transported to Woden Valley Hospital. The news hit the operations room at two in the afternoon. Danny apparently had a recurring medical problem, which worsened that Sunday and required hospitalisation. He was admitted for an overnight stay and was given intravenous drugs to settle his condition. The news sent the room into a panic. Did they postpone? Or was there an alternative? Would they only arrest Barry and leave Danny for Monday? Would they risk Danny finding out Barry had been arrested?

The room filled with discussion, as everyone debated the situation, offering various options.

As the room calmed, Ian Houghton, who had been seconded from the Brisbane office, made a suggestion. Barry Steer was to be arrested as planned. And the search warrant for Danny Williams' unit would be executed, as Danny's girlfriend would be home and could possibly destroy any evidence if she saw Barry being arrested.

During Barry's arrest, Joan would arrive and witness her brother being taken away. Police would then wire Joan and send her to Woden Valley Hospital to tell Danny about Barry. She'd also tell Danny that she knew all about the murder, hopefully soliciting some information from him. Then Brian and his team would arrest Danny at the hospital and take a bedside statement.

The team mulled the idea over. It could work. Ian's suggestion was accepted. It became known as plan B.

Police phoned Joan and explained the situation. She eagerly agreed to cooperate. As before, Joan was told that if she didn't want to take part she didn't have to, and the police would respect her decision. Joan assured them she understood her rights, and was more than willing to help.

The operations room became frantic as each phase of the arrest of Barry and Danny was organised and reorganised. Joan was briefed and ready.

By six o'clock, Noel and his team were in place at Stuart Flats. Barry's son had been picked up and surveillance reported Barry was alone in his unit. Corey Heldon was also part of the arrest team. As the officers quietly assembled outside Barry's door, Corey dialled a phone number on her mobile. Barry Steer picked up his receiver.

Police knew the layout of Barry's flat. They knew where his phone was, and when he picked up the phone they knew exactly where he was. It was a ploy to distract and isolate Barry.

As Barry tried to raise an answer from the caller, Noel, Andrew Gomsi and the team burst in, shouting at full voice for Barry to lie down on the floor. He was seated on his lounge, wide-eyed and frozen by all the commotion. Noel didn't want to give Barry a chance to even think about resisting arrest. He and Andrew rushed forward to restrain him. They needed to get Barry off the lounge and onto the floor.

Noel, however, found he easily lifted Barry off the lounge. It took Noel by surprise. He'd expected Barry to be solid and aggressive. Instead, Barry was gaunt and shaking with fear. For a moment, Noel thought he should apologise if he was too rough on Barry. He placed Barry gently on the ground, looking to Andrew and the other officers in disbelief. This was the hardened hitman?

Once Barry was handcuffed, Noel brought him to his feet. He told Barry he was under arrest for the murder of Ricky Conway and given the mandatory caution. Barry began to sob.

As Andrew Gomsi led the search of Barry's unit, Joan appeared on cue. She had been waiting in the grounds of St Paul's Church Hall, next to Stuart Flats, which had been chosen as the assembly point for all the police involved in the arrests. Ben and Brian McDonald had prepared her for her walk-on role. Joan didn't disappoint. She went to Barry's flat, acted suitably shocked by the police presence and obeyed their command to leave the premises. She returned to Ben and Brian, who then wired her for her visit to see Danny. She was on her way, with the two detectives and a surveillance team following close behind.

It was decided not to search Danny's flat as his girlfriend was not at home. They'd wait till they got the word from the hospital.

Noel explained to Barry the seriousness of his predicament. He told Barry he would be charged with murder, and while he might not have injected Ricky, he was still responsible. Noel made sure Barry understood he wasn't an accessory, as Barry had suggested to Joan he was. He was a murderer and would be looking at life. Barry, which was his right, asked for a legal representative.

Even though Noel had overestimated Barry, he was sure of one thing. During the weeks listening to Barry at his home it was apparent he loved his son. Police had heard Barry and his son playing together. They'd heard Barry wiping his son's nose, preparing him meals, and comforting the four-year-old whenever the child became distressed.

Despite his tough talk, Barry was a loving and caring father. He'd even told Joan he was planning to spend some of the money he would get from John on his son. Noel knew that Barry's love for his son might be reason enough for him to cooperate to reduce his potential sentence.

As Noel and Barry stood in the unit while police conducted their search, Noel noticed a small picture of Barry's son. He took the picture and told Barry that he could keep it with him. Noel didn't have to explain. Barry cried. He knew he wouldn't be seeing his son for a long time.

Corey Heldon and Noel drove Barry back to the Winchester Centre. On the drive, Barry turned to Noel and said, 'If I'm goin' down ... they're all goin' down with me.'

Joan reached the ward where Danny Williams was being treated. The duty nurse asked her to wait while she checked on her patient's condition.

With all the attention police had given Joan, praising her for her work in helping to gather evidence against Barry and Danny,

Joan was taking her role very seriously. However, she was also like a little kid with a secret who was busting to tell someone. Waiting for Danny at the nurses' station Joan wrote a note, according to Ben, and slipped it to one of the staff. The note read, 'I'm wired.' It's uncertain what the nurses made of Joan's note, or even if they understood it correctly, but she was eventually led to Danny.

Danny couldn't believe what he was hearing when Joan gave him the news. He jumped out of bed, putting his health second to his freedom. He made a phone call, asking for his brother-in-law to collect him and take him to Stuart Flats. Danny then spoke with the nurses requesting to be discharged.

Joan, meanwhile, left the hospital. Her work was done and she was allowed to go home. Ben, Brian and the surveillance team remained at Woden Valley Hospital, waiting to see what Danny might do.

It wasn't long before Danny's brother-in-law arrived. Danny's mother, Pauline, also drove up, having brought Danny's girlfriend. Pauline found Danny wandering down the corridor of the hospital. She could see he was sick and ordered him back to bed. Danny was insistent he had to leave, telling his mother the police were going to arrest him. She said they could arrest him at the hospital.

Mother and son argued, and Pauline finally asked, 'What have you done now?'

Danny gave his mother a direct answer. 'I killed the copper's wife.'

Pauline was in disbelief, and could do nothing but watch Danny leave with his brother-in-law.

When Danny's lift arrived, Ben and Brian headed for St Paul's Church Hall to rejoin the others. They had decided to take Danny at the flats. The surveillance team followed Danny and his brother-in-law, radioing their location as they made their way to Griffith.

While Danny had arranged to be taken to his home, he could have just as easily absconded with his brother-in-law's car and made a run for it. Danny could have also decided to confront John and request his money. The latter would have been a bonus to Operation Aquatic. Wherever Danny went the surveillance team kept a close watch. He was never going to escape.

Ben and Brian had reached St Paul's Church Hall and met up with the other officers involved in Danny's arrest. There were 10 in total. They listened as the surveillance updated their location.

'We're on Canberra Avenue, headed your way.' Danny was only minutes away from Stuart Flats. The officers readied themselves. 'Turning into Stuart Avenue …' Seconds away now. 'Left indicator on … they're turning into … the church car park!'

Pandemonium broke out amongst the officers as they scattered for shelter to avoid detection.

'You have never seen ten people move so fast in all your life,' Ben recalled. 'There were coppers jumping into bushes, hiding behind trees, plants, even blades of grass … anything for cover.

'Danny and his brother-in-law drove in and around the car park, then out again and on to the flats … we were sure they must have seen us … we were too obvious.'

Ben and Brian jumped into their car and raced after Danny, cornering him and his brother-in-law in the car park. Danny was ordered out of the vehicle, laid face down on the bitumen and was handcuffed. He was told he was under arrest for the murder of Ricky Conway. Danny was then taken to his unit where police executed their search warrant.

As his home was being searched, Danny, like Barry, realised there was no getting away with what he'd done. He told Ben he was willing to be interviewed and would tell the police everything he knew about Ricky's murder.

Because of Danny's medical condition Ben requested a Government Medical Officer be called to the Winchester Centre to examine Danny to be sure he was fit enough to take part in the interview. Ben and Brian conveyed Danny to the Centre.

At the Winchester Centre Noel and Corey interviewed Barry Steer, while Ben and Brian dealt with Danny Williams. Both Barry and Danny knew their situation was hopeless. They'd been caught and they were going to be going to gaol.

In preparation for the arrests, Noel had Corey Heldon put together the interview plans. She provided a folder for each of the suspects. On the first page was the suspect's name and what Operation Aquatic knew of them and their involvement in the murder. The folder also had link charts showing their relationship to the other suspects, audio tapes relevant to the particular individual, transcripts, surveillance and crime scene photos, and what information police hoped to gain from the suspect. Corey had tailored the folder so any member of the team could read it and, within ten minutes, get enough of an understanding of the suspect to conduct the interview.

Although Barry and Danny had said they would cooperate, once in the interview room, there was still a possibility they may have second thoughts and try their luck, believing the police didn't really know much and were relying on them to talk. Barry and Danny would soon realise just how much the investigators knew.

Corey witnessed the benefit of her interview plan first hand. As Noel began questioning Barry, Corey loaded the queued audio tape in the machine and pressed play. Hearing his own voice, Barry's face drained of blood and he turned grey-white. It was an interesting moment for Corey seeing Barry realise he had no secrets, and he had nowhere to hide. He was gone. Corey had never seen anyone react so stereotypically guilty as Barry had. It was as though he had said, 'You're too good for me, copper.'

Barry did speak with a legal representative. It's uncertain what the advice was. The weight of evidence against Barry was too great to propose any reasonable defence. His only option would be to plead guilty, help the police and hope the court looked favourably upon his contrition.

Danny believed he could see people's auras and initially had problems speaking with Ben and Brian. He said the two detectives had dark auras. Danny liked Noel and Corey, as they had light auras. Noel had a more practical explanation. It wasn't that Danny could see auras, as much as he knew what Ben and Brian thought of him and he didn't like it.

Barry and Danny both took part in taped record of interviews and made full and frank admissions of their involvement in Ricky's death. They were also prepared to further assist police in whatever way they could. Noel and the team revised plan B.

It was almost midnight and most of the team had been working well over 18 hours, but no one was going home just yet. There were two down, with two more to get.

Just how police would arrest John and Kathy now lay in the hands of Barry and Danny.

CHAPTER TWELVE

Sunday 27 to Monday 28 July 1997

The smell of fear

Barry and Danny gave police all they knew and more. They each confirmed John and Kathy's involvement in soliciting them, particularly Danny, to murder Ricky. The original plan was to kidnap Ricky and kill her. Then, as fate would have it, John heard the Area Mental Health Services team had seen Ricky after she attempted suicide on the Saturday afternoon. John contacted Kathy who then raced to Danny's flat and told him the job had to be done that night. It had to look like a suicide. They were paid an upfront fee of $2,500 and promised they'd get the balance a few days later.

The heroin was purchased from a mate of Danny's, Robert (not his real name). Robert not only sold the heroin that killed Ricky, but he had earlier sold two 'caps', 0.1 gram of heroin in each, to Kathy in April. Kathy had even asked if the heroin could be taken some other way than injecting it. Robert told her that it was possible to drink the drug. Kathy paid Robert $100 for the caps.

Barry and Danny committed the murder because, other than the fact they both needed the money, they believed Ricky was the 'slut' and 'bitch' John and Kathy described her as being. They'd never met Ricky or ever saw her at Stuart Flats, which is why Kathy had supplied them with a photo, map of the layout of the house and a key. Being a father, Barry sympathised with John.

At the time John was going through his Family Court battle, Barry had applied for contact to see his son. Barry was awarded his claim, while John lost. Barry thought John had been hard done by, hearing of course, only John's side of the story.

Around midnight on Saturday 3 May, Barry and Danny drove to the suburb of Evatt and parked in a cul-de-sac a short distance from Gollan Street. They went to Ricky's house, entered the premises by the back door, met Ricky standing in the hallway near her bedroom and ordered her back to bed. Ricky complied without a struggle.

To those that knew Ricky, her compliance was because her will had gone, she was emotionally exhausted and hadn't yet recovered to her former self. Had she been the person she once was, she would have given Barry and Danny a battle. She may even be around today to talk about it. Instead, all she could say as Barry and Danny prepared her to be injected was, 'Don't hurt me, I have two children.'

Danny injected Ricky twice. He used two separate syringes filled with heroin, but placed the needles in the same hole. While they waited for Ricky to die, they helped themselves to her fridge and drank two popper fruit juices. They also used the toilet. When they were sure their work was done, they packed up the syringes and left through the front door.

Ben described listening to Barry and Danny talking about how they killed Ricky as 'one of the most chilling things I have ever been involved in'. Though they were now confessing to their crime, there was still an amount of dispassion as they spoke. Ricky was just a job. They even commented that Ricky seemed to be expecting it, and accepted what was to happen to her.

Again, John and Kathy chose the night well. Ricky was at her lowest ebb, and they knew it.

Barry and Danny were shown the forensic photographs from the night Ricky's body was found. Barry commented that the bedding was not how he and Danny had left it. Asked if they noticed the keys in the lock on the inside of the front door as the exited, they said there were no keys.

Noel always had a theory that John might have returned to the scene during the night. Barry and Danny's admissions gave weight to that theory. He thought John might have deliberately left the keys on the inside of the door, to make it difficult for Phillip to gain entry. There were only three known keys to the house. John had one, Ricky another and Phillip had the third.

John's return would explain why Ricky's bedding was neat. Noel didn't think hired assassins would be so thoughtful.

Noel's theory would be hard to prove. He'd spoken to Ricky's former husband who installed the locks, to locksmiths, and even to John. As much as he would love to prove it, there was no supporting evidence. It would remain just a theory.

Barry and Danny agreed to help police in any way they could. Once their interview was complete, Noel, Brian and Ben explained how they could be of more assistance.

It was suggested one of them be wired. Police would then drive the pair to Gollan Street where Barry and Danny would knock on John's door. Once inside, they would tell John and Kathy that they'd been pulled in by the police and interviewed. They would inform John and Kathy that police told them that they were not far from arresting them for the murder of Ricky Conway. They were released because they didn't say anything and because police didn't have enough evidence. Naturally, they would ask John and Kathy for their money to skip town and hide out.

The plan was to get John and Kathy's reactions, to get them talking and hopefully put themselves in. Being early morning, John and Kathy might be too dazed to think straight and police just might catch them off guard.

Barry and Danny agreed to the plan. Barry was chosen to wear the wire and he and Danny sat in the back seat of the police car as Noel and Ben drove them to Gollan Street. It was very quiet journey. No one spoke. The remainder of the team raced to the location and set up positions around the house and the street.

In fact, Ben believes there were more police in and around Gollan Street that night than there were in the rest of Canberra.

It was about four in the morning on Monday 28 July, and the temperature was well into the minus figures. All the briefings took place inside the cars to keep warm. Noel explained to Barry and Danny what they were to say. The boys nodded. They would give it their best shot.

Barry and Danny walked up Gollan Street. They took their role seriously and rehearsed what they would say to John and what reason they'd give for arriving at such an early hour.

When they were in Gollan Street back in May, Danny had taken some heroin during the drive and was a 'little bit out of it' at the time. He couldn't recall which house it was. Luckily, Barry remembered. They walked up the drive and Barry knocked on the door. He knocked again. He saw movement come from a window and yelled in a hushed tone, 'It's only Barry and Danny, John.'

They waited but there was no answer. Barry knocked again; and again he told the occupants who they were. No answer.

Barry decided to plead, telling John they needed a quick word and that they needed to get out of town. Finally, the door opened.

Barry and Danny entered. The house was in darkness. Barry flew into a panicked rage, saying he would kidnap his son and leave town, that the police had interviewed him again and told him they were close to arresting him and Danny for Ricky's murder. He apologised for the early morning visit, explaining he waited till now to be sure the cops weren't following them.

Kathy did her best to calm Barry. Danny switched on the light and began making comments about the décor of the lounge room. 'So this is what it looks like.'

Danny suggested to Kathy she go back to bed. They'd come to see John.

John was quiet, but when he did speak he spoke in a low voice, loud enough to be heard by Barry and Danny, but not loud enough to be picked up clearly by the wire. Then again, Barry played his role so well, he didn't give either John or Kathy any opportunity to talk.

To Ben, Brian and Noel, who were listening in, it sounded like a one-way conversation. If only Barry would shut up!

Kathy finally quietened Barry down and gave him advice not to do anything to arouse police suspicion. She advised against kidnapping his son and to just go about his business normally, as if he had nothing to fear. Barry and Danny both asked about their money. They wanted any amount John could give them. They were getting out of town, regardless.

Finally, John spoke, saying he would arrange payment and call them in a day or two. Barry asked for the cab fare home and John walked into another room and returned, handing over a $50 note. John saw the boys to the door and they left.

As Barry and Danny reached the end of Gollan Street they saw Noel and Ben step out of their car. Barry turned to Danny and commented, 'I thought these blokes would have gone home … no such luck, hey Dan?'

Other officers appeared, helping take the wire off Barry and placing both men in handcuffs. They told Ben everything John had said to them, knowing he had purposely spoken softly to avoid any listening device. They also handed over the $50 note, which Ben bagged for evidence.

Having done their part, Barry and Danny were conveyed back to the Winchester Centre. Danny was later transported to hospital, where police formally charged him at his bedside.

It was John and Kathy's turn now. The police cordoned off the street and took up positions around the house, cutting off any escape route. Noel, Ben, Corey, Brian, Susan Ball and Detective Constable Matt Innes walked up the drive. The time was 4.30 am. There were no hushed tones accompanying the knocks. Ben didn't care who heard.

There were no lights on in the house. John and Kathy had retired back to bed. Ben pounded on the front door. There appeared to be no movement inside. Before Ben could knock a second time, a voice came from behind the door. 'Who's there?'

'It's the police, John. Open the door.'

John obeyed, allowing the officers into the house.

'We have a warrant to search the house … can you turn the lights on, John?'

Kathy and John stood in the lounge room. The officers huddled in the room and back out to the entrance. Ben handed John the search warrant and told him and Kathy to sit down. John and Kathy remained standing, either because of shock, or because they hoped it was all just a bad dream. Noel wasn't as patient. The long day was wearing and he ordered them to 'sit!' They did.

John read through the search warrant. Ben cautioned him, informing him of his rights to say nothing, that anything he did say could be used in evidence, and to call a solicitor or friend if he chose.

John hadn't quite comprehended what was going on, but he opted to contact a legal representative. All he understood to that point was that police wanted to search the house. Ben, again, wanted to be sure John knew his rights. Satisfied, Ben told John he was under arrest for the murder of his wife, Ricky Conway. John was in disbelief. 'No!'

Kathy had sat quietly, observing all that transpired between Ben and John. Ben turned to her and read her her rights. Kathy was bemused. Why would she need any legal representation? She looked to John for an answer. John told her to call a solicitor. She'd need one.

Kathy still hadn't realised what was happening, till Ben told her she too was under arrest for the murder of Ricky Conway.

With the formalities over, Ben sent the other detectives in to search the house. A call was made to Care and Protection Services for someone to pick up Alistaire, who was still alseep, and place him in care. Neither the police nor the earlier visit from Barry and Danny had woken him.

Ben told John he could wake Alistaire, get him dressed and ready. He was giving father and son some quality time together before they would have to be separated. Ben wasn't doing it for John, but for Alistaire. He knew the boy would most likely not see his father for a very long time.

Ben sat in the corner of the bedroom as John woke his son. Still half asleep, Alistaire listened as John explained he and Kathy had to go away and that some friends were coming to look after him.

For Ben, it was heartbreaking. He thought of his own children and how painful it would be to leave them indefinitely. Ben felt sorry for Alistaire. He'd lost his mother, and now he was losing his father.

The people from Care and Protection Services had arrived and waited outside. Ben was feeling some sympathy for John. After all, he was Alistaire's father, and it seemed what he had done was motivated in part by his love for Alistaire, however perverse his thoughts and deeds. Ben offered John the opportunity to take his son to the car and to have a final farewell. John stood up, stepped forward to leave the bedroom and said to Ben in passing, 'No … you do it.'

Ben took a minute to be sure he had heard correctly. Alistaire ran and dived at John's leg, wrapping both arms around it and crying for his father to take him. He wanted to stay with 'Dad'.

Ben pried Alistaire's arms loose and lifted him as he kicked and screamed to be let go. Once outside, Alistaire lost his energy and just sobbed. Ben held him tight, as he would his own children, and tried to comfort the distraught young boy. He was loaded into the car waiting for him and Ben watched as he was driven away.

Walking back into the house, Ben became overcome by a tide of emotion. He stopped, and took some deep breaths. Ben needed to compose himself. He couldn't believe John had just allowed Alistaire to be taken away like that.

'It was gut wrenching,' was the only way Ben could describe it.

Inside, Ben found John standing by the heater, acting as though nothing had happened. Not even a question or word about Alistaire. Again, Ben wondered why he had become emotional over John never seeing Alistaire again, when John didn't seem to care. He was as stony-faced as when the police marched through the door. What little sympathy Ben had for John disappeared at that moment.

During the search a piece of paper was found in a drawer of a dresser. The paper had handwriting on it, including Joan's name, her previous car's registration number, and abbreviated details about the night she had been detained by police. Kathy admitted it was her writing and that Barry (she didn't know his last name), a neighbour at Stuart Flats, had asked her to ask John if he could find out why his sister was stopped by police and her car searched. Kathy added that John didn't do anything about the request.

John denied knowing anything about the note and couldn't identify whose writing it was. It didn't matter. The note was crucial in substantiating one of Kathy's recorded visits to Stuart Flats where she spoke to Barry about the money he was owed. Just another little piece of the jigsaw.

Brian McDonald and Corey Heldon took Kathy away to the Winchester Centre. Noel and Ben remained with John while officers continued searching the house.

After a time, John decided he wanted to 'get it over and done with'. He agreed to leave the observation of the search to an independent officer not involved in the investigation. In this instance it was a Sergeant Sowden from Belconnen Police Station. Once Sergeant Sowden arrived, Noel and Ben drove John away.

It was around 6.30 in the morning. It was dark and the temperature outside was still in the minuses. All the windows in the car were wound up and the heater was on. Ben sat in the back with John while Noel drove. Within minutes into the trip, an unrecognisable stench engulfed the entire car. It wasn't body odour or flatulence. Ben and Noel put their windows down. The cold, frosty air was a pleasant relief to the offensive odour.

John didn't seem to care or notice. At the time, neither detective could identify the source. In hindsight, Noel and Ben both believe it was the smell of fear. While John kept an outward demeanour of being calm and in control, Ben is sure he was scared to death on the inside. They'd never smelt the odour before that night and they haven't smelt it since.

At the Winchester Centre, both Kathy and John refused to take part in a taped record of interview. They were formally charged and then contacted separate solicitors.

Later that morning John appeared before Magistrate Michael Somes. The duty prosecutor, Kerry Hempenstall, opposed bail. It was stated that John, by admissions of two of his co-offenders, was the mastermind behind the murder. It was raised that police had fears for John's own safety and that of his son, plus fears witnesses might be interfered with should bail be granted.

Magistrate Somes refused bail. He said there was a 'substantial body of evidence' that pointed to John's involvement in the murder, and he had 'severe reservations' that John would appear in court if released.

When Kathy McFie appeared before the court, she explained she suffered from chronic fatigue syndrome, angina and severe migraines. Magistrate Somes said her medical needs could be catered for while in remand and stated that Kathy had a 'particularly critical role to play' in the murder case.

The magistrate, again, found in favour of the prosecutor and denied bail. Both John and Kathy were remanded in custody and taken to the Belconnen Remand Centre.

Because John was a policeman he was placed in protective custody. Inmates tend to be violent towards former cops.

At around 4.30 in the afternoon of Monday 28 July, over 33 hours after starting their shift, the team of Operation Aquatic met at a local hotel to celebrate the arrests. It was customary after a big case. However, the celebrations were subdued and short-lived, as the adrenalin was spent and sleep finally took its hold. One by one, with having as little as a sip of a beverage, officers fell asleep at the table, and Ben fell off his bar stool. It was decided to meet up on another day, when their bodies had been replenished with much needed sleep.

CHAPTER THIRTEEN

Lives, loves and conspiracies

On 1 July 1996 John Conway was cruising in his patrol car, looking out for anyone who was flaunting the road rules — speeding, not wearing a seatbelt, or driving a defective vehicle.

Driving along Parkes Way, near Black Mountain Nature Reserve, just west of the city, a green Holden Gemini caught John's attention. Smoke billowed from the noisy exhaust. John switched on the blue lights and sounded the siren, indicating to the driver of the Gemini to pull over.

With the police car strategically parked behind the Gemini, John spoke to the driver. It was Kathy Marie McFie. This was their first meeting. Despite John's reputation for booking everyone he pulled over, earning him the nickname of 'Killer Conway', John took pity on Kathy.

Kathy explained she was looking to buy a new motor, a cheaper option to buying a new car. John offered to help her. He gave her his mobile number, telling her that when she found a replacement motor to call him and give him the details. John would run the engine number through the police computer to check if it was stolen. Being an engineer he even offered to check its mechanical condition.

Kathy was appreciative of the help and promised to call. She drove off with John's card in place of a defect notice.

Kathy was living at Stuart Flats in Griffith. She'd moved in about three to four years earlier, 1992 or 1993. Her only source of income came from a disability pension. Kathy lived alone, although she had a son from a previous marriage. She had divorced his father in 1979, and the son was now in his 20s and living his own life.

Stuart Flats is a small community to itself, with most tenants knowing each other and spending time together. This was true of Kathy and a neighbour in an adjoining block.

The neighbour was Pauline Williams, Danny's mother. She and Danny moved into the complex soon after Kathy, when Danny was a teenager. The two women would socialise and even attend bingo together every Tuesday and Thursday night.

After living in the flats for a couple of years, in late 1994, Danny's mother moved out, leaving the unit to her son and his girlfriend. Pauline still continued to see Kathy, keeping their bingo date. Kathy would occasionally drop in to see how Danny was doing and Danny would call over to Kathy's flat for a chat.

With Pauline gone, Danny allowed friends and associates to drop in and stay over. It became an open house. Danny's brother also became an occasional visitor.

Danny, as he would admit in court during his trial and that of John and Kathy, had been in trouble with the law since his juvenile days. He was addicted to heroin, taking up to a gram and a half a day, and committed various offences to feed his habit. Most of the offences were a means to supplement his unemployment benefits of $250 a fortnight. At times when he couldn't get any money for a 'hit', he'd borrow money from

Kathy. He would tell Kathy what the money was for and always paid her back.

A couple of weeks after being pulled over by John, Kathy kept her word and called him. John suggested they meet for coffee and from that time the two became friends.

Kathy and John began a sexual relationship in August. Kathy told Pauline all about John and how they were 'seeing a lot of each other', and 'making love most nights'. A week later Kathy received a call from Ricky, John's wife.

As previously stated, Ricky had found a greeting card to John signed by Kathy. Kathy had given John a coffee mug as a present. Ricky confronted John, believing he was having an affair. John denied the allegation. According to John, Ricky was always accusing him of having affairs. Ricky took matters in her own hands and phoned Kathy, warning her off and telling her that John was married and had a family. Kathy said she didn't know, and had she, she would have backed off right away.

What isn't clear to Ricky's family and the police was why, after this phone call, Ricky and Kathy became friends. Kathy became a regular visitor to Gollan Street from December. She even played babysitter to Alistaire. Ricky would share her thoughts, secrets and anxieties with Kathy. She told Kathy everything there was to know about her relationship with John. She trusted Kathy. Ricky even used Kathy as a reference, citing her as a friend, when making her application for sole parent's allowance after separating from John in March.

Meanwhile, Kathy was telling friends that Ricky was an alcoholic and was behaving cruelly towards her son.

To the outside world, however, it appeared that from December 1996, Ricky, John, Alistaire and Kathy were just one big happy family.

Ricky's family were less than impressed by Kathy's inclusion. They were suspicious, but Ricky wouldn't listen. Anna, Ricky's mother, found herself replaced by Kathy. During school holidays Anna would care for Alistaire, but now, because John insisted, Kathy was chosen to care for his young son. To Anna, this was just another of John's schemes to isolate Ricky from her family.

In October 1996, tragedy struck Ricky and the Reiners family, when Phillip, Ricky's father, died after a long battle with cancer.

In that month, Kathy McFie brought a new car. It wasn't brand new, but rather a second-hand white Mitsubishi Sigma. Still, it was in better condition than her old Gemini. When Danny asked about the Sigma, Kathy told him John had bought it for her. It cost nearly $3,000. Kathy also told Pauline, but added that she would pay the money back to John.

Around mid to late February 1997, Barry Steer moved into Stuart Flats. He and Danny became instant mates, despite their eight-year age difference. As Danny described it, he and Barry were 'thick as thieves'. They'd spend time in each other's flat, smoking marijuana and watching television. They'd even go together to score drugs or sell some 'gear' to make money.

Barry and Danny's friendship wasn't a situation where one had control over the other, but more because they shared similar interests and led the same lifestyle. Barry, like Danny, had also been in trouble with the police since his juvenile days. Unlike Danny, Barry didn't indulge in hard drugs. His poison was cannabis. He'd smoke between 300 and 500 cones a week.

Barry lived in the same block as Kathy, one floor above. It was another neighbour who introduced Barry to Kathy. At the time Barry moved in, he had applied to the Family Court seeking contact with his son. The circumstances are unclear but Barry's son was living in New South Wales, near Canberra. Barry, presumably, wasn't allowed contact by his de facto wife.

After Barry first met Kathy they had little to say to each other apart from giving polite greetings in passing. Eventually, though, they did begin to talk, mostly about Barry's son and the Family Court application.

It was March 1997 and Kathy introduced John to Danny and Barry. Barry remembers being introduced to John as Kathy's boyfriend. While they wouldn't always see John, the boys would notice his four-wheel drive parked on the premises. They also noticed John in the company of a young boy, Alistaire, but they never saw or knew of Ricky.

One day, Kathy, Barry and Danny's brother were cleaning out the communal storage room on the complex. Barry heard John's mobile phone ringing. Kathy didn't react.

'Aren't you going to get that?' Barry thought Kathy mustn't have heard.

'No … I know who it is,' came Kathy's reply.

John stepped out of Kathy's unit and joined them in the storage room. He told Barry the caller was most probably his wife, Ricky, and he didn't want to speak to her. John and Kathy then began talking about Ricky, telling Barry she was an alcoholic, a 'slut' and a 'bitch'. Barry was left with no doubt about how John and Kathy felt about Ricky.

Around late March or early April, the Family Court granted Barry conditional contact to see his son every other weekend. Barry was happy. Very happy. His fight to see his son and having gone through the Family Court processes gave him a common ground with John.

At this time, John had left Ricky and taken Alistaire, at the same time filing for custody. He'd also taken out a restraining order against Ricky on behalf of Alistaire. John was hoping for a win, to have full custody of his son, and Barry offered what support he could.

Things didn't go well for John. He lost, and Alistaire was

returned to Ricky. John was left in the same situation as Barry, only he wasn't happy about just having conditional visiting rights. Barry tried to talk to John, but his response was filled with anger and bitterness.

It was about this time that Kathy paid a visit to Danny's apartment. Danny was out, serving his periodic detention. Barry, Danny's brother and Robert were the only ones in the flat.

Robert had taken up residence with Danny and his girlfriend after being evicted from his unit in the Stuart Flats complex because he had failed to keep up with his rent and the Department of Housing took the action to evict him. Robert, like Danny, was a heroin user, and he was a regular dealer. He would buy a 'half weight', a half gram of heroin, then cut it up into smaller amounts known as 'caps' for his own use and to sell. The heroin would be packaged in small foil envelopes placed inside water balloons. The foils were folded to a size no bigger than an average fingernail.

Kathy had come to see Robert. She wanted to buy some heroin. She said she was buying the drug on behalf of a friend who wanted to give it a try, but that the friend didn't want to inject it.

Robert offered her some alternatives. 'You can have dragons ... put it [heroin] on a small piece of foil and put a light underneath and suck it up through a rolled note [money].'

Robert also told Kathy that the drug could be smoked or, of course, injected. When asked if it could be taken in a drink, he said it would taste bitter. Robert didn't recommend that idea, because Kathy would need about four or more caps to get stoned.

Nevertheless, Kathy bought some caps, 0.1 gram of heroin, for $50 each. Barry, who was in Danny's unit at the time, said Kathy bought two caps. Robert said he sold Kathy three. The amount is inconsequential. The fact is that Kathy purchased heroin.

John's penchant for hoarding things went beyond that of police badges and associated paraphernalia. He also collected numberplates. Danny owned two vehicles, both Sigmas. He either owned them, or another neighbour owned them and Danny had access.

The cars sat in the parking area of Stuart Flats. They were more decorative pieces than practical modes of transport, as the motors didn't work. Danny kept meaning to spend some time to get them mobile, but it never happened.

On one of the Sigmas was a unique NSW numberplate. It was a bicentennial plate, issued in 1988, specially struck to celebrate 200 years of European settlement in Australia.

Kathy approached Danny in his unit. Barry was there as well. Both Danny and Barry had been smoking cones. Kathy asked Danny, 'What are you doing with the numberplates on the back of that vehicle [Sigma]?'

'Nothing. Why, Kathy?'

'John collects numberplates … can he have it?'

'Yeah, yeah, not a problem, Kathy.'

Danny went to get some tools, while Barry walked with Kathy to the car. Removing the numberplate wasn't an easy task. The screws were old and worn. Barry just wrenched the plate free, bending it up and down to loosen it from the screws. Kathy asked Danny to deliver the prize to John, who was waiting inside her unit.

'Danny,' Kathy whispered. 'John wants to talk to you. It's rather important.'

'What is it about?' Danny queried.

'I can't say anything, but John wants to talk to you.'

Kathy led Danny to the flat, leaving Barry in the car park. Barry had planned to play a practical joke and 'spring' John taking the plate. After all, numberplates were the property of the Roads and Traffic Authority.

Barry sneaked behind Kathy and Danny, but by the time he reached Kathy's flat, everyone was inside and the door was closed. Barry realised they wanted their privacy, so he went back to Danny's unit for another cone.

Danny stood in the lounge area. He handed the numberplate over, and after some casual conversation, John said, 'I want something done about my Missus.'

John explained he wanted Ricky killed. He wanted Danny to find someone to do the job. Danny was disbelieving at first, but the reality sank in.

John apparently spoke about having Ricky kidnapped, killed and dumped.

Danny assured John he'd do what he could and get back to him. He left Kathy's flat, his head spinning from the conversation. He went home and shared a cone with Barry.

Danny didn't tell Barry straight away; he was still coming to terms with the situation. Eventually, he needed to confide in his friend. He asked Barry how hard it would be to kidnap someone.

'Why the bloody hell would you want to do that?' came Barry's reply.

Danny asked Barry if he would help him. Barry refused. He didn't want to get involved in any kidnapping, the risk of being seen was too great. Barry did ask why John wanted it done, and all Danny could say was that he hadn't asked any questions.

'Well, you'd better start asking,' was Barry's advice.

Danny still couldn't believe it. 'He wants me to knock [kill] his wife … oh, man, I don't know what to do.'

'Yeah, well, I wouldn't know what to do.'

'Well, I said I could organise it for him.' Danny felt obligated now.

'You'd better go and tell him you can't do anything.'

Danny thought for a moment, 'Well, I'll see what I can do first before I do that.'

Three days later Danny met John as he was carrying boxes up to Kathy's unit. On the stairway leading from the car park to the unit John told Danny to keep their earlier conversation to himself. John warned him to only speak to the person who would do the job. He didn't want any careless talk being his undoing.

Danny took Barry's advice and started asking questions, but John didn't have the time to explain. Danny didn't press the issue. John added that he wanted 'it' done soon.

'Yes, yes, I understand,' Danny hurriedly replied. 'I understand … I'll see what I can do. I can't do it overnight, but I can see what I can do.'

A day or two later Danny paid a social visit on Kathy. John and Kathy were curious how much money it would cost to have Ricky 'knocked'. Danny plucked a figure out of the air and told them it would be $15,000. John and Kathy were surprised at how cheap it was. It was a bargain.

'That's nothing, really, is it?' Kathy commented.

John and Kathy nodded to each other. They had the money, but they needed 'it' done that weekend.

'Well … I still haven't organised it,' Danny admitted.

'You'd better hurry up because this is the perfect time to do it,' Kathy explained. 'Ricky's eldest is going to the coast … Alistaire's going to be here and I'm going to be babysitting. John's going to be at the police station … that's his alibi.'

Danny appeared hesitant, despite his promises to help. Kathy then had an idea, 'They can't link you to it, why don't you do it?'

'It's not my scene, Kathy … but I'll see what I can do.'

'There's a bonus if you can get it done by Saturday,' Kathy insisted.

Danny and Barry's friendship was well known to John. If Danny were to tell anyone of John's request to kill Ricky it would be Barry. On the Wednesday or Thursday before the weekend of Ricky's death, Danny remembered a time when Barry stumbled into his flat, shaking and confused.

'Barry, what's wrong, mate?'

Barry collapsed on a sofa in Danny's kitchen. 'Nothing, man, nothing.' His demeanour said otherwise.

'I can help you out. Just tell me what's wrong.'

'It's nothing.' Barry wanted to be left alone.

'Is it your kid?'

'No.'

'Oh, what is it then? Tell me.'

Barry knew he wasn't going to get any rest. 'John's just put me up against the wall, man, he's just threatened me and I told him I didn't know nothing about it.'

Danny had heard enough and stormed to Kathy's unit. Kathy answered the door to the angry young man. Kathy tried to find out why Danny was so upset, but he wouldn't explain, he was there to see John.

As soon as John appeared, Danny released his anger, 'John, what's this big idea of attacking Barry … he knew nothing about it!'

John gave a cryptic reply, 'Oh, but you know what's going on anyway.'

'Yeah? What's going on, John?'

'You know what's going on … you'd better watch yourself … you better fuckin' watch yourself!'

They argued some more when John told Danny, 'Yeah, you'd better watch yourself or I'll take your girlfriend down with chloroform, so no one really knows … no one really sees anything.'

Danny took hold of the security screen door and bent it back, displaying his rage. He began yelling louder, inviting John to step outside. John and Kathy closed the door on him. He ran around the outside of the building shouting, 'Come on, John … just come out here …'

Drawn by all the commotion, Barry appeared and tried to calm his mate down, telling him to forget it and to get back inside. After a few minutes, Danny finally collected himself and joined Barry in his unit.

While this event was etched strongly on Danny's mind, Barry appeared not to have any recollection of it at all. Even so, Danny still seemed willing to help John and Kathy, despite the threats and despite it not being his scene.

What Danny was hesitant to do, was to tell John or Kathy that he would be doing the job, as he either didn't know anyone who could do it, or couldn't find anyone willing to do it. The money was certainly an incentive.

On Saturday 3 May, Barry was performing his community service in Queanbeyan and Danny was serving his periodic detention.

While working in a brick pit Danny had an argument with one of his guards. As punishment he was taken back to the prison and placed in a cell. Danny didn't handle the confinement well and began throwing furniture around and basically destroying his cell. The staff at the Correctional Centre released Danny, rather than deal with his violent behaviour. Danny left the centre sometime after lunch and headed straight home.

When Danny arrived at his unit he had a shot of heroin. Later in the afternoon Kathy paid him a visit. Her manner was urgent as she told him that 'it had to be done tonight'. Danny admitted he still hadn't organised anything as yet, but Kathy was insistent. She was sure he could find someone to have it done. Danny said he'd 'give it a go'.

According to Danny he had a conversation with John, either earlier or around this time, when John told him Ricky's death was to look like a heroin overdose. Danny responded, 'You're the paying man ... Well, that's the way it's goin' to be ... I'll tell these people.'

Kathy enquired if Danny had the heroin for the job. He didn't. In fact, he just used the last of what he had. Kathy showed him a white envelope containing a large amount of money telling him, 'This is yours ... give it to the people and get it organised.'

Kathy made arrangements to drive Danny to purchase the heroin he would need. As an incentive she also offered to buy Danny an extra half-gram for his personal use. Danny's eyes lit up. He needed to score. When Kathy left the unit, Danny counted the money. There was $3,000 inside, in $50 and $100 notes.

Barry had completed his day washing police cars at the Queanbeyan Police Station and was driven home by Joan. As he was stepping out of the car, Danny ran up to him, 'Can I borrow your sister's car? I need it tonight to do the job.'

Barry spoke with Joan, who agreed to lend her car. Barry, however, would have to drive his sister to her home and then return. While this was being done, Kathy was now ready to drive Danny to one of his suppliers.

Danny had teed up Robert to conduct the deal. He knew the supplier wouldn't deal with him, but Robert was a mate.

During the trip Kathy tried to convince Danny that he could do the job, 'Come on, Dan, you can do it ... you'll get away with it. They won't even think about pinning it on you ... you'll be clear ... you can do it.' Kathy assured Danny that John would keep a check on police communications and alert him if anything went wrong, like a neighbour calling triple zero.

Danny still protested, 'Kathy, I don't want to do this, all right ... it's not my scene.'

They reached their destination. Kathy gave Danny $500 to make the buy. He and Robert met his friend. According to Danny he paid $450 for two 'halves', pocketing the change. He also took the opportunity to shoot up. Robert's version is that they bought one half for $250.

In Danny's version, when they returned to the car, he told Kathy they would have to wait a few minutes, as he had promised to give his friend a lift into the city. Almost an hour later the friend appeared and they set off.

After the friend had been dropped off, Kathy, again, began trying to convince Danny to do the job. Danny had heard enough; he turned to Kathy and said, 'All right, Kathy, all right … it's going to be done tonight, all right!'

Robert can't remember giving anyone a lift. He just remembers driving straight back to Stuart Flats.

Back at his unit, Danny prepared the half gram of heroin. He mulled the drug, cutting the half gram up, placing some on a spoon and adding water, then using a syringe to mix it all together. When it was to his satisfaction, he drew it up into the syringe from the spoon.

Danny prepared three five-milligram syringes, each containing roughly the same amount. He left them under a glass ashtray and decided to see if Barry had returned.

Barry was smoking a cone and Danny joined him. He informed Barry, 'I've spoken with Kathy and told her I'm doing it … John's going to start work in about half an hour … it has to be done tonight.'

Danny explained that John's wife had been 'assessed as being suicidal' by the ACT Area Mental Health Service, and that her murder was to look like a suicide. He said he would inject her with enough heroin to kill her, and then asked if Barry would help. He needed Barry to drive him to the house and to 'stop her from screaming'.

'If you do that I'll give you $6,000,' Danny added as an enticement.

'Yeah … okay.'

Danny left and quickly returned with the white envelope he'd been given by Kathy. He counted out $1,000 and handed it to Barry. Barry would get the rest when the job was done. Danny wanted to see his mother and sister before heading off to do the job. Barry played chauffeur, and remained in the car while Danny visited his family.

Danny had gone to pay off some debts. He paid his mother, Pauline, $200 for an electricity bill. He gave his sister $600 which he owed her. Wondering how Danny had come into so much money, his family asked if he had 'robbed a bank'. Danny just told everyone to mind their own business. He wasn't going to tell anyone where or how he got the money.

Danny returned to the car with his brother. Danny's brother was now living with his sister, after moving out of Stuart Flats. The move came because he and Danny constantly argued.

In a more congenial mood, they told Barry to drive them to Civic. Barry parked in the car park and, again, waited as Danny and his brother went out to score. The two brothers bought three caps and shot them up together. Barry drove Danny's brother back to his home, and then they headed to Stuart Flats. On their way they stopped for petrol and Danny ran in to Woolworth's and bought two beanies, not an unusual purchase given it was autumn.

The beanies were changed into balaclavas, with Barry and Danny cutting eyeholes into each of them. Danny also had two pairs of gloves, a cotton pair and a leather pair he said were for gardening. They smoked a few cones and discussed what they would do to Ricky. Danny explained he'd use one syringe, but if that didn't appear to work, he'd use the second. All Barry had to do was restrain her and keep her from screaming. The third syringe was for Danny. He'd have it on their way to Ricky's house. Danny then went and saw Kathy.

It was about nine at night. Kathy gave him a recent photo of Ricky, a map of the interior of the house in Gollan Street with the address written on the back and a key for the back door. Danny had all he needed.

Barry looked up the address while Danny laid everything out on a table — the syringes, beanies, gloves, photo and the key.

Kathy decided to pay the boys a visit. She wanted to be sure they were still going to do it that night. Danny assured her they were and they were just about to set off.

Before they did, Barry wanted Kathy's phone number, just in case anything went wrong. Barry wrote it down.

Danny packed the syringes in a paper bag and wrote the number three on the outside, leaving the bag on the console of the car. As Barry drove off, Danny fell asleep, an effect of taking heroin. Soon afterwards Danny was jolted awake, when Barry had to brake hard as another car cut them off at a set of traffic lights. Once the drama was over, Danny went back to sleep.

Barry drove slowly up and down Gollan Street looking for the house. Once he'd found it he drove out of the street and parked the car in a nearby cul-de-sac. He shook his partner awake. Danny grabbed the syringes, took one out and injected himself. He threw the empty syringe down a drain. He and Barry then walked past the house, checking for any signs of occupancy, or if Ricky or the neighbours had any dogs.

There were no dogs, but Barry couldn't be sure if there was anyone home. The house was in darkness. Barry didn't want to break into an empty house. He decided they'd get Kathy to call Ricky and see if she was at home. Danny disagreed and suggested they go to the back yard and wait for a while to see if anything happened.

Danny climbed over the small side fence between the garage and the neighbour's. Barry went to the other side of the house and found some loose fence palings, which he moved apart and stepped through. They both waited by the above-ground swimming pool, staring at the house.

Barry had to wake Danny, as he began falling asleep. Nothing happened. Barry wasn't sure anyone was inside. He decided to go with his original plan and they returned to the car and drove to some local shops, where they found a public phone booth.

It's unclear who spoke with Kathy. Barry said it was Danny. Danny, however, said he attempted to dial the number, but was too out of it to complete the call, so Barry took the receiver. Danny could only support himself against the glass wall of the booth.

Whoever spoke to Kathy, they agree that they asked her to call Ricky's home after about 15 to 20 minutes. This was to give them time to be in place and observe when Ricky answered. They would then wait for her to get back into bed before going in.

Once they got back to the cul-de-sac, Danny had to be woken again. They grabbed the syringes, balaclavas, gloves, photo, map and key, and made their way back to the house. As they neared Ricky's house, they slipped the balaclavas over their heads and made for the back yard.

Oddly enough, Danny climbed back over the fence beside the garage, negotiating his descent carefully so as not to make any noise, when Barry just walked through the hole on the other side. In any case, they resumed their positions next to the swimming pool, waiting for Kathy's phone call.

A light was switched on in one of the rear rooms soon after the phone rang. It rang a few more times, then ceased. Barry and Danny waited till the light was switched off and went to the back door. Kathy had positioned Ricky for her death. The boys now knew which room was Ricky's bedroom, as they weren't able to clearly make out the map they'd been given.

Barry held the screen door open while Danny turned the key. They both walked inside, through the laundry, then down the hallway leading to Ricky's bedroom.

'How did you get into the house?' Ricky stood just outside her bedroom.

There was a moment's silence as Danny and Barry took stock of the situation. 'Could you go and hop on your bed,' Danny finally said.

To Danny and Barry's surprise, Ricky obeyed them. They followed. Ricky lay on her bed. The light in the bedroom was on and she stared up at the intruders. Danny took a syringe from Barry and showed it to Ricky.

'I have to give you this,' Danny told her.

'Why are you doing this to me?' Ricky pleaded in vain. 'Please don't. I have children and I have a bit of money.'

Barry and Danny looked at each other. Barry moved to the other side of the bed, pinning Ricky's arm down with his leg.

'Look, I'm sorry, but I have to give you this … I've been told to,' Danny explained.

'Yes, I understand …' Ricky's will had gone.

Danny swabbed her arm, and then injected her. 'Just go to sleep, you'll be all right … just go to sleep,' he told her.

Ricky closed her eyes. Barry and Danny waited. They even helped themselves to Ricky's cigarettes, drank two popper juices and used the toilet. Ricky made a noise, like a grunt or heavy breathing. They weren't sure if the one needle was enough. If they were to believe that Ricky was an addict, then it's possible she could have a high tolerance to the drug. They injected her a second time, placing the second needle in the same hole, trying to make it look like only one needle was used, and that Ricky had overdosed.

Danny sat on Ricky's chest, expelling her last breath of life.

Satisfied they had done their job, Barry and Danny packed everything up and headed out. They dumped the needles, balaclavas and gloves in separate locations as they travelled back to Stuart Flats.

On Monday 5 May, Danny had his mother drive him to Queanbeyan where he purchased a motorcycle and helmet for $900.

Barry caught up with Kathy, John and Alistaire in the parking area of Stuart Flats. John had to move his car because he was blocking a neighbour's parking place. He put Alistaire in the four-wheel drive, walked around the back and confronted Barry.

'What went wrong?' John demanded. 'Why didn't you make it look like suicide? You were told to make it look like suicide.'

'Well, that wasn't my department, you'll have to speak to Danny if you want to find out about that,' Barry defended himself.

That was the last time Barry ever spoke with John. After that, all communication was conducted through Kathy to protect John. All the boys cared about was getting the balance of their money.

CHAPTER FOURTEEN

Getting the pieces right

While John Conway, Kathy McFie, Barry Steer and Danny Williams were all locked up, there was still more work to be done to achieve a successful conviction. Based on the statements given by Barry and Danny, Noel Lymbery and his team needed to speak to more people to get corroborating evidence. They needed to verify what they'd been told by third parties.

One person of great interest to Noel and Ben Cartwright was Robert. According to Barry, it was Robert who had sold some heroin to Kathy McFie when he was staying at Danny's place. Robert had since moved, and Ben tracked him down at his current address. He spoke to Robert by phone first, explaining why he was calling and what they wanted to speak to him about. Robert agreed to help and both Noel and Ben met him at his home.

It was an interesting situation for Noel and Ben. Here they were about to walk in on a known dealer and start asking him if he'd admit to selling heroin to a murder suspect. His admission would normally have landed him in gaol. Given the seriousness and the importance of the case against John and Kathy, Noel sought an indemnity from prosecution that Robert not be charged with any offence relating to either of the defendants. The Director of Public Prosecutions granted the request. Robert, however, would still be arrested if any other offence was disclosed, such as being in possession of an illegal substance or if he admitted to other crimes outside of his dealings with John or Kathy.

Noel and Ben trod a fine line. They needed to speak with Robert. They needed his statement that he'd sold heroin to Kathy. They wanted him to show them the packaging, so they could compare it to the foils John allegedly found at Ricky's. What they didn't want was a reason to arrest him. No matter how willing Robert was, his cooperation would soon wane if he were to be placed in handcuffs.

Sitting in Robert's lounge room, Noel and Ben were getting all the information they required. Being police, they scanned the room as they talked. There were no drugs to be seen. They asked Robert if he could tell them how he packaged the heroin that he sold. He could do better than just tell them, he could show them. With that, Robert opened a cupboard and retrieved a foil. Noel and Ben gave each other a look. 'If there's any heroin in the cupboard or on the foil …' they thought.

It wasn't to be. Robert's house was clean, and the foil was for demonstration purposes only. Noel and Ben sat back, relieved, and watched as Robert performed his folding trick.

Robert admitted he knew Danny had been asked by John to kill his wife. He was in the unit when Danny walked in looking 'really agitated'. Danny asked him if he should do it and Robert replied, 'Look, I don't want to know … but if you do it, do it right and just leave me out of it.'

Robert had heard Danny and Barry discuss the murder, but he closed his ears; he didn't want to know anything about it.

Once they'd taken his statement and the sample foil, Noel and Ben left. They compared the foil to those John had surrendered to the drug registry, the foils he allegedly found at Gollan Street on 25 April. They were an exact match, right down to the folds. There was no doubt that the foils John handed in were purchased from Robert.

Police had three corroborating statements stating Kathy had bought caps from Robert — from Robert himself, Barry and Danny's brother. It should also be said Robert did not know, nor had ever met Ricky Conway.

Noel decided to get officers involved in conducting a final door knock of Stuart Flats. Now that everyone had been arrested, there might be some neighbours who were willing to talk, having been too scared to say anything to the police earlier. The door knock didn't reveal anything new, till a little old lady, Ruby, answered her door.

Ruby hadn't been spoken to during the first round. She had either been away when police called, or was missed by the officers. She knew most people in the complex. She had been living there for some time and she counted Kathy as one of her friends and thought Danny Williams was a 'very, very kind' boy. Ruby liked Danny a lot. Barry, on the other hand, wasn't someone she knew that well. In fact she didn't know his last name until she heard it on the news after he was arrested. When asked if she had met John Conway, Ruby said she had. Kathy introduced him to her, though he didn't say much. Ruby guessed he must have been married as she saw a little boy around with him on occasion. Kathy used to see Ruby quite regularly, but after she met John, her visits became less frequent. Eventually, Kathy did tell Ruby that John was married 'to a German woman'.

There was one time when Ricky apparently visited Stuart Flats. Ruby got a call from Kathy. She told Ruby that John's wife was on the steps and not to answer the door to her. Ruby had no intentions of doing so and locked her front door. She called Ricky 'the German woman', because Kathy had told her that Ricky had a lot of respect for Hitler. Ruby was from an era when friends and family had fought against Hitler and the Nazis. Telling Ruby the story about Hitler would hardly have endeared Ricky to her.

Ruby told police she had seen Barry Steer, Kathy and John together one day. It was 5 May. Ruby was able to be specific, because it was two days before her birthday and her daughter was visiting. John had apparently parked in her parking bay. While Ruby didn't have car, she did like it kept free for her daughter. She phoned Kathy to ask John to move his car. Ruby waited a while and checked, but John's four-wheel drive was still in her place. She then walked out of her unit and saw Kathy downstairs in the parking area. Kathy, John, Barry and Alistaire were all together. The three adults were in discussion. They were 'looking happy' according to Ruby. She even witnessed them laughing with each other.

Ruby interrupted the trio and asked that the car be moved. John helped his son into the vehicle and walked around the back to reach the driver's side. Kathy apologised and Ruby accepted it. She went back to her unit and her daughter arrived shortly afterwards.

Ruby's statement may not seem terribly enlightening, but it does put Barry, John and Kathy together, just one day after Ricky was found dead. Their behaviour together could be viewed as being very familiar with each other. It questions John being the grieving husband when he could be laughing with his babysitter and Barry so soon after Ricky's death.

It was also, most likely, the day Barry recalled when John pulled him up and asked what had gone wrong with making Ricky's death look like a suicide.

For Noel, Ben and the rest of team, Robert's and Ruby's statements were just more pieces in the ever-growing jigsaw.

They spoke to other people, finding out what they could about John and Kathy's relationship, and particularly Kathy herself. Kathy was an unknown. She had no criminal record, and hadn't done anything to attract the attention of the police. Family, friends and associates were all spoken to. Most saw Kathy as a gentle and giving person and couldn't believe she was involved with Ricky's murder in any way. Police also heard from some who had known Kathy and, because of soured relationships, depicted Kathy in a negative light. The team on Operation Aquatic got to know Kathy, but none of the information they received would help them with her conviction.

On the night John and Kathy were arrested police conducted an exhaustive search of the Gollan Street home. They were looking for anything that would implicate the pair in Ricky's murder, or show their association with Barry and Danny. The piece of paper Kathy used to write down details of Barry's sister being pulled over by the police was shown to both Kathy and John. John denied ever seeing it, but Kathy admitted it was hers.

Police found a lot of Australian Federal Police property and, more bizarrely, souvenirs from accidents. The items included police batons, leather jackets, pens, notebooks, badges and a person's coat that was worn in an accident. There were 1,125 numberplates found, some still in their paper jackets. Amongst them was a New South Wales Bicentennial plate. The holes where the screws went through had been damaged, and a corner was bent, evidence of the plate being forced off its vehicle. The plate would be identified by Barry and Danny as the numberplate they gave John on the day John approached Danny about killing his wife.

In the roof cavity of the house, police located boxes of audio tapes. Some had the AFP logo on them, while others were blank. They also had writing on them, dates and names. Noel and his team weren't sure of the relevance of the find and added the tapes to the other items, sending everything to the Property Office. If they needed them, they knew where to find them.

With the evidence Barry and Danny supplied police, a search was conducted to retrieve the needles, balaclavas and gloves which they had disposed of on their way home from Gollan Street. Barry and Danny told Noel that they had thrown the needles out as they drove along Ginninderra Drive, Kaleen. Ginninderra Drive is a main arterial road running east to west across the northern suburbs.

Corey Heldon was given the task of being the Field Officer. The Search and Rescue Unit were employed to walk the length of the Drive. They started at eight in the morning on 30 July and finished around one in the afternoon. The search area was just over a kilometre and they found 12 syringes. None of the syringes could be positively matched to those used by Barry and Danny.

Closer to their home, as they drove along the National Circuit in Barton, Barry told Danny to get rid of the balaclavas and gloves. Barry stopped the car beside a drain and Danny jumped out. With the items in hand, Danny reached into the drain. It was filled with dirt, so he buried the balaclavas and gloves under the soil and leaf litter. Danny hopped back in the car and the two headed home.

Federal Agent Bob Atkins from the Forensics Unit led the search of the drain. They pulled off the manhole cover, revealing the build-up of dirt Danny described. Brushing away the loose soil and leaf litter, they found the balaclavas and a pair of leather gloves, also known as rigger gloves. The second pair of gloves Danny and Barry used appeared to be missing. Photos were taken of the items while they were still in the drain, and then they were bagged for evidence.

Barry and Danny were being very helpful to Noel and Ben, supplying them with all the information they required and more. Noel and Ben have a similar approach to each other when interviewing offenders. Rather than playing the heavy and using scare tactics, they have found they get better cooperation being civil, presenting their suspects with the facts without throwing them down their throats. The exception was Ben's interrogation of John. Even then, Ben still didn't become overly aggressive, despite telling John he didn't believe a word he said and accusing him of murder.

Barry and Danny were in Noel and Ben's hands. They were caught and they knew they'd have to pay. Facing a murder charge, they both knew they could be sentenced to life. What the police needed was for Barry and Danny to agree to give evidence against John and Kathy. For their part, the Director of Public Prosecutions would ask the court to take into account their assistance and reduce their sentences. Barry and Danny accepted the deal and signed an agreement. They would testify against John and Kathy, and against each other. Should they not uphold their agreement after their sentencing, then they would be re-sentenced, facing the maximum penalty.

Barry and Danny agreed to plead guilty. This would be looked upon favourably by the court as their plea would save the court both time and money. Instead of a trial, Barry and Danny would face a sentencing hearing.

After John appeared before Magistrate Somes, Noel visited him at the Remand Centre. Noel was there to get his permission to gather some clothing and other belongings for Alistaire, who was in foster care. John gave his permission and still denied any involvement in or knowledge of Ricky's murder. He did tell Noel he would apply for bail as soon as he could. He wasn't going to spend any more time in the Remand Centre than he had to.

John kept his promise.

On 6 August both John and Kathy applied to have their bail reviewed in the Supreme Court. Police continued to oppose bail and Chief Justice Jeffery Miles heard the submissions. Noel Lymbery told the court police had recordings of conversations between John and Kathy talking about ways they could avoid attending Ricky's coronial inquest. Noel said the recordings included discussions about going interstate and feigning illness. John and Kathy also spoke about how they could discredit certain witnesses. Although the police recordings related to the inquest, it still demonstrated John and Kathy's willingness to avoid the legal process. Faced with a committal hearing, it could be considered that they would employ similar tactics so as not to appear.

Justice Miles adjourned the application for a later date, wanting to view the transcripts. Ben Cartwright informed the court it would be another six weeks till the prosecution brief was complete.

John Terence Conway, Kathy Marie McFie, Barry Steer and Daniel Scott Williams all appeared in the ACT Magistrates' Court on 11 August. Their appearance was for them to be formally told that the committal hearing would be held on 20 October.

No pleas were entered and there were no applications for bail. It was a just a formality, but it was the first time all four had been together since they were arrested.

Noel and Ben presented their brief of evidence against John, Kathy, Barry and Danny to Pip De Veau and Terry Golding. The two detectives knew Ms De Veau as a competent and valued prosecutor, while Mr Golding was a new barrister with the ACT Director of Public Prosecutions. He had gained his experience in the New South Wales courts, and was a well-respected barrister. Both lawyers were ready to prosecute Barry and Danny, but they had a bail application to see to before then.

With less than two weeks before the committal hearing, John Conway, through his defence barrister, Jack Pappas, lodged a new application for bail in the Magistrates' Court. Mr Pappas said he had fresh material relating to a surety and expert evidence from a Canberra psychologist, Dr Leigh Nomchong.

The police prosecutor had argued at the first bail application that John Conway was a risk to himself and possibly to his son. This time, Mr Golding submitted two letters written by John on 6 May, which had recently been found by Ricky's mother in the Gollan Street house.

After John had been arrested, Phillip Reiners contested his mother's will. The court ordered that Anna's solicitor become the new executor.

Soon after the decision, Anna employed a locksmith to change the locks on the Gollan Street house. While inspecting the interior, Anna found two letters written by John two days after Ricky had been found. The letters read:

'*Dear God,*

This is to introduce Ulrike Conway, my beautiful and loving wife. Please give her a comfortable future till I can be with her again. Ricky had a mortal problem with alcohol, but this would not bother her any more.

Your humble servant,

John Terence Conway.'

The second letter was addressed to Ricky with John promising to '*provide the best future for our son*'. It went on to say, '*I pray that you and I will be together in the near future without the mortal vices of mankind. I will never forget you. I will always have great love for you. Sleep well my bride.*'

Anna gave the letters to Noel, and he forwarded them to Dr Rod Milton.

* * *

At the bail hearing Dr Milton told the court that the letters were 'bizarre', and supported his original assessment that John could harm himself or his son. They showed John exhibited suicidal tendencies.

Dr Nomchong had recently interviewed John and said, 'I no longer consider him clinically depressed or a danger to himself or his son.'

When asked about the letters, Dr Nomchong quoted a passage where John had promised to *provide the best future for our son*. He believed those thoughts contradicted any inference that John would take his own life.

Mr Golding addressed the court, saying Ricky's murder was a 'planned, callous and sinister offence', and the bail application was 'frivolous' and 'perilous', given how close it was to the committal proceedings. He added that John was 'clearly a man who is capable of planning' and could leave the Territory before he was due to appear in court.

Magistrate Peter Dingwall refused bail. John would remain at the Belconnen Remand Centre till the start of the committal hearing.

On 13 October 1997, Barry Steer and Daniel Scott Williams appeared before Justice Ken Crispin in the ACT Supreme Court. They pleaded guilty to the murder of Ricky Conway. Though it was a sentencing hearing, submissions were still made by both the Prosecution and Defence. Representing Barry and Danny were Alyn Doig and Ray Livingston, respectively.

It was presented to the court that both men had been manipulated in committing the murder. Danny said he was 'blackmailed' as he alleged John Conway threatened to poison his girlfriend. Barry had been influenced by claims Ricky Conway was 'a bad mother and an alcoholic'.

Mr Livingston told the court John had 'manipulated two vulnerable men to achieve the death of his wife'. He described Barry as 'an inadequate man with a chip on his shoulder about the Family Court', and said of Danny that he was 'a hopeless heroin addict'.

Mr Doig suggested John Conway had 'picked his marks'. As an experienced police officer he had chosen Barry and Danny because of their dysfunctional backgrounds.

Terry Golding tendered the recorded conversations, where Barry talks of wanting to be a 'hitman' and how easy it was for him to have killed John's wife. Justice Crispin also heard Barry telling his sister that he would kill Danny if he 'dogged', and John Conway if he didn't pay the balance owing to them. The recordings did little to support Barry's claim of having been manipulated.

Terry Golding stated that Ricky's death was a 'cold-blooded killing of a blameless victim, primarily for money'. He added that 'the manipulation that was extended to the two prisoners was not to such an extent as to be mitigating', urging Justice Crispin to 'reject that there was any coercion at any time'. He did say, while Barry and Danny had committed the murder, John Conway and Kathy McFie had greater culpability for the killing.

Given Barry and Danny had signed an undertaking to testify against John and Kathy in their trial, Terry Golding made a submission to the court, suggesting a 50 per cent discount be given on their sentence. Justice Crispin adjourned the hearing to consider the submission and to deliver his sentence.

Justice Crispin gave his address on 16 October 1997. After outlining the evidence that had been presented by the Crown and the mitigating circumstances suggested by the Defence, the judge said that in his view 'the murder of an innocent victim by hired assassins should attract the sentence of life imprisonment'.

He explained himself by saying such a penalty would be warranted as 'the murder was premeditated'.

'Whilst the plan was essentially conceived by Mr Conway and/or Ms McFie, the prisoners also took an active part in the planning, arranging for the use of a car, the purchase of heroin and the provision of balaclavas and gloves. They also added the refinement of a telephone call to ensure that the deceased was at home. It was remorselessly executed. The victim's plea to be spared for the sake of her children went unheeded. When she did not die quickly, further heroin was administered. Then Mr Williams sat on her chest to hasten her death.'

The judge described their actions as 'pitiless determination'.

Justice Crispin also rejected the claims that Barry and Danny had been manipulated to commit the murder. There was no mention of any threats when they gave their record of interview on 27 July. When asked by police why they became involved, they gave various answers. They spoke of the money, the need to support their drug habit, and because they had been offered protection by John Conway.

Justice Crispin concluded on the matter saying, 'Having read Mr Williams' various statements carefully, I am not satisfied that any of these threats were made or, if made, played any significant part in Mr Williams' decision to accept Mr Conway's offer.'

With regard to Barry, the judge found, 'It seems clear from the record of interview with the police that money was the primary motivation for taking part in the murder though I accept that his belief as to the treatment allegedly being meted out to Mr Conway's child may have played some small part in his motivation.'

Justice Crispin still held the view that Barry and Danny should receive the maximum sentence for their part in Ricky Conway's murder. He did understand, however, that it was important to encourage people to provide assistance to the police to successfully prosecute all offenders. As Barry and Danny had agreed to testify against John and Kathy, the judge felt 'obliged' to reduce their sentences, however 'distasteful' it might appear to others.

The sentence that Justice Crispin imposed was 27 years, with a non-parole period of 18 years. He decided to reduce it by only one-third, reducing the sentence by nine years, and the non-parole period by six. He added, 'Any greater reduction would, in my view, shock the conscience of right-thinking members of the community.'

Barry Steer and Daniel Scott Williams stood in the docks. Justice Crispin then read their sentence. Both would be incarcerated for 18 years, with a non-parole period of 12 years, dating back to 27 July. The judge also asked that they be placed in the New South Wales Witness Protection program, as they were considered 'at risk'.

Barry and Danny were transported to the Belconnen Remand Centre, where they would stay till after the committal hearing of John and Kathy.

After the sentencing hearing, Noel and Ben went down to the holding cells under the court. They wanted to check on Barry and Danny and to give them their support. They even brought a treat for the boys — McDonald's hamburgers and fries. It would be a long time before either would ever taste a Big Mac again, and Noel felt it was a reasonable thing to do for them. After all, Barry and Danny were important witnesses for the prosecution.

To Ben's surprise, Barry was ecstatic. Not only for the burger, but also because he was expecting to get life. Barry shook both their hands and thanked them enthusiastically for all that they had done. Barry was looking forward to starting his life again in 12 years. He'd be 41 and he hoped to resume his relationship with his son. At the time, Barry was talking to a Family Court solicitor about retaining his right to have contact.

CHAPTER FIFTEEN

Sex, lies, audio tapes and anxious times

Prior to the committal hearing the police received a subpoena from John and Kathy's defence lawyers requesting all documentation and notes in relation to Operation Aquatic. This meant everything the officers had written down — official statements, records of interview and personal notes either in their diaries or on computer files — were to be handed over to the defence counsel.

This was not an unusual request. The defence lawyers, however, had also asked for copies of all the audio tapes that were found in the roof at Gollan Street.

The police had not given the tapes much attention, given all the other paraphernalia they had seized from the property. There were other matters that required their attention before listening to a bunch of cassettes.

As the subpoena was specific about the audio tapes, Noel and Ben decided they should take a closer look, or rather listen.

The tapes were recovered from the Property Office. Noel delegated the task of listening to and transcribing all the tapes to Corey Heldon. Because of the number of hours she had to spend sifting through the tapes and the methodical approach with which she applied to her task, the tapes became known as the 'Heldon tapes'. They would reveal a devious and manipulative plan to undermine Ricky's trust and confidence.

The cassettes were recordings of telephone conversations Kathy had with Ricky, John and other friends between February and April 1997. Thirty-nine tapes had been used to record Kathy's conversations with Ricky and John. The recordings showed Ricky being open and honest with Kathy about her relationship with John, how much she loved him, and how she hoped they could work their problems out. Ricky desperately wanted John, Alistaire and her to be a family. Her openness to Kathy came because she thought Kathy was a friend, a good friend.

What the tapes plainly showed Kathy doing was feeding her conversations with Ricky to John. It appeared that Kathy was trying to give John information that he could use against Ricky during his custody battle. Kathy would also talk Ricky out of notifying police when she alleged John hit and kicked her.

While Kathy heard how John was being abusive towards Ricky, and offered Ricky sympathy, she would tell John she didn't believe her. Kathy loved John and would do anything she could to help him.

Corey Heldon didn't transcribe every single conversation on the tapes, but she did transcribe those that were of particular interest with regard to the investigation. It took her two weeks. In Corey's words, 'It was the most depressing two weeks of my life ... from the moment I pressed play and hearing Ricky's voice, I knew there was something not right about this.'

Listening to the tapes affected Corey emotionally. She couldn't believe how 'wicked' and manipulative John and Kathy could be.

'Hearing her talk to Kathy as a friend, and knowing the outcome, was quite chilling. At the start Ricky sounded buoyant ... After the custody matter she was wanting to get her life on track ... be a better mother and sort out her employment ... you could hear the deterioration of her mind in her voice as the two [John and Kathy] manipulated her.

'To listen to that and to know it was real, that it wasn't a movie, wasn't made up, wasn't scripted ... that these people were taping her and getting some degree of enjoyment or pleasure ... I had a crisis of faith in people's inherent goodness.'

The committal hearing got underway at the ACT Magistrates' Court on 20 October, and would continue for the next four weeks. Committal proceedings are held to subject the prosecution's case to scrutiny, and for a magistrate to decide if the matter should be put before a judge at trial in the Supreme Court. The prosecution was led by Terry Golding, with Jack Pappas for John Conway and Craig Everson for Kathy McFie. They appeared before Magistrate Michael Somes.

On the first day Mr Golding outlined the case against John and Kathy. He spoke of Ricky's diary and the coffee incident, when John admitted to putting something in Ricky's drink to calm her down — the same day he alleged he found the foils of heroin. Mr Golding stated that John had been emotionally and physically abusive to his wife, and in a 'cruel and bizarre twist' his mistress, Kathy, had befriended Ricky. He also said that John had misled both Kathy and Ricky as to his relationship with the other.

Barry Steer took the stand, explaining how he and Danny had become involved with John and Kathy and how they had committed the murder. They were to be paid $15,000. Barry would receive $6,000 for assisting Danny, who would pocket $9,000 for injecting John's wife. Barry did say, when Danny was first asked to kidnap Ricky, that they discussed how they could poison her by connecting a hose to the exhaust of her car. Barry dismissed the kidnap idea as 'being too hard'.

Under cross-examination, Barry couldn't explain why there were inconsistencies in his testimony with what he had told police. He did, however, say that the statements and his evidence were true to the best of his ability. He told the court, 'I will go to gaol and do my penance and try and reform myself while I'm in gaol to get out and be a better person in society.'

Asked why he and Danny didn't leave the syringes at the murder scene to make it look more like a suicide, Barry passed the buck to Danny and replied, 'It wasn't my department.'

Other witnesses followed telling what they knew of the murder plan, how they had either overheard or had been told directly by either Barry or Danny. Danny took the stand and said he was 'too out of it' on the night of the murder. He even said he had fallen asleep on Ricky's bed after the first time he had injected her, only to be woken by Barry.

Terry Golding introduced the Heldon tapes, telling the court that the tapes would disclose the plan between John and Kathy to sabotage custody arrangements between Ricky and her son. Before the tapes could be played, Craig Everson objected. He said the material had been brought together contrary to the listening devices legislation.

In essence, it is illegal for anyone to tape another person without that person knowing they are being taped. Therefore, any such tapes would not be allowed to be used in either a court of law or for civil proceedings. It would be deemed, whatever evidence the tapes contained, to be inadmissible. There is an exception, however, under the *Listening Devices Act* that allows such material to be admissible if it is being presented in a court of law where the offence is punishable by imprisonment for life or for more than ten years.

Mr Everson also made an application to the court for the taped material to be suppressed on the grounds that it might be prejudicial. Magistrate Somes refused the suppression order, but hadn't yet ruled on the admissibility of the tapes.

Mr Pappas revealed to the court that, despite extensive enquiries by officers attached to Operation Aquatic, they had not traced the source of the $3,000 allegedly paid to Barry and Danny. He argued, 'There is no independent corroboration that Kathy McFie had paid the alleged contract killers $3,000 … It is integral to the story put forward by these two murderers that they were paid money with the promise of more to come.

'Proof of this alleged payment was absolutely vital to the prosecution's case, which paled without it,' he added.

Mr Pappas then applied for court orders to force the police to produce all financial documents relating to the four, as he believed the material was being deliberately withheld. Magistrate Somes refused his application. The police, however, did agree to produce the relevant documentation under subpoena. They believed John had paid the money from cash-only jobs he had done on the side, erecting sheds and garages for friends. Police had copies of receipts dating back to 1995.

Noel realised he needed a more thorough investigation conducted into John's finances. On the steps of the court Noel met a former colleague, Constable Richelle Jones. Richelle was an experienced officer, specialising in financial audits. As it happened, Richelle was back from maternity leave and was looking for work she could do from home. Noel quickly seized on the opportunity and told her, 'Have I got a job for you.'

On 20 November, four weeks after the committal had begun, the Crown prosecution rested its case against John and Kathy. Magistrate Somes was ready to deliver his findings, but was prevented from doing so when Mr Pappas made an application for bail. The magistrate told Mr Pappas that 'only in extraordinary' circumstances would he be prepared to grant bail. Both Mr Pappas and Mr Everson then made submissions for Magistrate Somes to disqualify himself from hearing the bail application, on the grounds of apprehended bias. The magistrate was not prepared to disqualify himself. He explained to the defence counsel that the application was for a review of bail, which had already been refused by himself and Magistrate Peter Dingwall. He would only consider the application if there was fresh evidence available.

With the bail matter resolved, Magistrate Somes asked John and Kathy if they had anything to say in relation to the charges against them. Kathy stood and read from a card, saying, 'I am not guilty and I reserve my defence.'

John also stood and simply said, 'Not guilty.'

Based on the evidence presented to the court, Magistrate Somes committed both John Terence Conway and Kathy Marie McFie to stand trial in the Supreme Court before a jury for the murder of Ulrike Conway, on or about 3 May 1997. He added that any bail application 'can be reviewed elsewhere if necessary'.

Christmas would come two days earlier for John Conway and Kathy McFie. On 23 December they appeared in the ACT Supreme Court for their fourth attempt at seeking bail. Justice John Gallop heard the matter.

All that was required was to satisfy the court that the two applicants would turn up for the trial and not commit any offence while on bail. The seriousness of the offence with which they were charged was not taken into consideration. They were, after all, innocent until proven guilty.

Justice Gallop said, despite facing the most serious of criminal charges, there was no reason to deny either the right to bail. He found that both had strong ties within the ACT, neither had a criminal record, and the fact that Kathy's parents were willing to post $50,000 cash as bail made a powerful case for her application. He also rejected Dr Milton's claims that John could cause harm to himself or his son.

John Conway and Kathy McFie were free, if only conditionally. John returned to Gollan Street, while Kathy went to live with her parents in Rivett, before returning to Stuart Flats.

John was to report daily to Belconnen Police Station, while Kathy was to report three times a week to Woden Police.

The news that John and Kathy had been granted bail was received with much angst and worry by most of the witnesses.

In Gollan Street, there were about six witnesses who had testified against John and Kathy at the committal hearing, and were to testify again at the trial. The knowledge John Conway had moved back into the street did not make them feel very comfortable. There were tense times as neighbours checked the area before leaving their house, hoping not to bump into John.

Ben Cartwright had his own concerns. John could come after him to exact revenge for what John would perceive as disloyalty. He and John had worked together in Traffic Operations Accident Investigations, and it was Ben who first put it to John that he had murdered Ricky. Ben thought John would give him the primary blame for being arrested.

John had met Ben's children, as Ben had met Alistaire, and all three attended the same school. Ben had to consider the possibility John might approach the school and threaten his two children. For Ben, the likelihood of this happening was real. He based it on his own knowledge of John and what Dr Milton had told the police.

Safeguards were immediately put in place. Ben contacted the local patrols and spoke with the principal of the school, making sure all teachers and staff kept an eye out and contacted police should John Conway enter the grounds.

The trial date had been set for May the next year. For the witnesses and Ben, it would be a long and anxious six months. May could not come soon enough.

As the months came and went, however, there were no incidents involving John and Kathy. They both fulfilled their bail obligations and kept a low profile until the start of the trial.

After the committal hearing, Barry Steer and Danny Williams were moved to Long Bay Correctional Centre in Sydney's east. They were placed in segregation, away from the main population, for their own safety. The arrest and subsequent committal were widely reported and, because they were giving evidence for the prosecution, they were at risk of assault by other prisoners. They could never be released into the general population, and would spend every year of their sentence in segregation. At least they had each other.

CHAPTER SIXTEEN

The trial

Press, radio and television journalists flocked to the ACT Supreme Court for the start of the trial against John Conway and Kathy McFie. It was 18 May 1998, one year and 15 days after Ricky's murder.

The cameras caught John and Kathy entering the court building separately. According to Ben, John and Kathy would drive in together, but go their separate ways into the building, so they could not be filmed together.

The trial was being heard by then Acting Chief Justice John Gallop. Fourteen jurors were empanelled. Twelve is all that is required, but in some trials, particularly those expected to run over a month, extra jurors are brought in to replace any that may fall sick or be discharged for whatever reason.

Once the jury had been selected, John and Kathy stood in the dock side by side as the indictment was read: 'You are both charged that you, on the 3rd day of May 1997 at Canberra in the Australian Capital Territory, did murder Ulrike Conway.'

John and Kathy both pleaded not guilty. They sat in the dock, their seats positioned together with a Corrective Services guard on either side, like bookends. Jack Pappas continued to represent John, while Kathy now had a new barrister, Richard Thomas.

Terry Golding gave his opening address, saying that the Crown's central evidence would come from Barry Steer and Danny Williams, outlining their recruitment by the accused and their part in Ricky's murder. He said there was a 'complex matrix of motive' for the murder, referring to John and Kathy's 'intimate sexual relationship' and the plans they were making for their future, which excluded Ricky.

Mr Golding admitted that John and Ricky had a troubled marriage and told the jury, 'It will emerge during the Crown case that Ricky Conway had a very real alcohol problem.'

Ricky's 'problem' had contributed to a 'degree of bitterness' between her and John. Mr Golding also spoke about the Family Court battle and said John and Kathy had chosen the date for Ricky's murder because they knew she was home alone and 'emotionally disturbed'.

Jack Pappas told the jury, 'The core of the Crown case is rotten … Barry Steer and Daniel Williams are thoroughly unreliable witnesses.'

Mr Pappas asked the jury to scrutinise Barry's and Danny's evidence carefully. 'John Conway's position in this trial is that those witnesses are criminals, thieves, drug users, addicts and persons previously convicted of fraud,' he explained.

'Mr Conway is a man of good character who had been a police officer for 12 years before his wife's death in May of last year … He says, "I didn't ask these men to kill my wife, I didn't promise to pay them money, and I didn't pay them money."'

The Crown began its evidence, tracing Ricky's movements from the Saturday afternoon when she had tried to borrow some rope to hang herself, to when her body was discovered by her elder son, Phillip, his girlfriend and Jacqui Dillon.

Patrick Kerr, one of the members of the Mental Health Crisis Team that was called to Gollan Street on the Saturday, described Ricky as being 'warm, pleasant and very cooperative'. He admitted she had had a 'serious alcohol problem for quite some time', but also spoke about how she had long-term plans to raise her son and was determined to retain custody. He left the house, satisfied that Ricky would not cause herself any harm.

Two of John Conway's work colleagues, Constables Darren Breatherton and Stephen Kent, told the court that John was a 'quiet chap' and they had never seen him angry or lose his temper at work. Darren Breatherton recalled being told by John that Ricky was an alcoholic, abusive and continually accusing him of extramarital affairs. He remembered an occasion when John told him that his son was trying to stop Ricky from hitting him, and she turned and hit their son. John also told him that the garage was the 'men's place' where he and his son could escape Ricky.

Stephen Kent had similar recollections of John describing his wife as being abusive to his son. John did say, after having moved out of Gollan Street in March 1997, that he 'felt free of her'. When John had received news of Ricky's autopsy, he told Constable Kent about the traces of heroin found in her body and that that had been a surprise to him.

Sergeant Larry Andrews revisited the conversation he had with John about a week before Ricky was killed. It was when they were working a Random Breath Test Unit together and John was disgruntled with having lost in the Family Court. He told Sergeant Andrews that he could 'see how people could kill Family Court judges, and their ex-wives'. John also expressed hatred for Ricky and concern for his son.

Barry Steer took the stand and recounted what he had told the police in his original statements and said during the committal hearing. He would be on the witness stand for nearly five days, as the jury listened to his testimony and heard the recordings police had made of Barry speaking to Danny, his sister, Joan, and Kathy and John.

Under cross-examination by Mr Pappas, Barry said he had received $1,000 from Danny and was expecting another $5,000 in only a few days after the murder. He stated he had intended to use some of the money to secure a future for his son, as well as fit his sister's car with new tyres so he could drive to see him. Mr Pappas enquired about the night of the murder, when Kathy McFie came to Danny's unit and asked if they were still going ahead with the killing. He asked if Barry had thought that the idea to kill Ricky Conway was Kathy's. Barry said he 'didn't come to any conclusions', and he didn't know 'whose idea it was'. He had been 'brought into it by Danny, and nobody else'. In one of the taped conversations with his sister, Barry does suggest it was Kathy's idea and that John was just going along with it.

Mr Pappas questioned the reliability of Barry's testimony. Barry told the court about the time after the murder when John asked 'what went wrong, it was meant to look like a suicide'. The conversation was not in Barry's original statement, taken on 27 July 1997, but came to him later. In his original statement he said he hadn't spoken to John after the murder. Barry admitted he hadn't remembered the conversation at the time he was questioned. His statement to police, with regard to that question, was wrong, but his memory had improved as time went on.

Danny Williams only had two and a half days in the witness box. Like Barry, Danny recalled the events of the night of Saturday 3 May when he injected Ricky with the lethal dose of heroin. He spoke about his meetings with John and Kathy discussing the murder, promising to ask someone to 'do the job', and travelling with Kathy to buy 'the gear'. He admitted he met up with John at the scene of an accident some weeks after the murder, though he didn't speak with John at the scene because John tried his best to ignore him. Danny also related the incident when John Conway allegedly threatened to 'chloroform' his girlfriend. Mr Pappas asked why he hadn't mentioned the incident to the police. Danny shyly admitted that it was, 'Probably because of my image.'

'You were afraid of looking a bit weak, were you?' Mr Pappas continued.

'You could say that,' Danny confirmed.

After a few more questions relating to other incidents where Danny said he and or his girlfriend had been threatened by John, but then admitted they weren't true, Mr Pappas stated to Danny, 'The simple fact is there were no threats.'

Danny denied it. The threat made by John to 'chloroform' his girlfriend was true.

Mr Pappas took issue with the way Danny recounted his conversation with John to Barry. In Danny's words, he told Barry that John had 'hinted' he wanted his wife killed. Danny explained he said that to Barry because he didn't want Barry knowing that John had put the proposition to him directly. Danny thought by using the word 'hinted' he was protecting John from any liability, and protecting Barry from having any knowledge of the deal. It confounded Mr Pappas, who then put it to Danny that John had never asked him to murder Ricky and never paid him any money.

Danny denied the statement, and when asked why he didn't just demand the remainder of the money from John he replied, 'Probably if he paid us, we wouldn't be here now.'

Richard Thomas questioned Danny's memory of events. Danny had testified to being 'on the nod' on the night he killed Ricky. Barry had also said Danny was falling asleep on the drive to Gollan Street and in Ricky's back yard as a result of his drug use. Danny admitted he did take a lot of heroin, and occasionally LSD, that it enhanced his view of the world and affected his moods. He also said he had memory problems because he was hit in the side of the head with a star picket at the age of 15, but had learned to compensate by developing a 'photographic memory' for 'some things'.

Mr Thomas questioned Danny's reliability, particularly as he had originally told police Robert was in the car with him when he and Kathy drove to buy the heroin. Danny later retracted the reference to Robert in his statement, as his memory improved. He agreed with Mr Thomas that at the time he was questioned by police he had not taken any drugs for three days and was quite sick. He didn't have withdrawal, as suggested by the defence counsel, because he didn't have any cravings. He was suffering pain in his abdomen and legs. He conceded his memory of the events leading up to the murder was 'confused' on the day he was arrested.

Danny was taken methodically through the questions and the answers he gave both the prosecution and John's defence counsel. Mr Thomas suggested that Danny's memory was 'jogged' by police and other people, which is why his account had altered. Danny denied the allegation. When Mr Thomas suggested the events involving John and Kathy talking about money and the murder had not happened, Danny simply said they. He also had an answer after Mr Thomas said that Kathy had not driven him to buy the drugs on the day of the murder. Danny replied, 'Well, she wouldn't let me drive her vehicle because I'm an unlicensed driver.'

Despite an exhausting and harrowing cross-examination by both Mr Pappas and Mr Thomas, Barry and Danny held up well. They didn't waver from what they had said happened. They were consistent with the bigger details, especially on conversations with John and Kathy, but varied on smaller issues, like who cut the holes in the beanies, whether Danny had lost the first half weight of heroin he bought initially, and who telephoned Kathy.

Barry, however, could not remember the incident Danny spoke of when John threatened his girlfriend, or having ever explained what the word 'chloroform' meant to his friend.

Robert testified about selling three caps of heroin to Kathy McFie and advising her of how it could be taken without injecting it. He added that on a separate occasion Kathy had said to him, 'Don't tell anybody about this because my boyfriend is a policeman ... if anything gets back to the police he could get in big trouble.'

When Mr Golding asked Robert what Danny had told him when he was in an 'agitated state', Robert recalled, '"I've [Danny] been asked to knock somebody off." His words were, "They've asked me ... John's asked me to knock off his wife."'

Robert didn't pay much attention and didn't want anything to do with it.

Mr Golding showed Robert the two foils John claimed he found in the Gollan Street house. Robert examined them, and stated that they were folded in the same way he normally folded foils containing heroin.

Jack Pappas referred to Robert's original statement he gave to Ben Cartwright, saying that Danny told him Kathy, and not John, had asked him to 'knock off' Ricky. Robert agreed to stand by his statement explaining, 'Back then, it was fresher in my mind.'

There was also the question of whether Robert was or wasn't in the car with Kathy and Danny the day they purchased the heroin that would be used to kill Ricky. Robert said he was. In fact, had he not gone with them to purchase the half weight, the dealer most likely wouldn't have sold it to Danny. The dealer knew Danny, but there was some bad blood between them.

Under cross-examination he told Mr Pappas that he only bought a half weight, not a full weight as Danny had claimed. He was also sure that there were only the three of them in the car, to and from the dealer's location. They had not driven the dealer anywhere after the 'score'.

Robert hadn't mentioned anything about the trip in his statement because he didn't think it important at the time and the police never asked him. He vaguely remembered Kathy mentioning something about John checking the computers, but could not recall the exact conversation that was had between Kathy and Danny. He defended his statement, saying he had not intentionally left anything out, and had only replied to the questions that had been put to him. If he had remembered the trip and the conversation he would have included it.

Mr Pappas pushed the point about remembering the portion of the conversation where Kathy told Danny 'John will check the computers.' 'But my question is, is it a recollection you think you have always had, or is it one that has just come back to you this morning?'

'I've always had it, but it's only come up now, because it is the first time I've been asked about it,' Robert answered.

Robert said he had never met or knew of anyone by the name of Ricky Conway.

Danny's brother was next in the witness box, and he gave similar evidence to that of Robert against Kathy, saying how he was in the flat when she purchased the heroin.

There was a lot of legal argument surrounding the introduction of Ricky's diary, and conversations she had with neighbours about the time she alleged John had slipped something into her coffee. It was referred to as being the 'coffee incident'. Included in this argument were the 'Heldon tapes', or at least a portion of a tape that involved a conversation between Kathy and Ricky.

The defence argued about the reliability of the evidence, questioning whether Ricky may have fabricated what she wrote and told other people to cast a negative light on her husband for any possible Family Court proceedings. There was also the accuracy of what the witnesses had to say. It was second-hand information and they could be misquoting Ricky. In short, it was nothing but hearsay.

The onus was on the Crown to prove that the evidence was not a fabrication or that it was not made in circumstances where there was a high probability that the evidence was not reliable. If they couldn't, then the evidence, the witnesses, diary and Heldon tapes would not be admissible.

To address the issue, Justice Gallop allowed Mr Golding to call each of the witnesses to give their account and for the diary and transcripts of the portion of the Heldon tapes, to be submitted to scrutiny in the absence of the jury. Having heard all the evidence, he then invited the defence counsel to make their arguments.

Ricky's recollection of events was found to be inaccurate by the defence. There were discrepancies between her diary and some aspects of the evidence given earlier in the trial. Even Ricky's reasons for keeping the diary were inconsistent. Some witnesses had said they had suggested to Ricky to keep the diary because it was a good idea, while Ricky told another witness that her solicitor had advised her to do so. The argument then was: how could anything coming from Ricky be taken as being reliable?

There was also the point that Ricky had not actually seen John place anything in her coffee or water, but rather suspected he had from its taste.

With regard to the Heldon tapes, Ricky is heard telling Kathy about the coffee incident, though there is no knowing when this call was made. The tape was marked in handwriting with a date, but it didn't correspond with the exact date of the incident.

There were a number of conversations on the tape spanning a large time frame, not reflected by the written date. Therefore, the conversation may have been made anytime after the incident.

The reliability of the witnesses was also in question, as most were friends of Ricky's and had a vested interest in what was happening between her and John.

The defence counsel were concerned by how Ricky had interpreted the coffee incident. In a call to the local police she spoke to an officer and told him that John had tried to 'poison her'. It was also the interpretation that the various witnesses had of the incident, even though she had told people that John had said to her he added the substance 'to calm' her down so they could talk. Ricky, however, never confronted John with this allegation, not giving him the right to respond. Had Ricky done so, and had the witnesses related the conversation, then the evidence might have been admissible as a demonstration of the relationship between the two.

Terry Golding rebutted the defence argument, saying that the evidence, the witnesses, diary and Heldon tapes would go to prove three things. One, that John was attempting to discredit Ricky for the purpose of any Family Court proceedings. Two, that John deliberately fed her heroin for the purpose of making Ricky appear to have ingested the drug prior to her being overdosed by Barry and Danny, thinking that an autopsy would show that Ricky had a history of heroin use and then possibly conclude that she had died at her own hands. Third, that the foils John alleged he had found at the house on the same day of the coffee incident would place Kathy, Barry and Danny together, showingly clearly their relationship and demonstrating to the jury that Barry and Danny had injected Ricky as ordered by John and Kathy.

Mr Golding believed that the defence would argue Barry and Danny had acted on their own in injecting Ricky, and that Kathy and John had not ordered them to do so. By linking the coffee incident to the foils and taking the evidence of Robert, Danny's brother, and that of Barry and Danny into account, the jury would see the two killers were acting under instruction. That being the case, then Kathy and John were as culpable in Ricky's murder as Barry and Danny were.

There had already been evidence introduced that Kathy had purchased heroin from Robert, and that the foils John handed in to the Drug Registry were the same as those sold by him. There was also supporting evidence from Barry and Danny's brother about the time Kathy bought the heroin and inquired how it could be administered. The fact Kathy had dealt with heroin and that Ricky had died from an overdose of heroin, for the Crown, proved a relationship between the defendants and the two killers.

Mr Golding addressed the issue of Ricky's reliability. With regard to an incident where her details of the event were found not to be proved, there was a recorded telephone conversation with Kathy in which Ricky admits to the exaggeration and says, 'It was the booze talking.'

Ricky's diary had on the first page a log of the amount Ricky had been drinking. It would be unlikely that Ricky would falsely keep track of the number of drinks she had. It showed Ricky was attempting to reduce her consumption. Then, if her account of how many drinks she consumed was accurate, it must be accepted that entries relating to other matters must also be taken as being correct.

One of the witnesses, Jacqui Dillon, saw Ricky on the afternoon of the coffee incident and commented on her friend's appearance, saying 'she looked very pale, drawn, and had bags under her eyes', adding weight to Ricky stating that whatever John had given her had knocked her out for some hours.

Mr Golding related another piece of evidence from Jacqui Dillon, who gave an account of Ricky confronting John over the coffee incident and John replying, 'I wouldn't do that to you because they would know it was me who had done it.'

Mr Golding believed this answered the defence's argument over demonstrating the relationship between John and Ricky, and was a relevant discussion in reference to the 'drugging'.

The defence contended that the evidence would not convince a jury on its substance, but rather because of the prejudice it contained. By drawing an association between Kathy purchasing the heroin, John tendering foils to the Drug Registry and Ricky dying of an overdose, while there could be other explanations for these separate events, the jury might come to a decision solely based on prejudice. The evidence, the witnesses, diary and the Heldon tapes, could distract a jury from the evidence already given by Barry and Danny, which, to the defence, still posed the question: 'did John and Kathy, or either one, ask them to murder Ricky?'

It may also be thought by the jury, if a connection could be made to either John or Kathy, that that person was acting on behalf of the other merely because of their relationship, when it could be that the person was acting independently. The jury might not discriminate between the separate actions and responsibilities of John and Kathy. Where they might find one defendant guilty on the evidence of Barry and Danny, they might assume the guilt of the other defendant based on the hearsay evidence and the prejudice it contained, rather than on the weight of facts. In other words, the evidence being presented was circumstantial, should it be accepted as the Crown proposed to present it.

Having spent most of the day debating the admissibility of the witnesses, diary and the relevant transcript of the Heldon tapes, Justice Gallop agreed to allow the evidence to be heard in front of the jury.

The judge's decision was a win for Noel and his team. Noel

and Ben saw the diary, specifically, as Ricky's own testimony against her husband.

The trial resumed. The jury heard how John had placed a bitter substance in Ricky's coffee, then a glass of water, one week prior to her murder. The evidence came from Ricky's neighbours, friends and her solicitor whom she told, and pages of her diary that were given to the jury to read. The telephone call between Ricky and Kathy in relation to the incident would be heard later, with the rest of the Heldon tapes.

The jury heard all the details, including Jacqui Dillon's recollection when Ricky had accused John of poisoning her. She also remembered seeing Ricky with a split lip, and Ricky saying she would file a complaint against John to Police Internal Affairs. Ricky later withdrew her complaint.

Another neighbour spoke of a conversation she had with John in 1996, in which John had talked about keeping the Gollan Street home. The neighbour had entered into an affair with John, and John basically told her he wouldn't continue the relationship if it meant Ricky might find out and he would lose the house. He certainly wasn't prepared to pay the mortgage with only Ricky living at Gollan Street. He told the neighbour that he would lose nearly $30,000 if he sold the house, which was more than the money he had borrowed from his parents to help pay for it in the first place. When the neighbour heard about the coffee incident, she advised Ricky to call the police.

There was another witness to substantiate Ricky's allegation. It was Constable Colin Dix from Belconnen Police Station. Ricky had called him on 27 April, two days after the incident. She told him what had happened and spoke with him for 20 minutes as he took down the details. He asked her what she wanted him to do about it, and Ricky said 'nothing'. She just wanted someone to talk to. Constable Dix agreed with Mr Pappas that, at the time, there was no solid foundation in Ricky's complaint. He had trouble keeping her focused on her account of the incident, as she would begin to talk of other things. He knew Ricky. Constable Dix had attended her address on previous occasions when she had called the station.

Lynette Corrigan and Joanna O'Donnell were two administration assistants who worked with John in Traffic Operations Accident Investigations. John told Lynette about having discovering the foils at Ricky's, and Lynette suggested he hand them in and get them tested. About a week before he was arrested, Lynette asked John who he thought had 'done it' and John replied, 'I have a fair idea.'

Lynette noticed a change in John's demeanour after Ricky's death, observing he had become quieter and withdrawn.

Two weeks before the murder, Joanna was in the office when John arrived with his son. Alistaire stood beside his father as John told Joanne he had to pull Alistaire and Ricky apart because they were fighting and that his son didn't want to go back to his mother.

Joanna remembered Ricky calling about once a day to speak with John. Ricky had even confided in Joanna that John had taken Alistaire from her and she wanted him back. John told her that Ricky was more interested in getting his money than she was in Alistaire.

On one occasion, just four days before her murder, Ricky called and Joanna put the call through to John. She could hear his end of the conversation. She heard him say, 'You're the one who's got everything,' then he slammed down the receiver.

Ricky called back just a few minutes later. Joanna did not hear any of the second conversation. Mr Pappas suggested that John's comments were made after he had left Ricky, which would explain why he was angry towards his wife. Joanna said she had

had similar conversations with John prior to March 1997, when he was still living at Gollan Street.

Ricky's elder son, Phillip, her mother, Anna, and sister, Gabby, presented their evidence. Phillip was the one to receive the most attention, particularly as the defence enquired about Ricky sourcing a contact for marijuana. Phillip admitted he knew a contact, Mark, and gave his mother the details, adding that it was for his grandfather, who was suffering from cancer. The marijuana was to be used to relieve his pain and improve his appetite. Phillip did remember his mother telling him that Mark had been at her place two or three weeks prior to her murder.

Anna spoke about how unusual it was to get a phone call from John, as he rarely called her. In her words, 'he ignored me'. The greeting was also different, in that he would normally just say 'Hello', but on Sunday 4 May he had greeted Anna with a 'Hi, Mum'. John said he had been trying to get hold of Ricky all day but had been unsuccessful. He wanted to know what to do with Alistaire's weekend clothes, because he was taking his son to school on Monday, as he had arranged with Ricky. Anna told John to try later as Ricky had told her she would be doing some gardening and may not have heard the phone.

Gabby told the jury that Ricky was upset the weekend of her death because she had found out John had engaged another solicitor. Ricky didn't know the reason why and it bothered her. Gabby related the coffee incident as told to her by Ricky, and informed the court that her sister had made appointments to attend a drug referral and alcohol centre and Alcoholics Anonymous the following week.

At the time of the trial, Brian McDonald had been promoted to Acting Superintendent, in charge of Woden Police Station. Terry Golding called Brian to introduce the recordings from the telephone intercepts.

The tapes were played to the court. The jury heard John telling an acquaintance of his, 'I don't think I've got a problem,' and that everything should be all right with regards to the police enquiry into Ricky's death.

John blamed Ricky's family for the allegations against him, saying that they were 'trying to find an excuse for their lack of concern'. He said his situation was 'very awkward, very uncomfortable'.

The jury heard conversations between John and Kathy, especially one where John tells Kathy of a mutual friend, Danny Williams, he saw at an accident scene.

Other tapes contained phone calls from Kathy to Barry, making arrangements to hand over some money at a mutually convenient location. A service station was chosen. The jury heard this tape after having been shown a video from the surveillance team that followed Barry and Danny to a petrol station where they met with Kathy. On a separate tape, Barry was heard speaking to a male, laughing as he said, 'What do you want us to do, lose sleep over it? I didn't know the bitch. There's no skin off my nose ... the only reason I'm losing sleep is because I haven't got paid.'

On day 12 of the trial it was Noel Lymbery's turn. Terry Golding introduced John Conway's taped record of interview during Noel's evidence-in-chief. According to Noel and Ben, they expected a grilling at the hands of Mr Pappas, as they would expect from any defence lawyer. They believed, in particular, Mr Pappas would accuse them of being single-minded in their pursuit of John.

Noel took the stand and explained the series of events that took place the night Ricky's body was discovered, the initial cursory search of the house and follow-up investigations of the property. The time came and Mr Golding presented four videotapes, the record of interview of John Conway, to be tendered as an exhibit. There was no objection to the tapes. The jury sat through six hours and 11 minutes of John answering questions on the afternoon and night of 7 May 1997.

They saw John becoming upset and crying at the mention of Ricky's name. They heard him telling the detectives that he loved his wife, and how he had hoped he and Ricky would have got back together, that she would stop drinking and they would become a family again. He denied he had ever hit her or caused her any physical harm. He denied that he and Kathy were having, or had ever had, an affair. She was nothing more than the babysitter. John denied having had any extramarital affairs while being married to Ricky.

The jury heard John's version of the coffee incident, how he had tasted something bitter in his coffee and poured it down the sink when Ricky was in the bathroom. It was then he found the two foils on the kitchen window and placed them in his pocket. He didn't know what the white powder was, whether it was an illicit drug or not.

Ben suggested that John had driven a wedge between Ricky and Alistaire, and undermined her authority by making the garage a 'safe haven' for 'men only'. John agreed in hindsight he may have, but said that there were always problems between Ricky and her son.

Later in the interview Ben had put it to John that he was involved in Ricky's death. He was asked how he organised it, where he bought the heroin, or whether he stole it. John denied all the allegations. He admitted he had a motive and a lot to gain, but 'wanted nothing more than to get back together with her'.

After the tapes had been played, Noel gave more details on the developments of the investigation from that point on— the identification of Barry and Danny and the covert operations that followed. He spoke about enlisting the help of the two killers to approach John in the early hours of Monday 28 July 1997, and how they handed a $50 note to Ben that had been given to them by John. Noel admitted that the scientific unit was unable to find any fingerprints on the note.

Mr Pappas questioned Noel about the investigations into Mark, who was a friend of the family's and a drug user who had stayed at Ricky's before she was murdered. He also wanted to know what the police knew of $3,000 having been taken from the Gollan Street address. Noel approached the issues confidently, saying that Mark was 'of interest' during the early days of the investigation, but eventually eliminated from their enquiries. The Operation Aquatic officers were satisfied that Mark had no connections to, or had ever used heroin, and what happened during his time with Ricky was corroborated through the taxi company he used to get to Gollan Street, and the pawnbroker who purchased the microwave Ricky had given him to sell. All these events happened during March 1997, and police, again, were satisfied Mark had not seen Ricky after that time.

Noel didn't know much about the missing money. Neither John, nor any member of Ricky's family had mentioned any missing money to police. The first time the police were aware of any suggestion that money may have been stolen from the house was when they overheard Barry talking to his sister. He told her that he had heard, after 3 May, that there was $3,000 in the house, and that it had gone.

Mr Pappas enquired if Noel and his team ever thought that Barry's and Danny's financial gain had come from taking the money on the night of the killing. Noel didn't agree with that assumption, due largely to the intelligence gathered before Barry's and Danny's arrests, where they were recorded admitting to other people they received money from Kathy prior to going to Gollan Street. In Danny's original statement he mentions

Ricky saying she had money, but Danny says they didn't believe her and never followed it up. They were both asked by police if they had stolen any money or any other items from the house on the night, and they said they didn't.

Mr Pappas put it to Noel that he had already concluded John Conway had killed his wife by 7 May. Noel rejected the assertion. He said he had sufficient information which gave him a suspicion of John's involvement in or knowledge of the murder, but that he was keeping an open mind. When asked if he thought it would have been advisable to stop Ben Cartwright from making accusations to John of having been involved in the murder, Noel disagreed.

When Mr Pappas suggested that Noel had also made blunt accusations to John, Noel again denied it. Noel explained that he said to John, 'You've got it all now,' but had not directly accused him of murder. He conceded that his wording was subtle, compared to Ben's.

Noel had appeared in court for almost three days. Given Mr Pappas' cross-examination of Noel on the record of interview, Ben was preparing himself for the worst. After all, he was the one who put those questions to John, and he would have to answer for them.

Mr Golding called Constable Corey Heldon and introduced the Heldon tapes. There was some objection to do with some of the content, but Justice Gallop ruled the tapes admissible in their entirety.

Ricky was heard on the tapes giving intimate details of her life, confiding in Kathy that she felt John was setting her up to take Alistaire away from her. She spoke of the violence she suffered, telling Kathy, 'I'm sick of being belted, Kathy. I'm sick of it … I'm sick of the violence, you know. I'm sick of what it's doing to Alistaire and doing to me, and, nah, it's just not worth it.'

Kathy offered support and advice saying, 'What are friends for?'

Then, during a conversation with John, Kathy told him, 'When she [Ricky] rang me late after you supposedly gave her a bashing, I told her not to call the police … Anyway, I'll give her a call and see how she is today … I'll offer my sympathy, as it were.'

John was heard laughing at Kathy's offer of sympathy.

Kathy even recorded herself speaking with the Care and Protection Services, alleging that Ricky had hit Alistaire with a belt and slapped him across his face. Officers from the Protection Services visited Alistaire at his school the next day. When Ricky found out she didn't know what to do and turned to her friend for advice. Kathy feigned shock, asking Ricky, 'How the hell did that happen?'

Ricky was close to tears, 'Somebody put in a report, didn't they, that I hit him last night.'

'Well, I'll be buggered,' was Kathy's response. Kathy then discussed with Ricky as to who would have made such an allegation.

Ricky even defended her friend Kathy to a next-door neighbour. The neighbour alleged that John had been trying for some time to get Ricky out of the house, and if she did go he would move in with Kathy. Ricky told Kathy that she said to the neighbour, '… no, you're wrong'.

Not everything was going Kathy's way, though. In one call to John, she told him that Ricky had discussed intimate sexual details. 'I can't believe that you would not give me the one thing I asked, and that is to be faithful to me,' Kathy pleaded. 'The fact that I have to speak to her and be civil to her because it's the best thing in the circumstances … is something I'm prepared to do … but I just don't want to hear that stuff.'

John responded by denying he had slept with Ricky, despite the fact the call was in February when John and Ricky were still living together as husband and wife in Gollan Street.

Kathy told John, 'I'll do whatever it takes to make you happy.'

Like the diary, the Heldon tapes gave Ricky the opportunity to present herself at the trial and give evidence against John and Kathy.

It was time to hear Ben Cartwright. Ben hadn't slept much the night before his appearance. He was expecting to be accused of being unprofessional and using bullying tactics against John. Terry Golding had warned him he was likely to receive a very hostile cross-examination from Mr Pappas over John's record of interview.

Ben had studied the full brief, including all 1,129 questions and answers, running through his mind the reasons why he asked John this and that, and more importantly, why he chose to treat John so aggressively.

Mr Golding led Ben through the series of events on the night of 4 May. He even asked Ben if he had noticed anything about the toilet in Ricky's house. Ben replied he noticed the toilet seat was in the 'upright position', which he thought was 'unusual'. Mr Golding asked Ben to read to the court John's first statement that he made on the Monday after Ricky's body had been discovered. Ben told the court he had made a recording, with John's permission, of the three messages Ricky had left on his mobile the Saturday she died. The jury heard the phone messages, how she was threatening to end her life, and telling John he and Kathy had 'won'.

Ben explained all that he was involved in throughout the investigation, including the arrest of Danny and John, and taking Barry to Gollan Street for a 'walk-through'. His evidence-in-chief was over. It was now Mr Pappas asking the questions.

Being a policeman, and having been involved in one of the most high-profile murder cases in the Australian Capital Territory's history, Ben felt the pressure. The investigation, his reputation, credibility and professionalism were all on the line.

It wasn't quite a 'make or break' situation, but Ben didn't want to be the one who had forgotten to follow a simple procedure or missed anything during the investigation.

Ben was handed a document and asked if that was a true and accurate transcript of the statement given by Danny Williams. Ben looked through it and answered that it was. Mr Pappas asked him to be sure. Ben was.

Mr Pappas then asked if Ben had made his mind up on 7 May that John was guilty of the murder. Ben denied he was completely convinced, but said he had his suspicions. Mr Pappas read the questions Ben had asked John about the murder. The first was 'Why did you kill her?' Then when John denied he had, Ben asked, 'Why did you organise her death?' Again John denied he had. Mr Pappas again asked Ben if he had made up his mind that John had killed Ricky considering the questions he'd asked. Ben stated as he had before, that he had his suspicions but had not made up his mind.

Mr Pappas sat down and Mr Thomas had no questions to ask.

That was it. Jack Pappas had only asked Ben a total of 11 questions. Five of the questions related to Danny Williams. Ben was amazed. He had had a sleepless night for nothing. It was done.

The relief was soon overshadowed by a feeling of it all being an anti-climax. Ben's testimony didn't even rate a mention in the *Canberra Times* the next day.

Ben attributes his easy time to the professionalism of the investigation. 'We had done what was required of us, a professional and thorough investigation. Every possible witness was located, a statement obtained, every thread of evidence located, documented, seized, exhibited and produced in a manner that was professional. There was no stone unturned and no line of enquiry that wasn't followed up.'

*　　*　　*

The case for the prosecution was nearly ended. There were a few other witnesses to clarify some issues raised during the earlier part of the trial. The witnesses included Karen, who was the first to bring Barry Steer to the attention of the police, Barry's sister, and Constable Richelle Jones.

Richelle had investigated the finances of John, Kathy and Ricky, and to a lesser extent Barry and Danny, dating back to 1994. Barry and Danny had little money, and what there was were mostly social security payments.

Richelle did uncover a number of bank accounts belonging to John, including some he had probably forgotten he had. Interestingly, John instructed some of the bank statements be posted to his work. It appeared Ricky would have been ignorant of his full worth. Also, the money John had requested from his parents to use as a deposit on the new house he planned to buy with Kathy was not money he was borrowing, but rather money he had previously placed in his parents' account. Over the years John had paid small amounts into his parents' bank, building a sizeable total of between $10,000 and $20,000.

Richelle's investigation into John's 'cash-only' building jobs, money from which was not deposited into any of his accounts, led her and the team to assume he would have had, at any time, a couple thousands of dollars in cash lying around the house. She could not say, however, where the $3,000 had come from that was used to pay Barry and Danny. There was no paper trail to link what Barry and Danny alleged with any money belonging to John.

Even so, the evidence presented by Richelle showed that John had access to money, enough to pay the $15,000 contract.

Another witness, a computer specialist employed by the AFP, had determined that John Conway had accessed a computer at the Woden Police Station on Saturday 3 May. He had logged on at 5.05 pm and retrieved information concerning the attendance of police at Gollan Street. The evidence could be collected because the AFP used a special audit program that recorded user key strokes for reviewing later.

With the prosecution rested, it was now time for the defence to present their case, and for John Terence Conway and Kathy Marie McFie to have their say.

CHAPTER SEVENTEEN

John Terence Conway

On Friday 19 June 1998, 43-year-old John Terence Conway of 35 Gollan Street, Evatt in the Australian Capital Territory, took to the witness box. This would be the first time the jury would hear John answering the allegations against him.

Mr Pappas took John straight to the point very early in the testimony. He asked John if he understood the caution police had given him when he was interviewed on 7 May. He did. He also understood that anyone under caution is usually regarded as a suspect in an investigation.

Mr Pappas then asked if he had lied about any matter. He admitted he had. John confessed that, while Kathy was his son's babysitter, the two had also entered into a sexual relationship.

Asked why he lied to police, John replied, 'I knew that if I had told them I was in a relationship, that would have made me look unnecessarily guilty, and I was also very embarrassed by the fact that I was in a relationship with somebody else while I was still married to Ricky.'

John had been in the relationship with Kathy since August 1996. They had met in July the same year. He told the court that his marriage to Ricky was 'rocky' and they had their 'tiffs', would make up and then argue again. In March 1997, after they had had an argument, Ricky called the police from a neighbour's house and, under Ricky's orders, John was escorted off the property.

Alcohol was the primary source of their problems according to John. He said Ricky's consumption was 'fairly frequent' and her behaviour towards him would change.

John explained to the court, 'When she'd [Ricky] been drinking to any extent she became abusive, primarily verbally and her temper seemed to become very, very short. Her tolerance to anything that was happening became almost negligible at times depending on how much she had consumed.'

John conceded that Ricky had tried to seek help with her drinking, attending clinics and was prescribed drugs. He couldn't remember exactly when, but she sought help several times during their marriage.

On 2 April, John saw Ricky in the hallway, holding their son tightly and he told her to 'let go'. She didn't. John then pulled them apart. He could see Ricky's temper rising, hurried Alistaire to his car, and then they left. Ricky and Alistaire had had an argument in front of the garage leading up to John's intervention, though John didn't witness the confrontation.

Later that day, Ricky spoke with a police officer and showed him her injuries, which included a split lip and bruising to her arm. Mr Pappas asked if John could have caused those injuries and he replied, 'I may have. I don't recall it, but at that time it may have happened.'

'Was the incident sufficiently heated for something like that to have happened?'

'I think it would have been, yes,' John replied.

John then agreed with Mr Pappas that he had downplayed the incident when talking to police on 7 May, explaining, 'I don't recall striking [Ricky] at that particular time but it is possible it may have happened. As I said I don't recall hitting her. I just don't recall it.'

John denied knowing Barry Steer or Danny Williams any better than to just say hello and goodbye to in passing. He denied ever telling either of them about Ricky, or ever calling her an 'alcoholic', 'bitch', or 'slut' in their presence.

John did admit to telling Kathy about collecting numberplates. He said the New South Wales bicentennial numberplate, presented in court, was given to him by Kathy one evening. He then denied having a conversation with Danny Williams that day.

On the issue of Ricky filing a complaint against John with the AFP Internal Investigations Department, John said he wasn't sure when he had found out about it. He did not accept, as stated in court by witnesses, that he had promised to drop the restraining order against Ricky if she withdrew her complaint. John dropped the order after speaking with the Deputy Registrar at the Family Court just prior to proceedings. He said he was unaware the complaint to Internal Investigations had been withdrawn till 'a long time after' the Family Court hearing.

John had learned of Kathy's tapes, the Heldon tapes, sometime in April 1997, just before Ricky's murder. Kathy had brought them to John's attention, but he couldn't recollect why or what conversation they had about it. He did remember his reaction, 'I suppose [I was] confused as to why they were being done. Just confused really, I suppose'.

John also recalled, 'The last time I listened to any of those tapes was prior to Ricky's death'.

John related the same version of events of what happened on 25 April with the coffee incident, as he had done when speaking with Ben Cartwright in his record of interview. The one difference was, he accepted he had taken the foils for a specific reason, saying, 'Because I recognised the two foils as something that may have related to a narcotic substance ... I thought if they were anything narcotic I may be able to use them at a later stage in a Family Law Court proceeding, if necessary.'

Referring to the accident that involved a diplomat's Mercedes and a van, John remembered Danny Williams being at the scene. He heard Danny say 'A good prang, eh?' John looked around, but ignored him. Asked why he didn't speak to Danny, John replied, 'Because when he made the comment I thought he was an idiot.'

John admitted telling Kathy later that day of his meeting with Danny, as heard on the Heldon tapes played to the court. Mr Pappas wondered why John referred to Danny in such an oblique way. John answered that he wanted to see if Kathy would know who he was talking about. He said there had been a discussion between Kathy and him, some months earlier, that if anything happened around Stuart Flats Danny would be the first to poke his nose in.

On 5 May, the day after Ricky's body had been discovered, John said it was then that he first knew he was a suspect in the investigation. He told the jury that it was the way Ben Cartwright spoke to him and something Ben said that made him aware. He couldn't recall 'precisely' what it was that was said, but he knew by the manner in which Ben conducted the interview. John was talking about the time he gave his first statement.

In relation to the purchase of Kathy's Sigma, John stated that he had lent her $2,000. He gave her some advice about the car, but ultimately it was her decision to buy it. The money John lent to Kathy came from cash he had and withdrawals from different accounts. At least $1,000 of the amount he lent was in cash.

When Barry Steer and Danny Williams called on John on the morning of Monday 29 July, John claimed he wasn't in the lounge room the whole time. He did not recall a conversation between Barry, Danny and Kathy about how much money the men were owed. He said he left the room twice. One time was to check on Alistaire, making sure he hadn't been woken by the intrusion, and the other time was when he retrieved $50 to give to Barry and Danny for their taxi fare. Barry and Danny left just a few moments after John's return. He denied owing Barry or Danny any money, but he knew Kathy had lent them some of her money. He told her he wasn't happy with the situation.

John was vague when asked if he remembered any of the conversation in the house where Barry told John about police suspecting him and that John 'had something to do with' his wife's murder. John did, however, have some memory of being asked to pay money.

Mr Pappas ended his evidence-in-chief by asking, 'Have you ever been convicted of any criminal offence?'

'No, I haven't.'

'Did you ever directly, or indirectly ask Barry Steer or Danny Williams to murder your wife?'

'No, I didn't.'

'Did you ever offer to pay money to either of them to murder your wife?'

'No, I didn't.'

'Did you ever ask Katherine McFie to do that on your behalf?'

'No, I did not.'

'That is, request that your wife be murdered, and at your request that it be done for money?'

'No.'

During John's presentation of his testimony, he spoke quietly. So soft was his voice that there were several occasions when he was asked by Justice Gallop to speak up and repeat his answers.

Mr Thomas was somewhat bemused by John's insistence on speaking with Ricky on Sunday 4 May. He had taken John back to earlier testimony where he admitted that he would allow his mobile to ring out, knowing it was Ricky calling him, and that he would ask work colleagues to tell his wife he wasn't there when she called. Mr Thomas thought John would have considered it a relief not to hear from Ricky on the Sunday.

John stated he tried to get in touch with her because he was worried for her welfare. Mr Thomas reminded John that he had spoken with Sergeant Sly the day before and suggested to the officer that Ricky was just seeking attention and not seriously contemplating suicide. If so, why the concern on Sunday?

'It wasn't so much the suicide, it was what had happened to her overnight. Just whether she'd been drinking,' John explained.

Mr Thomas continued, '… you decided on Sunday morning to be concerned about her?'

'No, this is the first time she hadn't contacted me during the morning,' John explained.

'I put it to you that would have been a relief rather than you rushing off to contact her?'

'It was a relief not to hear from her very first thing in the morning, yes,' John admitted.

The time Danny Williams attended the motor accident, followed by John's conversation with Kathy was another point of bemusement to Mr Thomas. John agreed with Kathy's counsel that he didn't speak with Danny because he didn't want his sergeant to know he knew him. John knew of Danny committing break and enters, but wasn't sure if he knew he dealt in heroin at that time.

Mr Thomas didn't think it made any sense that John would refer to Danny being at the accident in oblique terms and expect Kathy to know who he was referring to months after they had

had a conversation about him. It made perfect sense to John under the circumstances.

'So, it was just pot luck that she happened to know who you were talking about?' Mr Thomas queried.

'I suppose so … I hadn't given it much thought.'

Mr Thomas accused John of having double standards. John had admitted he had spoken with Ricky about a reconciliation and moving to Queensland, after he had left Gollan Street in April. He was also, however, having a similar conversation with Kathy while staying under her roof and allowing her to care for his son. He told Mr Thomas that his 'ultimate desire' was to go to Queensland with Ricky.

'You say that you loved Ricky above all else. Is that what you want this court to believe?' Mr Thomas asked.

'Yes, yes, that's correct.'

'Kathy was simply someone who was there, conveniently, there for your assistance?'

'Yes, that's correct,' John answered.

Kathy sat in the dock, quietly sobbing. John's admission was not what she had wanted to hear, or had believed to be true.

While in the Belconnen Remand Centre during October or November 1997, John had written a note expressing his feelings for Kathy. John had actually given the note to Kathy while they were in the centre. It started with, *Kathy is not guilty of the two charges laid upon her*, and ended with, *Kathy is my life now and always*.

Due to an objection by Mr Pappas, only the first and last sentences were read to the jury. Still, the note did demonstrate John's affections for Kathy.

The question from Mr Thomas was, what had changed by the end of 1997 for John to give his undying love to Kathy, when he had promised it to Ricky?

John said 'it has changed'. He still said he loved Ricky on 7 May when he spoke to police, but had given his love to Kathy in late 1997. Mr Thomas suggested that the change of heart came about because Ricky was no longer available. John agreed, 'in a manner of speaking'.

Mr Thomas didn't accept that that was true. He put it to John he had written the note in an attempt to manipulate Kathy, to keep her on his side, knowing he would need her to help him beat the charges. John denied the allegation. He never manipulated Kathy, but he did admit he never told her about wanting to get back together with Ricky, because he 'didn't want to'.

John didn't see that as manipulation. He accepted he had led Kathy on and 'two-timed' her, but he didn't believe that was the same as manipulation. John also rejected the testimony of the neighbour, who said she had had an affair with him, that John broke the affair off for fear of Ricky finding out and for fear of losing his house.

When asked if the note John wrote in the Remand Centre, stating that 'Kathy is not guilty', was an admission of his guilt, John denied it.

When Terry Golding had his turn to cross-examine John Conway, he started with the Heldon tapes. One of the tapes included recordings from John's mobile message bank. The messages were from Ricky left on Saturday 3 May. These messages were earlier than the one Ben Cartwright had recorded from John's message bank.

On the Saturday morning Ricky had called John six times asking him to call her back. With each call Ricky became more and more exasperated with John's non-response, finally threatening to talk with her solicitor and contact the police. She wanted to talk to Alistaire and reminded John that she never stopped him talking to his son, however early or late it was he called. She expected the same courtesy.

One message Ricky had left at 12.21 that afternoon was, 'This is about the tenth call I've made today to talk to Alistaire. I haven't had one opportunity to talk to him, John. Not one. I know you and Kathy are humping. I don't give a shit about that anymore, but I would like to talk to my son. If you don't get him to ring back I will get onto my solicitor, and I mean it …'

Ricky's next message was simple. She left it at 2.48 in the afternoon and said, 'Will you please ring me back? It's very important. Thank you.'

Ricky had been calling since nine that morning. Just after three, after the last message was left, she had become depressed and asked her neighbour for a piece of rope.

In John's original statement on 5 May, he told the police that Ricky had called several times on the Saturday and asked to speak with Alistaire. John claimed the conversations were amicable, but Ricky didn't speak with Alistaire because her son didn't want to talk with her.

The Heldon tape demonstrated a different scenario.

The reason why Terry Golding asked about these particular recordings was because John had given Ben Cartwright access to his mobile message bank, which portrayed Ricky being depressed and crying, and saying she wanted to die and join her father. John had never alluded to or offered these earlier messages left on his machine. He had wiped them, but not before making a copy on the audio cassette.

John admitted to the court that he recorded the earlier messages while in his office on the Saturday afternoon. He accessed his mobile messages again at around 11 that evening and heard the later messages from Ricky. He didn't erase those.

John, however, said he had forgotten about the earlier messages when giving Ben Cartwright access to his message bank.

Mr Golding put it to John, 'It wouldn't be the case, would it, that on the week following the death of your wife, you were trying to create some sort of an impression about your wife's vulnerability and susceptibility to suicide?'

'No, that's not correct.'

'This wouldn't be a deliberate red herring that you were simply trying to set up to divert the police's attention from what you knew to be the fact?'

'No, that's not correct.'

'That you had deliberately organised, through the accused person Kathy McFie, Mr Williams to kill your wife?'

'That's not correct.'

Mr Golding addressed John Conway's phone records that showed he had called Kathy soon after having accessed the computer in the Woden Police Station. The call lasted 36 seconds, and John said it had gone to Kathy's answering machine and he just left a message. After 20 minutes he phoned back, got the answering machine again, but didn't leave any message that time. Kathy eventually called back and John said he only asked about Alistaire.

It was alleged by Mr Golding that the calls were more sinister than John had suggested. Mr Golding believed that 'five minutes' after John had learned of his wife's welfare from the police computer he called Kathy to arrange with Danny for the murder to take place that night. Again, John replied that that was 'not correct'.

Mr Golding believed John had encouraged Kathy to lie and deceive Ricky for his purposes. John denied he had. Transcripts from the Heldon tapes were read, where Kathy tells John she would do anything for him and wished their situation was different, especially when she has to listen to Ricky talk about making love to John. After hearing the conversations, John admitted it sounded like Kathy was deceiving Ricky for him, but he denied it was intentional.

Under cross-examination, John now recalled the conversation he had with Kathy about why she had made the tape recordings. She apparently said she taped Ricky and John because she 'couldn't understand' why Ricky would tell her one thing and John was saying another. He wouldn't be drawn by Mr Golding to admit he knew of the tapes before April, when it had 'come as a shock' and 'confused him'.

In early March 1997, in one of the Heldon tape conversations Kathy told John that she had taped Ricky, but that the quality wasn't good. 'The tape hadn't turned out' how she wanted. John agreed that was probably the first time he learned of the tapes, but still argued he didn't really know about them till April. That was when he first 'saw' them.

Mr Golding was a little confused. There appeared to be a time when John first learned of the tapes, when he first heard the tapes, and another when he first saw the tapes. John clarified his point by saying that he hadn't paid much attention to the phone call when Kathy mentioned taping Ricky. Yet, as Mr Golding pointed out, Kathy was expressing her love to him, and he was returning his love to her, but he didn't hear her mention anything about tapes.

John stood by his original statement that he didn't know of the tapes till April. John admitted he supplied Kathy with the cassettes, at least the ones marked with the AFP insignia, but never asked why she wanted them. He didn't give them to her all at once, just a few at a time. He also never listened to any music that Kathy may have been recording on them.

Returning to the taped record of interview John undertook on 7 May, Mr Golding asked if he lied about his relationship with Kathy, which was question 22. He did, as he had already stated to his counsel, Mr Pappas. Mr Golding then asked if he lied when he answered question 1121. That question was, 'Have you told any lies during this taped record of interview?'

John admitted he did. John also agreed to Mr Golding's proposition that he had begun his taped record of interview with a lie and ended it with a lie.

Mr Golding took John through other answers he gave in relation to Ricky's family. John had told Ben and Noel that he had developed a close relationship with Ricky's father because his parents lived outside Canberra.

Conversations taped by police revealed John having a less than affectionate feeling towards Ricky's family. When talking with his parents about what would happen should he die suddenly, John stressed that they were not to bring Alistaire up 'the German way', because he didn't like the way the Reiners treated their kids. He also warned his parents that if they lost custody of Alistaire, they'd never see him again. Mr Golding then suggested that John's response to questions about Ricky's family were lies, and his answers were an attempt to have police believe he was close to the Reiners.

As Mr Thomas had done, Terry Golding accused John of deceiving Kathy by telling her he loved her when, in fact, he loved Ricky. He put it to John that he lied to Kathy 'every day'. John could only answer he 'wasn't sure how often', and admitted to loving Ricky. Mr Golding tested John's devotion to Ricky by referring again to the Heldon tapes.

The conversations between Ricky and John were more hostile than cordial, with John at one time accusing Ricky of possibly giving him a sexually transmitted disease and talking to her about divorcing her.

John defended himself by telling Mr Golding, as he had told police in his interview, that he still hoped his marriage was 'salvageable'. Mr Golding could not see any love or devotion being displayed in any of the phone calls between John and Ricky.

Mr Golding also suggested John lied when he told police where he had gone after leaving Ricky in March. He said he had slept in his car and then moved in with an elderly couple he had met who understood his situation. What he admitted to was not telling Ben and Noel that the elderly couple were Kathy's parents, and that between sleeping in his car and moving in with the couple, he spent some time with Kathy at her flat.

John didn't see it as a deliberate lie to police, but just not a 'complete answer'.

Despite John telling Ben and Noel he was in daily contact with Ricky, Mr Golding had already proved that his phone records didn't support such a statement. John argued he did see Ricky, or that Ricky would call him.

John's records, however, showed that he let Ricky's calls go to the message bank, and he would ask work colleagues to tell Ricky he wasn't available. John had also been absent from the house after 26 April to when he picked Alistaire up on 2 May.

John insisted that he did speak with Ricky on the telephone on a daily basis. Mr Golding asked if he ever told Kathy about the communications. John said he didn't.

Mr Golding again accused John of 'deceiving Kathy' on a daily basis. John agreed he had deceived Kathy, but wasn't sure how often he told her the lies.

It was Mr Golding's turn to examine the note John had written in the Remand Centre. He read another line from the note, saying, '*I was too stupid or blinded by other factors to see this love,*' followed by another, '*I have realised what my feelings are for her and what her feelings are for me. I realise now that I am now and have been, for more than a year, in love with Kathy.*'

John admitted he hadn't appreciated Kathy's love until after their arrest. Despite hearing the Heldon tapes with Kathy professing her love and telling John she'd do anything for him, John said he 'hadn't taken a great deal of notice' of what she was saying. John had said that while he admitted deceiving Kathy, he still loved her. He clarified the point again for Mr Golding explaining he just didn't realise 'how much' he loved her.

Throughout the cross-examination, Mr Golding would refer to answers John gave in his 7 May interview with police, and the answers he gave the jury under Mr Pappas' examination. There were a lot of inconsistencies. John told the jury he hadn't seen any confrontation between Ricky and Alistaire before separating the two in the hallway on 2 April. He told police he had.

John admitted his answer in court was a lie.

John had said he didn't know Ricky had dropped the complaint to Internal Investigations till well after the Family Court Hearing when asked by Mr Pappas. In his interview with police, John admitted to knowing at the commencement of the Family Court proceedings that Ricky had dropped the complaint.

John couldn't tell Mr Golding when he precisely knew. It was something he couldn't explain.

When Ben Cartwright enquired about the coffee incident, John gave his version of events against those recorded in Ricky's diary. He asked Ben, 'Do we have to go into this?'

John admitted to Mr Golding that he had asked that because he was reluctant to discuss with police his suspicions about Ricky's drug use. Yet, as heard by the court during the Crown's case, he had told six people, including two non-police officers about finding the foils on the kitchen window. Mr Golding believed it was another 'red herring', and that he was setting up his wife as a drug addict.

John denied it, but admitted he never knew Ricky to use heroin. Mr Golding then accused John of trying to 'create a false trail to deflect the police inquiry from the murder'. John denied it.

Mr Golding also picked up on John's reasons as to why he had collected the foils. In his testimony John said he wanted to use them in the Family Court, believing them to contain a narcotic. However, when explaining to Ben Cartwright on 7 May why he had taken the foils, he told Ben he didn't know what the white powder residue and foils could be, but that he was just curious about them.

John admitted he had lied to police. The reasons he gave in court were true. Mr Golding put it to him that he lied to police about that, because he was intending to give the police the impression of being naive in relation to illicit drugs. John denied it.

During John's record of interview, there were up to 1,200 questions and answers. Mr Golding suggested to John that there were a number of lies he told police during that interview. John agreed there 'were a few'.

Mr Golding had taken him through most of his answers to number 373, and asked if he needed to continue to expose more of John's 'falsities'. John conceded again.

The point Mr Golding made to the jury was that, although John admitted to lying to police about Kathy, he also lied about other things. John argued that any false answers he gave weren't intentional.

Mr Golding reminded John about the conversations he had with Kathy, where she stated she would do anything for him, 'anything to make him happy', and that John knew she was vulnerable. He then suggested that John had recruited Kathy to serve his 'cowardly interests'. Those interests being 'the assassination of his wife'. John answered that it wasn't correct.

'And you deliberately recruited her to recruit one other extremely vulnerable resident of Stuart Flats?' Mr Golding continued.

'That is not correct.'

'And at this stage you have taken the conscious decision to simply abandon her to her own fate?'

'That's not correct,' John repeated.

Justice Gallop interrupted proceedings to clarify a point. He addressed John and asked that if the testimony of Barry and Danny were to be accepted, '… do you suggest that she [Kathy] might have been acting on her own account, independently of you?'

'I'm not aware of anything happening as far as that's concerned,' John replied.

'But if it did happen …' Justice Gallop continued, '… it would have to be independently of you, is that what you say, you had nothing to do with it?'

'I had nothing to do with it.'

Terry Golding referred back to the police phone tap that covered the conversation John had with Kathy about seeing Danny Williams at the car accident. He was curious, as Mr Thomas had been, that Kathy would know who John was referring to. Equally, he was curious how John knew Kathy had understood who he was subtly referring to without her mentioning his name.

Mr Golding asked, 'Well, was it the words, "Mm, did you speak to him?" did that give you the clue that you were referring to Danny Williams?'

'I don't recall.'

'Certainly not, "Yeah, fair enough," seems to be pretty opaque, doesn't it, in the sense that there's no suggestion there of Danny Williams being the person to whom you were referring?'

'I don't recall what gave me the impression that she understood who I was talking about,' was John's answer.

At the time of the conversation, John was involved in assisting the Criminal Investigations Branch in a covert operation and the installation of listening devices. He had made mention to Kathy about a file he left at home and whether she had read it. She had. The file was from the investigation he was involved in and contained information on listening devices.

Mr Golding believed that John was warning Kathy about there being listening devices in their home, as he knew he was a suspect in the murder. John admitted to knowing he was a suspect, but it 'never entered his head' that there were listening devices in his home or car.

Giving evidence about the night he and Kathy were arrested, John told Mr Golding that he let Barry and Danny in, but did not think it was the 'right place' to do anything when Barry said he wanted to skip town because the cops knew he was involved in 'this murder'.

'What, you were going to ring the police after he'd left and say, "Better get on to this bloke, he's about to skip the town"?' Mr Golding enquired.

'No, we'd set up a phone call for him later. I was going to contact the police later that morning and tell them what had happened.'

John claimed the conversation went quickly, and he wasn't sure he heard Danny asking for 'a couple of grand', despite agreeing to pay them the money later in the week. He just knew that Barry was 'somehow involved in the murder' and the conversation 'went on from there'.

John admitted that he had gathered Barry was talking about Ricky's murder early in their conversation, though her name had not been mentioned.

'You must have been outraged?' Mr Golding suggested.

'I wasn't real happy with the idea,' John agreed.

Mr Golding continued his cross-examination and after a while decided to review what he had learned. He asked John, 'So, just so that I understand you and so the jury understands you, these two men, whom you barely knew, one of whom you know was a criminal and the other you didn't like, at four o'clock in the morning arrived at your house, awoke you and gratuitously offered you, as a policeman, information that they had murdered somebody?'

'That's correct.'

John said he didn't make any protest or ask any questions because they were giving him information that he would take to police. He was 'setting them up'. He couldn't, however, explain why or when he realised they were talking about Ricky, or why they came to visit him in the first place.

When Mr Golding asked what John was thinking and feeling when Barry referred to Ricky by name, John couldn't remember. He couldn't tell Mr Golding if he felt shock, anger or was 'flushed' with rage.

Just after Barry mentioned Ricky on the tape, he asked John when they'd collect their money, and John answered, 'Kathy's got your phone number, hasn't she?'

John argued his response was all part of his plan to set up Barry and Danny. He also denied being in the room at the time Kathy assisted Barry and Danny with coming to an agreed value of how much money was owed to them.

On the tape Kathy suggested the money owing was $10,800. John couldn't explain why it appeared to be an 'extraordinary coincidence' that Kathy would come to the exact amount Barry and Danny had testified was owing.

John defended himself by stating that he was away from the room when Kathy and the two men gave the most damning of evidence. John also drew a blank when Mr Golding pointed to Barry's parting remarks about getting rid of the evidence, throwing the key away, and 'shit like that'.

It was obvious from the recording that John was seeing Barry and Danny out the door. He told the court that he gave them the $50 note to 'get them out of the house quietly'. John didn't think it was an extraordinary thing to have done, despite admitting he didn't like Barry and knew Danny to be a criminal. Not to mention they had both just told him they killed his wife.

John denied he had conspired with Kathy to murder his wife. He denied getting Kathy to buy heroin and help recruit Danny Williams to murder his wife, or to seek out other people to commit the murder. He denied feeding heroin to Ricky in a cup of coffee, for the purposes of deceiving the police, so that traces of heroin would be discovered during an autopsy and lead them to think Ricky had had a prior history of using the drug.

John denied the charges against him.

Ben Cartwright sat in the court during John's testimony. He observed that John displayed no emotion, no feelings and no empathy. John gave his responses like 'a brick wall answering questions'.

Ben added, 'He came across as the cold fish that he was.'

CHAPTER EIGHTEEN

Kathy Marie McFie

On 24 June 1998, just after John Conway had finished his three and a half days in the witness box, Kathy McFie was invited to the stand by her counsel, Mr Thomas.

Kathy, as John had done, denied any knowledge of, or having anything to with, the murder of Ricky Conway. She admitted to knowing Barry Steer and Danny Williams and lending them money on occasion, the largest amount she lent being $30. She also admitted that John had paid the substantial amount on her new car, the Sigma purchased in October 1996, but she added that she paid him back from money she received out of a compensation claim. Her story was verified by her bank accounts.

In August 1996, John and Kathy had begun a sexual relationship. She had heard their relationship described in court as an 'affair' and resented that stigma.

Kathy understood from John that he had separated from Ricky, and had moved out of the Gollan Street house and was living elsewhere. A couple of weeks after their relationship started, Ricky phoned Kathy and told her that John was back, living with her and Alistaire. Kathy questioned John about this, and he told her he had moved back for the sake of his son.

Ricky and Kathy continued their phone relationship, eventually becoming friends, and Ricky invited Kathy to her house on 31 December.

During their developing friendship, Ricky would tell Kathy intimate and personal details of her relationship with John. Kathy, again, was told by John that he was sleeping on the lounge, but Ricky was stating otherwise. When Kathy confronted John with what Ricky had told her, John denied it. Kathy never told Ricky about her relationship with John, because John had asked her not to.

Kathy told the court that when she started visiting Gollan Street she witnessed some incidents she found 'disturbing'. She gave as an example times when there were 'verbal altercations' between Ricky and John in front of Alistaire, which she said were not good for their son to have witnessed. John and Ricky apparently agreed, but their behaviour didn't change.

With respect to the Heldon tapes, Kathy explained that she had recorded Ricky and John because of the confusing explanations John gave about Ricky claiming that they were sleeping together. John would give Kathy an explanation, and then when she confronted him again, he would argue she didn't understand him, or tell her 'I didn't say that like that.'

This left Kathy unsure as to what the truth was, so she decided to tape the conversations with both parties to be sure of what they were saying. She also thought she could play them back to John if he ever tried denying what he had said.

Kathy was asked if she had ever played the tapes for John, and she replied that she had, but it was some time after she had began the recordings. Kathy stated she didn't get much of a reaction from John when he heard the tapes.

As heard during John's examination, the first of the Heldon tapes revealed Kathy talking about her love for John, and giving him her commitment that she would do anything for him. Kathy admitted she did love John, that she was committed to him, but not enough to murder his wife.

Contrary to John's evidence, Kathy told the court that she made him aware of the tapes in March. She had told him about their existence, and she attempted to play him one of the conversations. John appeared not to be interested so she switched off the machine.

While John was living at Kathy's parents' place in April, they would sit around the dining table with maps and other materials planning their move to Queensland. Kathy's whole family knew, as did her friends. It was a big move for Kathy as she was very close to her parents and her son who all lived in Canberra.

Kathy wasn't aware John wanted to reconcile with Ricky. She wasn't aware that John was having a full relationship with his wife and her at the same time. When Kathy heard those admissions in court, she said she felt 'not very good'.

Kathy conceded that John had lied to her.

Kathy denied having ever bought heroin from either Robert, Danny's brother, Danny or even Barry. She couldn't offer any reasons why they would say she had, and didn't know of an occasion which may have been confused with them thinking she had purchased heroin. Kathy also denied taking any trip with Danny to buy the narcotic from a dealer.

Mr Thomas questioned Kathy about her phone call to the Care and Protection Services, as heard on the Heldon tapes.

Kathy told the court that there had been an incident where there was an altercation between Ricky and Alistaire at the Belconnen Mall. Kathy was with them at the time. Police apparently attended. Two days later a person from the Care and Protection Services turned up at Gollan Street and made enquiries about the incident. Ricky gave her account and Kathy, who was at the house at the time, 'backed it up'. Ricky thanked Kathy for not saying 'what happened'.

A week later, or thereabouts, Kathy witnessed another incident between Ricky and her son and she decided she couldn't keep quiet any longer, so she made the call. She asked not to be identified to Ricky because she wanted to keep contact with Ricky, to help both her and Alistaire.

Kathy was taken through the transcripts of the listening devices recordings, particularly the conversations between her and Barry.

Kathy admitted that Barry wanted to borrow some money because he was having his son stay with him, and that she had said she'd speak with John. She never asked John for the money because she knew he didn't like her to lend money to Barry.

Kathy stated she couldn't remember any other conversations with Barry Steer to do with money. She didn't know what Barry meant when he said, 'I said to Danny is [*sic*] I said to you to leave it go until you can save up a lot, 'cause it's no good to us getting dribs and drabs, we've got bills we want to sort out, shit like that.'

Kathy didn't understand why he was mentioning money, or why he would tell her what he told Danny Williams. She also didn't know why he said later that he told Danny he hadn't seen her in a couple of months.

Kathy explained she used the public phone box because she didn't want John to know she was calling Barry. She had agreed to lend him some money and knew that John wouldn't have been pleased if he found out. She would slip out of the house when she could to call Barry.

The meeting at the service station was arranged for Kathy to lend Barry $20. She wasn't expecting Danny, and was very apprehensive giving money to Barry in front of Danny. She said she had problems getting Danny to repay her. She slipped Barry the $20 when she offered him a cigarette. Kathy explained that the 20 minutes or so she was in the car was spent talking about Barry's son, Alistaire and 'just general things'.

Mr Thomas completed his examination by asking if Kathy had ever had a criminal record, had ever come to the adverse notice of police, or had any minor traffic infringements. Kathy denied the first two, but agreed she did have a minor traffic infringement.

Under cross-examination by Mr Pappas, Kathy said that she had tried to help Danny quit his drug habit, as she knew it was hurting his mother. She didn't know he was taking heroin, only that he seemed addicted to marijuana.

After Danny's mother left the complex, Kathy admitted to only visiting Danny in his flat 'twice in the last two, three years'. The reasons Danny gave her for borrowing money was to buy cigarettes and groceries. She'd have never lent Danny money to buy drugs as she was trying to stop him, for his mother's sake. She denied Danny had ever said to her he needed the money because he was 'hanging out for a hit'. The only reason Kathy gave for lending Barry money was because he had come to her door once and asked.

Mr Pappas pressed Kathy on her motives for keeping in contact with Ricky after John had moved back into the house. Kathy said that it was Ricky who continued to call her and she didn't encourage it. Initially Kathy wasn't happy with Ricky calling her, but they soon developed a friendship.

Kathy stated she kept her contact with Ricky because of her concerns for Alistaire, and because she wanted to help Ricky with her drinking. Mr Pappas suggested that the reason for the contact, particularly as the Heldon tapes showed, was because Kathy wanted to gather material to convince John to leave home and be with her.

Kathy admitted she did want John to leave Ricky, but denied ever encouraging him. She didn't have to. John had told her that was what he was planning to do.

Mr Pappas referred to Kathy's devotion and love for John, and how hurt she must have been listening to his wife talk about their sex life. Kathy admitted it was distressing hearing Ricky talk about having had sex with John, but John denied it and she believed him.

Kathy stated she didn't know how she felt when John left Ricky in March, but she was relieved and, at the same time, still concerned for Alistaire. About a week after John had moved out, however, Ricky told Kathy she had had sex twice with John one night. Ricky also told Kathy she and John were talking about reconciliation, and that she would sign a contract to give up drinking to have John back. Kathy argued that Ricky would change her mind 'one day to the next', and that Ricky had also told her that she hated John and never wanted to see him again.

Kathy agreed with Mr Pappas that the reason why John returned to Gollan Street during March was because of Alistaire. Mr Pappas suggested it must have been a relief for Kathy that John had taken Alistaire away on 2 April. It meant John had no reason to return to the house. Kathy accepted the proposition, and said she still worried about Ricky and her drinking, but she was glad she wouldn't have to put up with the phone calls.

Ricky told Kathy after 2 April that she would fight for her son. Ricky was determined, and would do whatever it took to get him back. Kathy denied being concerned that, if John lost the Family Court battle and Alistaire went back, he would return to his wife and Kathy's plans to have John would 'come unstuck'.

As history showed, John's last contact with Ricky was on 25 April. He took Alistaire back on the 23 April and stayed the night, then returned the next day at Ricky's request, as he did again on 25 April.

When John went to see Ricky on 25 April, Kathy said she wasn't happy. She didn't know why he had to go there and then. She explained they were both in bed when Ricky called and John left half an hour later. He stayed the whole day and spent the night, returning to Kathy on the morning of 26 April. Kathy agreed she was feeling hurt and confused, but denied she saw her relationship with John 'going down the drain'.

Mr Pappas asked if Kathy wanted to drive a wedge between Alistaire and his mother, so she could get him out of the house and have both John and his son. Kathy denied the allegation. She believed Alistaire was better off with his mother, if only she would stop drinking. She also said she wasn't sure she could cope with bringing up a seven-year-old, but if she had to she would. It wouldn't be something she'd do by choice.

Kathy had several conversations with Alistaire over the phone, as heard on the Heldon tapes. In one conversation Kathy is telling Alistaire that he might have his 'own pool' and he 'won't have to worry about Mummy', asking him 'How does that sound?'.

The pool reference, according to Kathy, was made because Alistaire was upset about not being able to use the pool at Gollan Street. Ricky would not allow him the use of the pool if he were being naughty. Kathy, however, felt Ricky used the pool as a 'bargaining tool' and she didn't agree with Ricky's methods. She was telling the young boy that 'one day' he might have his own pool. She was not, as Mr Pappas put it to her, suggesting to Alistaire that he live with her and John. She was simply trying to calm a distraught boy.

The second conversation revolved around Alistaire's birthday. Ricky had apparently asked Kathy not to attend. Kathy thought it was because she got on better with Alistaire than Ricky, and Ricky didn't want to be embarrassed in front of the other mothers. Kathy tells Alistaire that Ricky doesn't want her at his birthday, saying 'Mummy's being a bit mean' and 'that's not very nice, is it'. Asked if Alistaire was upset when she made these comments, Kathy couldn't remember.

Mr Pappas asked Kathy about the police recording of a conversation she had in Barry's flat. Kathy is heard mentioning $4,000, the amount Barry claimed to be owed. The conversation isn't clear and there are a lot of words that are inaudible.

Kathy could not recall why she referred to that amount of money. She did know that John's Family Court costs were over $4,000, so she thought she might have been telling Barry about that. Barry then tells Kathy that he said to Danny, 'I'm frustrated too, Danny … you already had your pay, Danny.'

Kathy could not understand what Barry was talking about. She agreed with Mr Pappas that she didn't ask Barry at the time, but changed the subject and began talking about a bill she owed.

'That bill I got today … I've got nothing,' is what Kathy said next in the conversation.

Mr Pappas asked if she was in fact responding to Barry, and not changing the subject as she had said. Kathy denied it. She denied it was something she said, that she'd 'plucked out of the air'. She didn't know why she said it, but she agreed she knew Barry was talking about money.

Mr Pappas was insistent that Kathy and Barry were discussing the money she owed him and Danny for killing John's wife. Kathy denied it.

Justice Gallop then interrupted proceedings. He addressed Kathy and began explaining how advocacy works, telling her that it is not Mr Pappas asking her the questions, but rather John Conway through Mr Pappas. Like her counsel and the Crown, Mr Pappas didn't have a personal interest in the case, but was being directed by his client.

Kathy said she understood.

Justice Gallop was satisfied and handed the questioning back to Mr Pappas.

Kathy was taken to another conversation recorded between her and Barry on 21 July, the day the police held the press conference and the media descended on the Gollan Street address.

Kathy was in Barry's flat again and he told her why he thought the police pulled over and questioned her sister and searched her car. Barry explained Danny was dealing from her car when they were both parked in a car park one day.

Barry referred to it by saying, 'You know, and I'm sitting in the [inaudible] spot and someone comes over and says, "hello", you know, because I know them. I don't give a shit. If they want to use, that's their problem. I don't give a shit.'

Mr Pappas asked Kathy to explain what the conversation referred to. She told him that Barry and Danny are in a car park and they've met someone they know, but that Barry had a problem with them. She wasn't sure what else Mr Pappas wanted from her.

Mr Pappas asked her directly, 'What do you think the reference to "if they want to use" is all about? Do you think that's someone using the car park, do you?'

'I don't know,' Kathy replied.

'You don't think it's got anything to do with using heroin?'

'Yes, that could be it,' Kathy conceded, although she denied it had anything to with Danny specifically selling heroin.

Mr Pappas reminded Kathy that she didn't ask any questions of Barry during the whole of the conversation, yet in court, she appeared to be very puzzled by what Barry was saying. Kathy told the court she didn't understand the conversation and she knew nothing about it.

On the next page of the transcript she tells Barry about 'being in the wrong place.'

Barry then says, 'On show at the wrong place'.

Kathy agrees with him and Barry adds, '… everyone around them goes down with them'.

Kathy couldn't explain to Mr Pappas why she said what she said. She had 'no idea'.

The continuation of that conversation was when Barry told Kathy that he and Danny would wait for a large amount to be paid, rather then in 'dribs and drabs'. Kathy denied knowing the meaning of that phrase. Barry then told her that it would take her about ten weeks to save some money, and Kathy replied that she only had three dollars.

Mr Pappas put it to Kathy that that was an agreement between her and Barry to save some money over ten weeks to then give to the men. Kathy didn't agree that the conversation meant that, because she didn't owe them any money. Even so, Kathy couldn't explain what the conversation was about or what it meant.

Mr Pappas asked Kathy if she was afraid to answer the question 'frankly and honestly', because if she did, she would be convicted of murder. Kathy didn't understand. Mr Pappas asked the question again. Kathy didn't agree. She didn't know how better to answer the question, because she didn't know what the conversation meant. All she knew was that it was about money.

Justice Gallop interrupted again. Hearing her answer to Mr Pappas's question, Justice Gallop didn't think Kathy really understood what was happening to her. He felt he needed to explain again why Mr Pappas was putting the questions and allegations to her. He said to her, 'Mr Pappas, counsel for John Conway, is cross-examining you with a view to establishing in the mind of the jury that you are responsible for this murder alone and not him, not Conway.'

Kathy looked back at the judge and replied, 'I've just gathered that.'

Justice Gallop then explained that should the jury agree with the cross-examination, it could mean she would be found guilty and John Conway could be acquitted. He emphasised his point by adding that that was what Mr Pappas was 'aiming at'.

Kathy was stunned. 'I don't understand that.' With the realisation, she broke down in tears as her emotions engulfed her.

Mr Thomas then asked for an adjournment to speak with his client. He needed to talk with Kathy further about what Justice Gallop had told her.

After the adjournment, Kathy was unable to continue with her testimony. Court was adjourned till the next day.

With the court resumed, Kathy was asked to explain how it was that Barry and Danny, in their statements to police, could tell them that she had withdrawn $200 from the bank on 18 June, when she had stated she only paid Barry $20 at the service station meeting.

According to police records, the detectives on Operation Aquatic didn't access Kathy's accounts till after 28 July, and after Barry and Danny said they had received $200 from Kathy.

Kathy had already said in court she didn't tell either of them how much she had withdrawn, or even told Danny she was lending Barry money. She slipped the money to Barry with the cigarettes, concealing the loan so Danny wouldn't ask for any money. So, how did they know how much she had unless, as Mr Pappas proposed, she had paid them $200?

Kathy said she told them she'd been to the bank, because she had problems remembering her PIN. She made a joke of it. She argued that she couldn't have had $200 on her anyway, because she had withdrawn the money before going shopping with Alistaire.

Kathy hadn't answered the question.

Mr Pappas pressed the issue again. In the end, Kathy said she might have told them. She couldn't remember. Mr Pappas then asked if Danny had heard she was carrying money did he ask her for some that night?

Kathy said he didn't.

Mr Pappas went back to the conversation where she and Barry were discussing money, and she said she didn't have any, and then she discussed a bill John had to pay. The bill was a phone bill belonging to Ricky and amounted to over $500. Kathy and Barry seemed to argue over whether the bill had to be paid or not, as Ricky was dead. Kathy explained to Barry the bill had to be paid.

Barry then told Kathy, 'Dig her up and ask her for it.' He laughed and added, 'That's what I say, dig her up and ask her for it.'

'That was a dreadful thing to say about your dead friend, wasn't it?' Mr Pappas suggested.

'Yes.'

'And did you say to Barry, "My goodness, Barry, don't speak ill of the dead in that way"?'

'No, I didn't say anything like that. I didn't respond in any way to it,' Kathy admitted.

Mr Pappas asked if Kathy had shown her annoyance at Barry, made some sort of a facial expression that she didn't appreciate the comment. Kathy said she might have, but she couldn't remember. She did remember she 'didn't like it'. Kathy also said she didn't enter into any discussion about what Barry had said, because Alistaire was 'close by'. She didn't want to talk about it anymore. She left Barry giving him the cheerio, 'All right, love. Catch ya.'

Despite Mr Pappas suggesting that Kathy had left on amicable terms with the man who had denigrated her friend, Kathy defended herself by saying, 'I say that to everybody.'

When asked if, on 28 July, it had taken her by surprise to find Barry and Danny admitting to Ricky's murder and implicating John and her, Kathy agreed. Mr Pappas, however, suggested it was because the two men were saying it in front of John, and it was for that reason that Kathy was surprised.

Kathy said it had taken her a while to realise what they were saying, and she couldn't remember saying much that night. She then corrected herself and said she 'probably did say more'.

Kathy could recall the conversation she had with Barry and Danny that night. She couldn't, however, remember why she was adding up amounts of money. She didn't know what the references were to $4,200 and $10,800.

Kathy admitted she couldn't remember most of her day in court, or the former week, let alone something that happened a year ago.

Mr Pappas put to Kathy that John was absent from the room when she had her conversation about the money. John had stated he left the room twice while Barry and Danny were there. Kathy only remembered John leaving the lounge room once, but she still couldn't even be sure of that.

Kathy denied she had conspired with Danny, knowing he was vulnerable, to kill Ricky so she could have John and Alistaire. Mr Pappas suggested she wanted to eliminate any temptation John would have to return to the matrimonial home to be with his son.

Kathy became visibly upset during the questioning and Justice Gallop even offered her time to collect herself. She declined and carried on.

Mr Pappas ended his cross-examination by asking Kathy to give the court a reason why Barry, Danny, Danny's brother and Robert would have lied in their evidence against her. Kathy couldn't say. She said she didn't understand why they, her accusers, had said what they said.

Before Terry Golding could ask his first question, Justice Gallop wanted to be sure Kathy was able to continue. Jack Pappas' cross-examination had left her flustered. She assured Justice Gallop that she didn't require a break. She was 'fine' to continue.

Mr Golding revisited a lot of the areas John's counsel had covered. He even apologised to Kathy for doing so, knowing how distressed and upset she had been. He explained, however, that he had to re-examine the same areas because John had deceived her 'something terribly' in the early part of 1997.

Kathy agreed. If she thought his comment would mean she would get an easier time, she was soon sorely disappointed.

During her initial testimony and her cross-examination. Kathy had told the court she knew very little about John's financial position. Mr Pappas had accused Kathy of wanting John's money, which she denied.

Mr Golding presented a telephone intercept where John was asking Kathy to give him the number of a Commonwealth Bank account. Kathy was heard going through a 'green folder' extracting a number of different bank and credit union accounts in her search. It appeared to Mr Golding, from the conversation, that at that time Kathy was well aware of John's financial situation.

Kathy denied it. She argued she only knew John had 'something like seven accounts' from evidence presented in court. She said she 'didn't take much notice' when she went through the file. It was none of her business. She was just 'trying to find something for him'.

Kathy told the court she was prepared to live with John 'in a tent' if it meant being with him in Queensland. Her wanting John had nothing to do with his money, the house, or even Alistaire. She just wanted to be with him.

Mr Golding asked Kathy if she remembered what John had bought Ricky for her birthday. Kathy did. It was a bottle of liqueur. Cointreau. On another occasion, Kathy took over a bottle of sparkling wine.

Kathy didn't think anything of John's gift at the time. She also argued that if she hadn't taken the wine, Ricky would have bought herself a cask.

Mr Golding thought Kathy was concerned about Ricky's drinking. She was, but she admitted she would on occasion 'sit and have a drink with her'. She did her 'best to discourage' Ricky's drinking, because she knew the difficulties that arose between Ricky and her son when she drank.

Mr Golding saw Kathy's actions as a deliberate attempt to 'sabotage any relationship that Ricky Conway had with her son'. Kathy denied it. She argued that she took wine over because it was better that Ricky drank a 'small amount' rather than a cask.

Kathy was asked if she remembered the particular time Mr Golding was referring to.

Kathy answered that it had 'happened many times'. She then corrected herself and said it only happened 'twice'.

Kathy's subterfuge in lending Barry $20 without John knowing was 'a ridiculously complicated arrangement' according to Mr Golding. Kathy said it wasn't. She had 'done that many times before with other people over different things'.

'For the sake of $20 you drove halfway across Canberra to meet covertly with a murderer?' Mr Golding enquired.

'I drove from Evatt to Dickson which takes less than ten minutes. I wasn't prepared to go all the way to Griffith to give him some money,' Kathy explained.

When asked why Barry was making sure Kathy had called him from a public telephone, Kathy said that Barry knew John didn't like her lending money, and that he would have 'gone crook' on her if he knew.

Kathy made two calls, one at midnight, and another a couple of days later at 9.30 pm. She had told John she was going out to get cigarettes. Barry asked her on the second occasion about the public phone, apologising that he hadn't checked with her the first time she called.

Mr Golding was more than bemused by Kathy's explanations.

'These arrangements, these arrangements are for purposes of you loaning him $20?'

'Yes.'

'This is not a deal that's going to bring down the Indonesian economy we're talking about here?'

'No.' Kathy added, 'When you're on a limited income $20 is a lot of money.'

Kathy admitted that she had told Barry, as caught by the telephone intercept, that she had to 'borrow the money'. She told the court she had said that because she didn't want Barry knowing she'd been to the bank, because she didn't want it getting back to Danny.

Mr Golding reminded Kathy she had, less than two hours earlier, told the court she had told Barry she'd been to the bank. Kathy agreed she did tell both of them when she met them in their car at the service station. She stayed with them for 20 minutes, and told them she'd been shopping, which is why Danny didn't ask for any money. She handed the money over to Barry surreptitiously at the end of their meeting.

Mr Golding couldn't believe that Danny, knowing there was no money to borrow, would go for a drive with Barry and sit in a service station with him and Kathy just talking for 20 minutes. Plus, Danny wouldn't have known why they were there because he wouldn't have witnessed the transaction between Kathy and Barry as she described. Danny would have been wasting his time.

As Mr Golding tried to go back over what Kathy had told him, her telling Barry she 'borrowed', and then that she'd been to the bank, he stopped himself. He paused and admitted he was 'confused'.

Kathy agreed, she was confused too. She couldn't explain why Danny was there or what he was thinking. She hadn't been expecting him.

Phone records were produced and shown to Kathy. The records revealed a phone call from Gollan Street to Barry Steer's phone at seven in the morning on 18 June, the date she met Barry and Danny at the service station.

At 8.30 on the same morning, police taped John and Kathy having a conversation. John had called from work. Kathy told John that she 'tried that number' but that there was no answer. John commented, 'Not from home?'

Kathy responded with, 'Yeah, I wasn't gonna speak, I just wanted to see if there was an answer … but it rang out.'

Kathy couldn't remember the conversation. She denied John's comment was made telling her not to use the home phone and to use a public phone. She didn't know what he meant.

Kathy accepted that the phone record showed a call to Barry's. She accepted the police transcript as being correct. But she still couldn't remember the conversation. She also couldn't say why she would call someone if she weren't prepared to talk to them.

In another telephone conversation later in the day, Kathy told John about forgetting her PIN and having to withdraw the cash over the counter. She said she had the number written down back at her flat. John responded, 'Yeah, well, I wouldn't suggest you go back there … unless it is necessary … not for a while.'

While John was telling Kathy not to go back to Stuart Flats, Kathy could only say 'mm'. Because of her lack of response, Kathy thought she 'probably didn't register' what John was talking about.

Mr Golding felt John was warning Kathy to stay away from the area where the two men were who had murdered his wife. Kathy denied that was the case. She said she had 'no problem' going to her flat when she wanted.

Mr Golding reminded Kathy she had acknowledged John's comment with 'mm', and the fact he said not to return 'unless it is necessary' gave his proposition some basis.

Kathy still wouldn't accept what was being put to her and explained she was more than likely not listening.

On 17 June, the day before Kathy paid Barry the money, Barry and Danny gave testimony that they had driven around Gollan Street and left a message on one of the cars belonging to Kathy and John.

Kathy had told the court earlier she found a note under the door of her flat when she returned to collect the mail on 16 June.

Either way, it was the message that led Kathy to call Barry on 18 June. Mr Golding decided to find out whose version was true.

To find out, Mr Golding had Kathy look at the transcript of the telephone conversation she had with Barry at 9.30 in the evening on 18 June. Kathy told Barry, 'Um, with that message last night, I presume … I had to presume it was yours.'

Mr Golding asked Kathy what 'last night' meant and she admitted it was the day before, 17 June. Kathy said she made a mistake when talking with Barry. She was referring to 16 June. Two days earlier.

Barry, however, didn't pick up on the mistake either and just said, 'Uh hum, uh hum, that wasn't a problem …'

Kathy could only agree with Mr Golding that Barry must have understood her, that she was referring to the message she found under her door on 16 June.

Kathy apologised if she 'got a word wrong' but she was just referring to a message Barry had left. She couldn't understand its importance. She strongly denied ever getting a message left on her or John's car. 'No, I don't agree with that!'

Kathy also had difficulties understanding that there was anything wrong with the original statement she had given to police. It was suggested to her by Mr Golding that she had deliberately not told Constable Susan Ball that she was in a sexual relationship with John, because it could be seen as a motive for them to have killed Ricky.

Kathy still didn't understand. In fact, she didn't know what business it was of the police to enquire about her personal details. She was never asked about her relationship, and she told the truth when she said she and John were friends. If she were asked about the relationship, she still wouldn't have given any details.

Mr Golding wondered if Kathy understood Mr Pappas when he put it to her that she had killed Ricky to have John?

Kathy said she was 'blown away' when she heard that, but she didn't agree. She 'wouldn't do anything to hurt anyone', no matter what her grievances. She would not and did not kill Ricky Conway. She also denied ever having enlisted Danny Williams to 'do her dirty work', as Mr Golding phrased it.

Like Mr Pappas before him Terry Golding took Kathy through the Heldon tapes. There was something in nearly every conversation that showed John and Kathy's contempt for Ricky, Kathy deceiving Ricky, and Kathy manipulating Alistaire.

The tapes were an edited version of what had been recorded, and Kathy argued there were other conversations that showed her 'nicer' side. She had done a lot more for Ricky than what the police had produced in the way of surveillance material and the Heldon tapes.

Mr Golding was happy to concede that might be true. He asked Kathy that if there was material that demonstrated that her relationship with Ricky was caring and positive, why hadn't her counsel produced it?

The Heldon tapes were tendered as an exhibit and accepted by the court, yet there were no other recorded conversations from the tapes submitted by the defence to counter the prosecution's version.

Kathy just said there was, though there was no answer to Mr Golding's statement. He continued going through the transcripts of the tapes, almost line by line.

Kathy denied recruiting Danny Williams to kill Ricky Conway. She denied buying heroin and giving it to John for him to put into Ricky's drink and/or foodstuffs. She denied receiving from John $3,000 to pay Danny for the contract. She denied phoning Ricky's house on the night of 3 May while Barry Steer and Danny were waiting in the back yard of 35 Gollan Street.

She denied all the charges put to her.

Just before Kathy could return to her seat, Mr Thomas wanted to clarify some of her testimony. He got Kathy to elaborate on some points that he felt Mr Pappas and Mr Golding had not allowed her to explain.

One of the arguments Kathy gave about not having much of a memory for events and conversations was because of her illness. Mr Thomas asked her to address the jury and to explain what she meant. Kathy suffered from chronic fatigue syndrome, and two of the symptoms of the condition are a lack of concentration and memory loss. This was her excuse for not remembering a lot of the surveillance and other material Mr Pappas and Mr Golding had put to her, and why she said she probably wasn't listening when some of the people were talking to her in those tapes.

During Kathy's cross-examination there were times when the proceedings were adjourned for her counsel to submit objections to Justice Gallop. The jury were excused and Kathy was told to take her seat next to the co-accused, John Conway.

Before John's testimony, Kathy and John sat side by side with an officer next to them. After hearing John's evidence, and with what Kathy had endured, the seating arrangements changed.

Kathy and John still sat in the dock together; however, the guard was now between them. Their image of solidarity was broken.

CHAPTER NINETEEN

Puppets, medleys and mosaics

On 29 June 1998, the ACT Supreme Court had heard all the evidence, both from the prosecution and from the defence, in the trial of John Conway and Kathy McFie. It was now time for each counsel to address the jury with final remarks, highlighting what evidence proved their case.

Mr Richard Thomas referred to Romeo and Juliet, the story of two lovers prepared to die for each other, saying that Kathy may have 'loved too well'. While Kathy demonstrated her love for John, John returned nothing but 'manipulation and control'. John Conway had 'completely betrayed' Kathy.

Mr Thomas believed the note John wrote and gave to Kathy in the Remand Centre, which said 'Kathy is not guilty', was a 'powerful admission' by John of his guilt.

Although John didn't write 'I am guilty' that's exactly what he was saying. It was also a very 'cynical attempt to manipulate' Kathy and ensure her continued cooperation.

The inconsistencies in both Barry Steer's and Danny Williams' evidence could only cast reasonable doubt on Kathy's involvement.

Mr Thomas said that Kathy was 'caught up in a net of intrigue worked by the arch puppet-master, John Conway'. He described Kathy as having little understanding of the events taking place around her.

'Control is what this case is all about,' Mr Thomas suggested to the jury. 'John Conway was quite happy as long as he was in control.'

In conclusion, Mr Thomas asked the jury to look at all the evidence and all the testimony and the credit of the witnesses, and said from that they would find 'a reasonable doubt that Katherine McFie was knowingly involved in this murder'.

Mr Jack Pappas began his address saying that Mr Thomas' speech reminded him of when he was a young boy. He remembered he would race home, don a pair of Mickey Mouse ears, switch the television on and be 'transported to Fantasyland'.

Mr Pappas went on to argue against the Crown and Mr Thomas' case, illustrating his points with references to popular songs. 'History Repeating' by the Propeller Heads and Shirley Bassey, 'Things That Make You Go Hmm' by C & C Music Factory and Paul Robeson's 1940 hit, 'It Ain't Necessarily So'. Justice Gallop interrupted Mr Pappas and asked that he 'stick to the evidence in this case' and not give his personal opinions.

Mr Pappas believed that Kathy had a powerful motive to kill Ricky Conway, 'born out of jealousy' and 'born out of the desire' to have John.

Because of John Conway's double dealings with his wife and Kathy, Mr Pappas proposed that it weighed heavily on Kathy's motive, giving rise to 'the notion of a woman scorned, or a woman treated badly'.

Mr Pappas argued that the police investigation was 'blinkered' in going after John Conway, from as early as 7 May. The police had formed a view about John's involvement and then proceeded to 'flesh out preliminary guilt'. Mr Pappas suggested the police had a case 'in theory', then tried to make the evidence fit their theory.

The money paid to Barry and Danny had never been sourced. The investigation was unable to 'uncover any movement of funds' to account for the alleged payment.

Like Mr Thomas, Mr Pappas questioned the reliability of the evidence given by Barry and Danny, and accused the prosecution of portraying John as an evil 'mastermind'. John had little to gain financially from the murder. Ricky had no life insurance, no mortgage insurance, and he was left with the burden of having to continue paying the mortgage on the house.

It was conceded by Mr Pappas that John could be viewed as 'sleazy', 'disreputable' and 'immoral' in his treatment of 'his wife, in relation to Kathy McFie, and women in general'. John had not denied his 'duplicitous actions'. This did not mean, however, that John Conway had hired two killers to murder Ricky Conway. Mr Pappas reminded the jury that John's morality was not on trial. He was not being charged with lying to Ricky; 'he has to live with that'.

At the close of his address, Mr Pappas mentioned 'a famous criminal trial in America only a few short years ago', the O J Simpson trial, where 'there was an ill-fitting glove' presented as evidence. In that trial, Simpson's lawyers finished by telling the jury, 'if it does not fit, acquit'.

Referring to what Mr Pappas believed were inconsistencies and pieces of evidence that 'didn't fit', he left the jury with his own admonition, 'if in doubt, leave him out'.

Much to the relief of the jury, Terry Golding explained that he was not going to 'exhaustively' review all the evidence. Instead, he wanted to draw the jury's attention to 'compelling' pieces of the evidence, which he would ask them to 'carefully consider'.

Despite John giving evidence of his love for Ricky, Mr Golding told the jury that John Conway had 'nothing but contempt, if not hatred' for his wife. The accused treated his wife 'appallingly' both physically and emotionally. John was 'dragged kicking and screaming' to admit his sexual involvement with Kathy, after 'overwhelming' evidence from witnesses and listening devices.

Mr Golding defended the police investigation, asking the jury not to be 'deflected' by Mr Pappas' criticism. The police were not on trial. He reminded the jury that it was a murder trial and not 'some Agatha Christie novel'.

Mr Golding also rebutted Mr Pappas' proposition that he had tried to portray John as a mastermind. He said he didn't submit to the jury that John was 'a clever man at all'. John's choice of assassins spoke 'eloquently to the contrary'.

Both Barry Steer's and Danny Williams' evidence under cross-examination was 'unshaken', according to Mr Golding. While they were not witnesses of 'choice', they both stuck to the core allegation of the Crown case, that John had asked Danny to kill his wife, and that after the murder John had asked Barry what went wrong, 'why didn't you make it look like suicide'. Barry's and Danny's evidence incriminated both the accused.

Mr Golding said that John's motives for killing Ricky were 'a complex mosaic'. It wasn't simply 'sexual forces at play within the relationship of the three'. John's marriage had gone 'seriously wrong' and he had committed himself to Kathy. While John did not have much to gain financially, Ricky's death meant he was free from other responsibilities, such as maintenance that would have accrued had she lived and kept custody of Alistaire. Mr Golding believed that John's son was a powerful factor in the way he 'viewed the possible resolution of the problem that confronted him'.

The surveillance recording of Kathy calling Barry from a public phone box to organise the meeting at the service station was played to the jury. Mr Golding wanted them to hear it again, to follow it with their copies of the transcript, and decide if they believe Kathy was only lending Barry $20.

Even more compelling was the tape of Barry, Danny, Kathy and John, recorded on the night of their arrests. The arithmetic done by Kathy matched the exact amount owed to Barry and Danny for the murder. The evidence, Mr Golding said, was 'absolutely transparent'.

After the final submissions, Acting Chief Justice John Gallop spoke to the jury of their obligations. It had been seven weeks and they had heard over 100 witnesses.

Only one juror of the 14 originally empanelled had been released on the second week for medical reasons. For the purposes of deliberation, only 12 jurors were required. A ballot would be held the following day to decide which juror would be excused. It was the first time in ACT court history that excess jurors were present at the end of a trial.

Still with 13 jurors, Justice Gallop began directing them on the evidence, presenting both prosecution and defence evidence for their clarification and consideration.

The following day, after the final addresses were made, the prosecution and defence counsel met in the judge's chambers. Justice Gallop was informed that one of the jurors had been seen in the company of a former boyfriend of Kathy McFie's. The concern was that the former acquaintance might have relayed information to the juror that would prejudice their decision.

Justice Gallop called the jury and informed them of the development. He asked if any juror had information from the ex-boyfriend that might affect their ability to give a true verdict.

No one from the jury spoke. Justice Gallop accepted the situation and continued with his directions.

After addressing the jury, the ballot was held and the thirteenth juror was chosen. Justice Gallop offered to exempt the man from being called for jury duty for five years. The man declined. He said he would be 'honoured to do it again'.

Justice Gallop's address had taken the whole day, so he retired the jury till the next sitting, Monday 6 July 1998.

At 10.00 am on the Monday the jury were asked to deliberate. By 4.30 in the afternoon the jury foreman sent a note through to say they had reached a verdict.

The courtroom was packed with relatives, friends, police and the media. Ricky's and Kathy's families were present throughout the proceedings, but no one from John Conway's family had been observed attending the court. Not even on the day of the verdict.

The clerk of the court asked, 'How say you, is the accused John Terence Conway guilty or not guilty of the charge that he on or about the 3rd day of May 1997 at Canberra in the Australian Capital Territory did murder Ulrike Conway?'

'Guilty,' the foreman read.

'How say you, is the accused Kathy Marie McFie guilty or not guilty of the charge that she on or about the 3rd day of May 1997 at Canberra in the Australian Capital Territory did murder Ulrike Conway?'

'Guilty.'

There were elated yells of 'yes' as the verdict was read. John Conway remained stony-faced, while Kathy McFie became distraught. As custodial officers led her down through the trapdoor to the holding cells, she screamed back, 'John, tell them I didn't know! Tell them I didn't know!'

Outside the Supreme Court the Reiners family were tearfully relieved. It had been over a year since Ricky had been murdered and their life turned upside down. Ricky's sister, Gabby, told the waiting media, 'This had been a long and painful 14 months. The revelations made in court about Ricky's character and habits have been false and distressing to us all.'

Anna Reiners said that she always held the hope that the trial would have a positive outcome. She added, 'We can start the healing.'

Justice Gallop sentenced John Conway the next day. He said the evidence was clear that John was motivated by an intense loathing for his wife. He added, 'The evidence also establishes that Mrs Conway maintained her dignity right to the end on her last and darkest day. I am satisfied on the whole of the evidence that she was a fine person and a devoted mother and she certainly did not deserve to die.'

Justice Gallop called John's role in the murder 'cowardly', exploiting Kathy's devotion and getting her to facilitate the killing. John's only goals were for Ricky to die and for him not to be caught.

The trial judge praised the professionalism of Noel Lymbery and Ben Cartwright throughout the investigation, and their hard work in eventually catching both John and Kathy. Justice Gallop believed John had tried to 'humbug the police and hoodwink the jury', but it did not work. Everyone had seen through John's masquerade as a devoted husband.

'The accused Conway has shown no remorse or contrition for what he has done … He is supposed to have been upholding law and order and serving this community and yet he has committed one of the worst crimes that anyone in the community can commit,' Justice Gallop said.

John's conviction fell into the worst category, which allowed for life imprisonment to be imposed. Justice Gallop had to determine his sentencing with reference to two issues. The first was the sentence handed down to Barry Steer and Danny Williams by Justice Crispin. They were originally sentenced to 27 years, but that had been reduced by a third for their cooperation with authorities. The other was Justice Gallop's concern that with life, no minimum period of non-parole is given. He thought a Parole Board might review the case and allow John out before he felt John should be released.

John was asked to stand in the dock, then Justice Gallop delivered his sentence. 'I sentence you to 24 years' imprisonment and I fix a non-parole period of 18 years'.

Kathy McFie was sentenced two days after John. She was given 20 years' gaol with a non-parole period of 12 years. Justice Gallop found she was less culpable than John. Her actions were driven by her devotion to her lover.

'It was Conway's idea to have his wife killed and he enlisted McFie as his lieutenant … I regard him as more culpable and I sentence her accordingly,' Justice Gallop explained.

After any trial the accused have the right to appeal, be it the conviction or the sentence handed down. With respect to this trial, the different parties, including the prosecution and Barry Steer and Danny Williams, lodged no fewer than six appeals.

John Conway's counsel lodged an appeal against the conviction, citing 18 points where it was alleged the trial judge had erred. The main point was the direction from the judge to the jury with regard to the evidence of Barry Steer and Danny Williams against Kathy McFie, which was also used as corroborating evidence against John Conway.

Then there was the exchange between Justice Gallop and Kathy McFie while she was giving her evidence. Mr Pappas felt that Justice Gallop should have discharged the jury as requested, and his failure to do so led to a miscarriage of justice.

The Heldon tapes were another point, with John's counsel arguing it was 'hearsay' evidence and should not have been allowed.

Kathy McFie's counsel also argued the jury should have been discharged, but for a different reason. Mr Thomas believed the judge should have released the jury after he had learned that one of the jurors had been seen with an ex-boyfriend of the accused.

The Crown lodged their own appeal against what Mr Golding saw as a 'manifestly inadequate' sentence imposed on Kathy McFie. Mr Golding submitted to Justice Gallop at the time that it would be an error if he did not impose a significantly higher sentence. Justice Gallop believed the sentence he gave was adequate.

To add to the list, Barry Steer and Danny Williams also appealed the severity of their sentences.

In September 1999, the Full Federal Court spent four days hearing all the appeals. Justices Jeffery Miles, John von Doussa and Mark Weinberg reserved their decision, returning on 10 April 2000 to deliver their 127-page judgment.

The three judges were unanimous in rejecting all the grounds for each of the appeals, except one. On that, it came down to a two to one majority in favour of a rejection.

That appeal was the one lodged by the Crown asking for a significantly higher sentence for Kathy McFie. Justices Miles and von Doussa agreed with Justice Gallop's reasons for sentencing Kathy McFie. Justice Weinberg believed there was a case to increase Kathy's sentence to 22 years with a non-parole period of 14 years.

The Department of Public Prosecutions accepted the decision and didn't pursue their appeal to a higher court.

John Conway's counsel took his appeal against the Federal Court decision to the High Court of Australia, the last stop in the appeal process.

Acting Chief Justice Mary Gaudron and Justices Michael McHugh, Michael Kirby, Kenneth Hayne and Ian Callinan were asked to rule on what had been presented to the Federal Court. The main point was whether corroborating evidence from Barry Steer and Danny Williams against Kathy McFie could also be used against John Conway under the co-conspirators' rule.

In February 2002, five months after the appeal was lodged with the High Court, John Conway learned that his appeal against his conviction was rejected. The judges upheld the decision of the Federal Court and stated, 'The evidence of what was said and done by and in the presence of the appellant [John Conway] when Steer and Williams called on him and McFie in the early hours of 28 July was rightly described by the Full Court as devastating. His explanation of his conduct was incredible ... His conviction was inevitable.'

The matter was now at an end. John Conway will remain in prison until he is eligible for parole. The earliest John Conway will be released is 18 May 2016. Kathy McFie will be eligible for parole on 29 June 2010 and Danny Williams on 27 July 2009.

Kathy McFie served her initial years of detention at Mulawa Correctional Centre in western Sydney. In 1999 she was featured in a Nine Network documentary, *Doing Time*, looking into the lives of prisoners behind bars. It appeared Kathy had adjusted to prison life quite well, and become a 'mother hen' type figure, helping new inmates settle into the system.

CONCLUSION

Operation Aquatic was one of the most successful high-profile homicide investigations for the Australian Federal Police. At its peak there were 73 police officers following up enquiries, manning listening posts, maintaining surveillance and conducting valuable, but tiring, door knocks. Some officers were only required for a day or two, while others were there from start to finish. At the helm, leading the investigation through each of its dramatic twists and turns, were Noel Lymbery and Ben Cartwright.

At the Supreme Court trial the Crown presented 113 witnesses. Of those, 88 were civilians and 25 were police. The trial lasted for seven weeks and one day.

It was an interesting situation for Noel and Ben, because their case against John Conway and Kathy McFie, and the subsequent presentation by the Crown to the Supreme Court, relied on the testimony of convicted felons.

John Conway was a police officer with 12 years' experience, holding a highly respected position in society. Kathy McFie was an average citizen without any police record. Kathy just had a minor traffic infringement against her name. Yet, they were charged, tried and convicted for murder on the basis of information given by two self-confessed drug addicts and part-time dealers who had also confessed to murder. Even some of the supporting witnesses' backgrounds were questionable.

Even so, a jury of six men and six women accepted, as Noel and Ben hoped they would, that the witnesses, despite their histories, were telling the truth.

It wasn't only the witnesses who sealed the conviction, it was the work by the whole team in conducting surveillance, and approaching each line of enquiry with the thoroughness and competency expected from a police officer. As Ben put it, all the I's were dotted and T's crossed.

The work conducted by Richard Thrift's surveillance teams, and the officers manning the listening posts under Brian McDonald, cannot be emphasised enough. It was they who compiled the major evidence against each suspect through covert observation and taping relevant conversations. There were 15 listening devices employed, most operating over a 24-hour period and relying on the dedication and professionalism of those officers manning the listening posts under extreme conditions and with little rest.

Another factor that helped convict John Conway and Kathy McFie was Ricky. Through her diary and the Heldon tapes, the court heard her side of the triangle that had developed between her, John and Kathy. Ricky spoke to the jury, told them of her love for her son, and the fear and anguish she experienced in her relationship with her husband.

Ricky convicted John and Kathy from the grave.

After Operation Aquatic, Noel Lymbery remained with Belconnen Crime Unit for some time before going back to Witness Protection. Ben Cartwright has also moved on. He is now Superintendent of the Protective Security Liaison Officers (PSLO). Still a part of the Australian Federal Police, the PSLO are federal agents dedicated to obtaining intelligence and performing liaison duties at the 11 counter-terrorism first response airports around Australia.

Ben's involvement in Operation Aquatic hasn't ended either. He has written articles for journals about the investigation into Ricky Conway's murder. He has also presented the subject to specialist forensics and law enforcement organisations across the country. Operation Aquatic is viewed as an excellent example of diligent police work.

Ben and Noel still have a close relationship with the Reiners. It isn't uncommon for either of them to call Anna and share a cup of strong coffee with the family. Likewise, the Reiners family know that if they have any questions or need to talk, Ben and Noel are only a phone call away.

But why? Why would John and Kathy contract anyone to murder Ricky? The reasons are speculative. Dr Rod Milton suggests it was John's controlling nature and arrogance, exemplified by his hoarding and social inadequacies and the inability to develop close friendships with people. After the Family Court hearing John had lost custody of his son. Perhaps, more importantly, he had lost to Ricky, meaning he had lost control of his life. What happened during the custody battle was enough of a trigger for John to want to regain control, and for him to implement a devious and manipulative plan. With Kathy's help, John undermined Ricky's self-confidence and set her up for her eventual death.

Police believe money was also a contributing motive for John. After all, he would have been forced to pay alimony to Ricky and may even have had to contribute to the mortgage of a house he was no longer living in. Ricky would have received 18 per cent of John's wage. Should John's first wife also want her share for their child, John would have been instructed to pay 27 per cent of his wage to his ex-wives.

What of Kathy's involvement? Her part in Ricky's death was undeniably played out in court through the surveillance tapes and the conversations she bizarrely recorded herself. But why do it? She loved John, and most likely, had seen John as a 'knight' rescuing her to take her to a better place. That better place being Queensland, well away from Stuart Flats.

The one question remains, whose idea was it to kill Ricky? Was Kathy going along with John, blinded by her love? Did Kathy make the decision, having, what she believed, was a contact in Danny who could have the job done? John and Kathy know the answers, and neither is saying.

John and Kathy were given the opportunity to contribute to this book. A letter was sent to each one, informing them of the book and inviting them to comment. An express post, self-addressed envelope was given to both with which they could make contact. The NSW Department of Corrective Services returned John's reply express envelope, explaining it was a contraband item. They did say that the letter was forwarded to him, but as yet he has not replied.

Kathy did make contact through a welfare officer. While she agreed to speak, she had more questions than answers. Kathy requested a copy of the manuscript before being published. The request was denied. She was concerned over what had been written about her and what affect the book may have on her family. Her concerns were addressed, and she seemed to accept how the book would portray her.

When Kathy made her initial contact, she referred to John in conversation as 'her partner'. It seemed a strange phrase to use, given the circumstances of the trial and how John had attempted, through his legal team, to have her be held responsible for Ricky's murder. Kathy, however, would not say what her current feelings are for John, or give any information on whether there is an on-going relationship. She was, however, surprised John had not responded to the letter. Kathy also wouldn't give any comment on the events surrounding Ricky's death, her involvement, and subsequent arrest, trial and conviction. She did admit that she believed she was not portrayed fairly by the media or the police, but she wouldn't say anything more.

After the trial, Anna Reiners told the media it was now time for the healing to begin. Her youngest daughter was her sunshine, and with Ricky gone, Anna's life had grown dark. Anna had a light stroke in 1997, in no small part due to the treatment Ricky had received at the hands of John Conway. Ricky's murder and the trial had continued to take its toll on her health, as the allegations of Ricky's drinking and poor relationship with her son became front-page news.

Time doesn't heal all, and it is evident when speaking with Anna, Gabby and Ricky's elder son, Phillip, that there's no amount of time that will totally heal the pain they feel or come close to filling the void left by Ricky's sudden death.

While in foster care, Alistaire would periodically visit his mother's family, helping to develop a close and loving bond. Alistaire is now living with Anna where he is also getting the support and love of his brother, aunty, uncle and cousins. The Reiners are slowly becoming a complete family again.

Sometime in 1999, Barry Steer wrote to Anna, expressing his remorse for killing Ricky. The letter read:

'Dear Mrs Rieners [sic],

Would you please take this time to allow me to apologise for intruding into your life by writting [sic] *this letter to you. However, over the last eleven month* [sic] *the magnitude of what I have done to you and your family by my actions has reached a point where I must express my deepest sorrow to you. I know that I can never apologise to you for what I have done but I just wish to express in some small way my remorse.*

John and Kathy had convinced me that not only was Ricky an alcoholic but that she was bashing young Alistaire. Due to my own childhood where I was severely bashed by my father this struck deeply within me. Over the next six week period both John & [sic] *Kathy kept at me with these lies. Also they kept telling me that Ricky was harassing them. When Danny finnally* [sic] *approached me and said that John had asked him could he arrange the death of Ricky to look like a suicide, my state of mind about Ricky, because of what I had been told, was such that I believed that Ricky would have deserved it.*

After committing this horrendous crime and leading up to my sentencing I started to learn the truth about Ricky, just how good a mum she was and the problems she was having with John. Then the day before my sentencing my solicitor gave me a copy of your's [sic] *and your family's victim impact statements. This had an horrendous effect on my being as the full impact of what I had done finally hit me.*

I now fully understand just how stupid I was in believing what John & Kathy had told me. Unfortunately this cannot undo what I have done and I will always have to live with that. All that I can ask is that you try to understand just how terribly sorry I am for my actions. I know that no matter how much I apologise I can not undo my actions.

I will never be able to ask for your forgiveness and I would be extremely honoured if at some time in the future you were able to express to me just how much you dispise [sic] *me for the anguish and pain that my actions have brought upon you and your family. I know that words can never heal the pain but perhaps some time in the future you may be able to say to me that you understand my remorse.*

I have taken this opportunity in an attempt to express to you my deep and utter remorse at what I have done, would you just please try and find some understanding in your heart for me

Barry Steer'

On 27 November 2000, Barry Steer was found hanging in his cell. He had committed suicide. The reason is believed to be a letter he received stating that he would not be allowed to see his son again. There's been no official confirmation.

Danny Williams has never contacted the Reiners. He still remains in protective custody in Long Bay Correctional Centre in eastern Sydney.

John Conway and Kathy McFie have also never contacted the Reiners. John has never had any communication with his son. He has served his time in maximum security and is now classified as a minimum-security prisoner. John is currently serving his time at Goulburn Correctional Centre in the New South Wales Southern Highlands, not far from Canberra.

Ulrike 'Ricky' Conway was a good mother. She was a good mother to Phillip and she was a good mother to Alistaire. She kept a tidy house. She put her sons' needs ahead of her own. She saw they were fed, clothed and had shelter. She tried to shield them from life's pain and ugliness. Was she an alcoholic? Ricky enjoyed a drink and a smoke. She didn't drink every day, and she didn't always drink to excess. She drank to fill a void. She drank to replace the love and tenderness she desired, but had been refused by John. All Ricky wanted was a husband who loved her and for them to nurture a happy and healthy family together. She wanted what she had had as a child for her own children. For whatever reason, she chose her men badly, and her simple desire, sadly, became an unobtainable dream.